FINANCING INFRASTRUCTURE

FINANCING INFRASTRUCTURE

Who Should Pay?

Edited by

RICHARD M. BIRD AND ENID SLACK

Published for the Institute on Municipal Finance
and Governance at the Munk School of Global Affairs

by

McGill-Queen's University Press
Montreal & Kingston • London • Chicago

ISBN 978-0-7735-5146-6 (cloth)
ISBN 978-0-7735-5147-3 (paper)
ISBN 978-0-7735-5244-9 (ePDF)
ISBN 978-0-7735-5245-6 (ePUB)

Legal deposit fourth quarter 2017
Bibliothèque nationale du Québec

Printed in Canada on acid-free paper that is 100% ancient forest free
(100% post-consumer recycled), processed chlorine free

McGill-Queen's University Press acknowledges the support of the Canada
Council for the Arts for our publishing program. We also acknowledge the
financial support of the Government of Canada through the Canada Book
Fund for our publishing activities.

Library and Archives Canada Cataloguing in Publication

Financing infrastructure : who should pay? / edited by
Richard M. Bird and Enid Slack.

Includes bibliographical references and index.
Issued in print and electronic formats.
ISBN 978-0-7735-5146-6 (hardcover). – ISBN 978-0-7735-5147-3 (softcover). –
ISBN 978-0-7735-5244-9 (ePDF). – ISBN 978-0-7735-5245-6 (ePUB)

1. Infrastructure (Economics) – Canada – Finance – Case studies.
2. Infrastructure (Economics) – Government policy – Canada –
Case studies. 3. Municipal finance – Canada – Case studies.
4. User charges – Canada – Case studies. I. Bird, Richard M., 1938–,
editor II. Slack, N. E. (Naomi Enid), 1951–, editor

HP120.C3F56 2017   363.0971   C2017-904861-9
                                            C2017-904862-7

This book was set by True to Type in 10.5/13 Sabon

Contents

Tables and Figures

TABLES

FIGURES

Preface

Financing Infrastructure: Who Should Pay? is about who should pay for municipal infrastructure, with a particular emphasis on making the users pay. Much of the discussion to date has focused on asking federal and provincial governments to pay for municipal infrastructure ... and with some success. Few have suggested that the revenue for new infrastructure should mainly come from the people who benefit from the infrastructure. This book attempts to change that narrative by emphasizing the economic and other advantages of making users pay. The various chapters consider user-fee financing for infrastructure in general and for specific infrastructure (such as transit, water, and sewers) in selected jurisdictions in Canada, the United States, and Europe.

Earlier versions of most chapters were presented as papers at a conference of academics and practitioners organized by the Institute on Municipal Finance and Governance (IMFG) at the Munk School of Global Affairs at the University of Toronto in October 2016. IMFG is a think tank at the university that focuses on the fiscal and governance challenges facing large cities in Canada and around the world. It sparks and informs public debate through the publication of papers and books such as this one, and it engages the academic and policy communities through public events and round tables.

This book will be of interest to policy makers at all levels of government as well as the academic community and members of the public who are interested in understanding how to pay for the growing municipal infrastructure all agree is needed. It will help readers understand why charging user fees makes sense, how we should determine how much users should pay, and where charging is done well and where it can be improved. The book suggests some ways to convince politicians and the public of the importance of pricing infrastructure correctly.

In addition to the individual chapter authors, we would like to thank
other participants at the conference who provided useful comments on
the draft chapters: Ben Dachis, Herb Emery, Drew Fagan, Adam Found,
Kyle Hanniman, Harry Kitchen (also an author in this volume), Mel
McMillan, and Joe Pennachetti. We also appreciated comments from
conference observers: Mathieu Bélanger, Alan Broadbent, Chris Gian-
nekos, Phinjo Gombu, Rob Hatton, Kate Manson-Smith, Oliver Jer-
schow, Andrea Roberts, and Carole Saab. We are grateful to Selena
Zhang, manager of programs and research at IMFG, for organizing the
conference and overseeing the publication of this book with McGill-
Queen's University Press.

Richard Bird and Enid Slack

FINANCING INFRASTRUCTURE

1

Financing Urban Infrastructure:
Should Users Pay?

RICHARD M. BIRD AND ENID SLACK

Politicians and officials at all levels of government seem to agree with most citizens that Canada's urban infrastructure needs to be repaired and extended. Aging water systems need to be fixed, sewage needs to be adequately treated rather than just dumped into the nearest water source, roads and bridges need to be repaired, urban transit must be updated and extended, and public housing as well as schools, health centres, and government offices need to be brought up to current standards. Although such concerns are not limited only to urban areas, it is in and near the larger urban areas in particular that major infrastructure investment is most needed to accommodate expanding populations.

We all agree that something needs to be done. But who should pay for it? Even the largest and richest cities seldom think they have much room to raise additional revenue from the property tax, the only real fiscal instrument available to them. Smaller and often poorer municipalities definitely know that they cannot pay for new infrastructure. What can be done? The answer seems obvious: turn to the federal and provincial governments for financial support. These levels of government, it is argued, can and should increase transfers to finance new local infrastructure, facilitate and encourage new and innovative forms of public–private partnerships (P3s or PPPs) to finance larger projects, or at least permit local government to access new forms of revenue on their own initiative, perhaps in the form of imposing surcharges on existing provincial or federal taxes in order to finance investment, notably in rapid transit.

However, although some encouraging words have been heard in response from federal and provincial governments, some promises made, and even some federal money pledged,[1] no level of government seems willing to tell people that in the end they are going to have to pay for any increased investment in public infrastructure. It is of course not surprising that citizens are generally unwilling to pay more taxes or that governments are prone to play "pass the buck" when it comes to who should pay for what infrastructure. Nonetheless, it is a bit odd. We do not as a rule decide to build public infrastructure simply because it looks nice or because someone in power thinks it would be a good thing to do for some reason or another. Presumably, we do so because we need it to provide particular public services at a certain level for those who live in (or may choose to live in) a particular place. Cities – a term used here as shorthand for the often complex mix of political and fiscal institutions that provide urban public services – are in the business of providing a mix of services, most of which require physical infrastructure to be produced. Logically, the first place any business, even one conducted within the sphere of the public sector, should look for revenue to refurbish and improve the services it provides is to the people for whom they are provided.

WHY USERS SHOULD PAY

A democratic society does not tell people where to live or what to eat. Nor does it necessarily pay all or even any of their bills when they make decisions on these matters, although it usually does establish through its governing institutions the rules and regulations (e.g., health and safety rules, land use planning) within which such decisions are made. Societies may also choose to redistribute income and wealth to some extent in part to ensure that everyone is able to pay for what we as a society determine through our inevitably imperfect political institutions is a reasonable level of food and shelter. Canada has an elaborate – if not fully satisfactory or complete – system of interpersonal transfers, mainly at the federal level, intended to move us towards this goal. Sometimes we go even further when it comes to public services – those provided wholly or partly through the public sector. Various equalization programs, though again far from perfect, are in place at both the federal–provincial level and the provincial–municipal level to help every government bear some of the cost of providing such services without having to impose an unreasonable burden of taxation on its residents. Finally, in Canada we also provide services that are largely financed through the public sector (such as education and health) and are provided free (up to some point) to everyone, even though most of the benefits clearly accrue to those who receive the services, because we consider that it is beneficial to society as a whole for everyone to have free access to such services. There is a lot of redistribution – perhaps not always sensible or even in the right direction – going on in the Canadian public sector.

But this reality does not mean that everything done through the public sector should be judged mainly in terms of its distributive impact. Nor do any of the arguments for redistribution or for subsidizing certain publicly provided activities just mentioned imply that it is any more sensible to require someone else to pay for all or part of the cost of transporting someone from where they live to where they work or for the water they may use for a shower before they leave home than it is to expect someone else to pay for the food they may eat between these activities. Assuming that Canadians as a whole acting through their federal and provincial governments have made at least an attempt, albeit imperfect, to establish a reasonable distributive baseline for citizens, then the right baseline rule for municipal governments wishing to make the best possible use of the resources at their disposal is to ensure that, whenever possible, people pay for what they get. Ideally, therefore, the full cost of providing such urban services as water and sewerage, streets and roads, transit, parks and recreation, and the removal and disposal of solid waste should be paid by those who use these services.

At present, however, with a few limited exceptions – especially with respect to water and transit and to a lesser extent solid waste and parking – such services are largely supplied for free. Since none of these activities is costless, the result is simply to shift the burden to someone other than the direct beneficiary. Even when prices are charged, as for parking on some streets for example, they seldom bear any relation to the real economic costs that parkers impose – not only the increased congestion imposed on other street users but also the cost of building wider streets so people can park in the first place. Sometimes, so long as the costs are borne by local residents through local taxes, the effects of poor pricing may not be too economically distorting – everyone uses streets in some way. Often, however, mispricing public services in this way may be not only unfair – whether considered against conventional normative standards or what Sheffrin (2013) calls "folk justice" (i.e., how ordinary people as opposed to "experts" view fairness) – but economically inefficient. Reducing the efficiency with which scarce public resources are used will, by definition, reduce the total size of the pie available for use and hence the potential well-being of everyone. But people are seldom aware of this cost since it is invisible – it is what does not happen when resources are wasted – and hence seldom mentioned in political discourse.

Failing to charge properly imposes hidden costs in several ways. Those who make use of public services (such as underpriced water or free roads) tend to use more services than they would be willing to pay for if they had to face the full cost. They may be happy as a result, but their happiness comes at the cost of wasting resources that could be put to better (more socially valued) uses. Moreover, this initial misallocation often results in still further waste as political institutions pour still more resources into additional urban infrastructure in response to demands for more and better services from both current users and those who – understandably – think they too should receive similar subsidies. Finally, since in the end virtually all public services that are not paid for by user charges end up being financed by taxes – a point to which we shall return – the initial efficiency losses from mispricing public services are even greater than the monetary amounts involved because taxes impose additional efficiency costs.

This last cost – the increased inefficiency in how society employs resources when it finances public activities through taxes rather than charge financing – may be offset to some extent by the way in which the (reduced) output is distributed. This argument has two legs, each of which has a (potentially) measurable aspect. The first, already discussed, is the social cost imposed by inefficient pricing. The second is the possible offsetting social gain from improved distribution that such pricing may yield. However, as noted above, any undesired distributive effect from charging may often be offset with less distortion through small adjustments in the existing array of transfer and tax policies. Presumably those who think mispricing public services is the best way to redistribute must see considerable value in hiding subsidies, have little faith in the ability of political institutions to deliver the socially desired amount of redistribution through more direct policies, or both. The first of these arguments may have some merit. It seems reasonable to attach value in terms of human dignity to the more respectful treatment associated with non-discriminatory rather than targeted redistribution, although this concern was more important when targeting required visibly singling out recipients than it is in the current age of the internet. The second argument for the distributive virtue of mispricing appears to rest on the belief that those who make the argument know better than society – or at least better than the political institutions we have developed to reflect and implement social intentions – what is really socially desired. This argument is obviously debatable: since the only way we have to weigh such values is in terms of the costs that we as a society are willing to pay to achieve them, in the end the only way we have to assess competing normative assessments is through the invariably imperfect workings of our political institutions. Criticizing the distributional results thus amounts to criticizing the procedures that produced them – no doubt always a useful and even necessary exercise for the long-term improvement of society, but not one that can be further pursued here.

Summing up, whether we are considering providing a service like refuse removal or buying the garbage trucks or building the roads and bridges they travel on, the first answer to the question "Who should pay?" should always be "users" – and preferably through direct user charges when feasible. However, two additional points that need to be considered when it comes to paying for urban infrastructure relate to timing and the relevant "user" population. If a bridge is intended to provide services for one hundred years, the relevant user population is obviously quite different than it would be if we were providing refuse collection service on a particular street every second Tuesday. Similarly, considering the waste treatment process as a whole, both costs and benefits may impact many more people than those who put the garbage out in the first place.

The first of these points – timing – suggests that the appropriate way to cover the costs of many infrastructure projects may often be to spread (smooth) the tax impact over time for reasons of both equity and efficiency: as we discuss in the next section, this is in fact the main choice to be made in considering how best to "finance" (as opposed to what we call here "fund" or pay for) infrastructure. While we think that users should definitely pay to the (usually considerable) extent possible, the fact is that there are many different ways in which infrastructure investment can and should be financed. The key point to keep in mind in discussing investment finance, however, is that it is important not to let the financing decision obfuscate what is really going on in terms of who is paying for, and responsible for, what.

How one deals with the second point – the external costs and benefits arising from individual decisions, such as to drive on a given road at a given time – critically depends on how the institutional context (the governance structure) is organized and on the roles played by different levels of government in financing urban public infrastructure. Again, however, the important point is to ensure that there is full public accountability with respect to who is responsible for what, how well they are playing their role in the infrastructure game, and who is really paying in the end. Although perfection in this respect is not possible in a world in which interjurisdictional spillovers mix with intertemporal concerns like those mentioned in the previous paragraph as well as interpersonal (and interjurisdictional) distributive issues like those discussed earlier, the main take-away message delivered in this book is that charging whenever possible has the considerable virtue of reducing the confusion, obfuscation, and general "noise" that too often characterizes discussions of infrastructure finance.

GETTING THERE FROM HERE: CONCEPTS AND ISSUES

The chapters contained in this book broadly discuss the extent to which and the manner in which the issues set out above are dealt with in a variety of different real-world situations. A common theme in many of these accounts is the inadequacy of the data. We do not have good estimates of the extent and nature of the infrastructure deficit within any one province, let alone across the country, and we are not able to make reliable comparisons across national borders.[2] We have even less comparable and reliable information on the extent to which users pay for public infrastructure, in part because different jurisdictions define infrastructure in different ways and report infrastructure finance very differently. In fact, as a close reading of some of the chapters in this book reveals, at times similar language and concepts are used to describe and measure very different activities, while at other times essentially similar activities are described and measured very differently. Here, for example, we use "funding" when discussing who ultimately pays for public infrastructure investment (that is, either users or taxpayers) and "financing" when describing the various ways in which such funds may be channelled to investment projects – user charges, local taxes, development charges, and various value capture schemes or transfers from provincial or federal governments or borrowing either directly or through various forms of public–private partnership arrangements.

Still, no matter what words or numbers are used, several messages emerge from most of the cases discussed here. One such message is that although economists frequently argue that users should pay, people and politicians are not listening. Much infrastructure is often financed by grants and subsidies so that – as is perhaps politically desired – it is seldom clear who is paying for what and when. The unfortunate result is that too much is often spent on the wrong infrastructure, which is one reason it is so difficult to measure the infrastructure deficit accurately. When user charges are imposed, all too often the only rationale is to produce some revenue with the result that even identifiable and congestible public services where pricing is relatively simple and its efficiency value is greatest are usually poorly priced. Neither consumers nor public providers get much useful information from such prices, and the result, again, is wasted resources and perverse incentives to provide still more underpriced services.

Some more positive messages also emerge, however. The most obvious perhaps is that reliance on user charge revenues appears to be increasing in a number of jurisdictions, although, as just mentioned, this result seems less likely to reflect the dawning of any light about the economic value of increasing pricing than simply a shift to more "chargeable" services (as with higher education in the US) or the increasing difficulty of increasing taxes noticeable in both the US and Canada. However, even though most charges have likely been introduced (or increased) almost entirely for revenue reasons, there are some promising exceptions, ranging from the singularly careful way in which Switzerland prices water, wastewater, and solid waste services to the recent introduction of stormwater pricing in some Ontario jurisdictions. What continues to be largely missing in North America, however, is any parallel to the extensive development in Switzerland of a legal and accounting framework that permits the proper discussion and implementation of the appropriate division between taxpayers and users in paying for such services.

A first step in improving outcomes when it comes to user charges for municipal public infrastructure – the principal focus of this book – is to clarify and understand the terminology. What is infrastructure? What is public infrastructure? What is municipal public infrastructure? As the following chapters indicate, all these questions may be and often are answered in different ways in different places. Broadly, however, the municipal public infrastructure with which we are principally concerned here may be understood as the built (or engineering) "hard" infrastructure – bridges, roads, waterworks, sewage plants, transit systems, etc. – needed to deliver services for which local governments are usually largely responsible, regardless of whether local governments own such works or whether they are built or operated by other public or (even regulated) private organizations.[3] In Canada, most such works are carried out directly by municipal governments, subject to the regulatory and organizational context established by the provinces. Some other countries hive off some such activities – notably with respect to water but sometimes transit systems, airports, parking facilities, etc. – in separate utility companies, generally publicly owned in the US though often private in some countries such as France and the UK. In all countries, there are often strong network and sometimes hierarchical relations between national, regional, and local service providers, frequently with very different arrangements in different sectors and sometimes in different regions. The heterogeneity of even this restricted universe is one reason why comprehensive and comparable treatment of infrastructure investment is elusive everywhere.

It is equally difficult to pin down just what is meant by user charges or fees, which may have many different labels in different sectors and places. Broadly speaking, we use "public pricing" and "user charges" as synonyms to mean charges to identifiable direct users of the services provided by a particular infrastructure investment – the person who opens a tap and gets the water, drives across the bridge, or rides the subway or bus. We argue that such charges should offset not simply the current operating costs of providing the service – a common aim widely accepted with respect to such services as water and transit – but also, importantly, the full life-cycle monetary costs (including capital costs), as well as expected future monetary costs (such as future upgrades and expansions).[4] Of course, direct users should not be charged for externalities – benefits accruing to others as a result of providing the service in question (an example is the use of water for the fire service). If the beneficiaries of such externalities are local, local general taxes like the property tax may be an appropriate source to pay for this portion of the service. If the benefit net is cast more widely, the burden may be appropriately borne by regional, provincial, or even national taxpayers.

Summing up, public infrastructure investment projects can ultimately be funded only by users or taxpayers. However, such projects may be carried out through many different forms of public-sector organizations, private companies, or a variety of public–private arrangements. The best way to design, build, operate, and maintain infrastructure may vary considerably depending on both the characteristics of the investment in question and the relevant organizational, regulatory, financial, and environmental circumstances as well as the technology available. There is no one answer to the question of how best to organize, finance, and implement infrastructure investment. But from the perspective of using scarce public resources as sensibly as possible, there is one ingredient that is common to all reasonable answers: namely, users should as much as possible be clearly responsible for covering that part of the full cost that is attributable to their use.

Not nearly enough attention is paid to ensuring that the investments made are those that people not only want but are willing to pay for or that infrastructure is properly used and maintained. The key to connecting what is done, how well it is done, how appropriate it is, and how well it is used is to ensure that those who decide, those who benefit, and those who pay are largely the same group. Unfortunately, given the inevitable human preference for someone else to pay and the understandable reluctance of politicians to face their constituents directly with the fiscal consequences of their decisions, there is usually no substantial constituency supporting more "user pay" infrastructure investment. Developing sufficient support for more sensible policy in this respect is unlikely to be simple. If outcomes are to be improved, there is more than enough for everyone involved to do:

- Federal and provincial governments should ensure that there are clear legislative guidelines for establishing sensible charging policies, maintaining the essential accounting systems, reporting the results publicly, and gathering and analyzing the information to ensure that the system is properly applied. Ideally the substantial work necessary to create the appropriate regulatory environment should be carried out in close collaboration with the regional, local, and even private agencies charged with delivering the services in question. It should also be preceded and accompanied by extensive (and in all likelihood prolonged) public consultations.
- Where intermunicipal or regional–local (e.g., in metropolitan urban areas), or even provincial–local (e.g., in rural areas), arrangements seem needed for good performance, the necessary legal and accounting requirements would again have to be put into place, adequate support and training provided to all involved, and as much prior consultation as necessary provided to develop a supportive collaborative coalition. In some areas, it might take decades to develop and implement such arrangements; in others, existing structures and systems may make the task less arduous.
- On the financial side, while there may certainly be a role for institutions like a federal "infrastructure bank" and for stronger provincial

institutional support for both local direct borrowing and for establishing public–private partnerships with respect to infrastructure in order to facilitate and keep as low-cost as possible the debt incurred by municipal service providers, care should be taken to ensure that local (and provincial and federal) taxpayers are made fully aware of the share of the costs they are expected to bear relative to those imposed on direct users. Any subsidies provided by higher-level governments (i.e., paid for by provincial and federal taxpayers) should be explicitly stated and justified in terms of the estimated (and reported) share of project benefits borne by non-users.

• Similarly, while local governments and their agencies should be encouraged to explore such techniques as development charges (on potential new users) and various value capture schemes (on existing users) as well as borrowing to smooth the fiscal impact of chunky investment projects, any support they receive should explicitly require them to develop and implement an appropriate charging system to ensure that direct users pay their share of the project cost appropriately as well as to report regularly and fully exactly who is paying for what and why.

Prescriptions like those just mentioned are unlikely to seem feasible to many involved in the real world of the public sector. They are also likely to be hard to sell to people who have as a rule never really been told that not only should they pay for what they get but that they in fact already do so – although not in any sensible way that would ensure that they are actually getting what they should for what they pay. Perhaps the only way to begin to change attitudes might be if politicians and officials were prepared to accept that their own lives should become more difficult because they need to work a lot harder to be more credible and trustworthy. For example, people are more likely to buy into a charging scheme if they feel that their interests and concerns have been understood and taken into account in a credible way. More information about what is going on and why may help but is unlikely to do the job on its own unless serious, credible, and continuing efforts are made to engage and communicate with all those who feel they are affected by some project or other.

Not everyone will get on board. But for any major project to succeed one has to try to create at least a minimal coalition of support. Starting small, and delivering the goods as promised on time and within budget is one way to start building public trust. Earmarking funds for new investments that people can actually see and benefit from may be another.[5] People do not like change; they seldom believe those who tell them that change is good for them; and they perceive concrete losses much more clearly and feel them much more strongly than they do nebulous general gains well down the road. The path to establishing a more sensible role for user charges in financing public infrastructure is thus unlikely to be straight, level, or easy. Nonetheless, it is a road with which those who would like to achieve a more effective, equitable, and efficient public sector should become more familiar.

ORGANIZATION OF THE BOOK

In chapter 2 Enid Slack and Almos Tassonyi make the basic economic case for setting prices equal to marginal cost. When people can consume a service without having to pay its full cost, they tend to consume and demand more than they would if they faced the true cost. Improper pricing (or no pricing at all) thus leads to costly overinvestment in infrastructure. If roads are not priced correctly, they become congested as more and more people who do not pay the full cost crowd on them. To relieve the congestion, users demand more roads. And so it continues, as inadequate pricing results in more congestion and still more demand for new roads. The solution seems obvious: price properly in the first place. However, few Canadian governments at any level set fees in a way that is efficient. When municipalities, for example, actually charge for services, they tend to set fees that will generate as much revenue as possible but are unlikely to reduce demand sufficiently to ensure that scarce public-sector resources are used as efficiently as possible.

Slack and Tassonyi describe how user fees are employed for a number of services – water and wastewater, stormwater management, solid waste collection and disposal, transit, parking, and roads – by municipalities across Canada. They also describe other funding and financing mechanisms used to pay for services and infrastructure – property taxes, land value capture taxes, development charges, intergovernmental transfers, borrowing, and reserves. Although municipal user fees have been on the rise in Canada in recent years, especially for water and waste water and more recently for stormwater management, few cities in Canada charge for roads and bridges, and, for those services where user fees are levied, marginal-cost pricing is rarely used. They conclude that better pricing is needed to link those who benefit from infrastructure with those who pay but that for local (and other) governments to implement proper pricing for infrastructure, users and citizens in general will need to be persuaded that it is a good idea, a theme discussed further in the last chapter of this book.

The next three chapters focus on user fees for specific types of infrastructure (water, wastewater, and transportation) in four Canadian provinces – Ontario, Quebec, British Columbia, and Alberta. In chapter 3 Harry Kitchen delves into the pricing of water and wastewater in Ontario, looking at where we have come from and where we need to go. The increase in water prices over the last twenty years, he argues, reflects the fact that water is increasingly being recognized as a scarce resource and that financing infrastructure has become a major policy concern. Initially spurred in part by a serious public health crisis arising from a poorly run municipal water system in the Ontario town of Walkerton, water pricing has improved in a number of ways in Ontario municipalities. Meters and volumetric pricing are now commonly used and full-cost recovery is the accepted goal. Although there is no consensus on what full-cost recovery actually means, amortization of capital costs and asset management plans are increasingly required. Residential water prices per cubic metre more than doubled from 1991 to 2009, but pricing is still not efficient and does not always promote conservation. Inefficient pricing continues to add to the demand for expensive and unnecessary infrastructure.

As water becomes scarcer, efficient pricing will be even more important for conservation. Efficient pricing of water would include a multi-part tariff to accommodate capacity constraints, economies of scale, periods of peak load demand, greater use of meters and volumetric pricing for sewer use (instead of surcharges on water bills), and user fees based on the volume of water runoff for stormwater systems. For smaller and remote communities to adopt efficient pricing, amalgamation or regionalization of smaller systems into one large utility may be necessary as might some privatization of water and sewer systems. Kitchen also suggests that in addition to acting as a coordinator and planner of water utility systems, the province should take on the responsibility of regulator to approve increases in water prices to pay for operating and capital costs. Moreover, any provincial transfers to municipalities for water should be conditional on municipalities setting efficient prices.

In Quebec, unlike Ontario, municipalities still use property taxes to pay for at least part of the costs of water and sewer use. Indeed, as Jean-Philippe Meloche and François Vaillancourt note in chapter 4, charges for water are relatively less important in Quebec municipalities than in municipalities elsewhere in Canada, accounting for only 17 per cent of municipal revenues. Less reliance on water charges can be attributed, at least in part, to the low level of metering in Quebec – in 2014, only 13 per cent of housing units were equipped with water meters. The authors estimate that charges for water, sewage, and wastewater cover less than half of the operating costs. For the City of Montreal, where for historical reasons most water has long been tax-financed – a practice that appears to have influenced behaviour in the province as a whole – that estimate is only 10 per cent, although the authors note that it is difficult to understand the true role of charges in Quebec owing to some terminological and classification confusion between taxes and charges in the available data. Greater use of user charges appears to be generally accepted as appropriate for commercial, industrial, and institutional users, but there continues to be debate in Quebec about charging for residential water use.

Turning to transit, however, Quebec cities appear to be similar to those elsewhere around the world. In Montreal, for example, users cover 36 per cent of transit funding. Although not common, user charges exist for two bridges and part of one expressway in Quebec, all of which are provincial responsibilities and public–private partnerships. Meloche and Vaillancourt emphasize the interaction between road pricing and transit pricing and suggest that road charges should account not only for the direct costs but also for pollution and congestion. Options to do so include gasoline taxes linked to intensity of use, tolls on access points that differentiate by time of day and location, parking fees that differentiate by time of day and location, or kilometre charges using GPS technology that are also linked to time and location.

Before discussing user fees in western Canada in chapter 5, Lindsay Tedds sets out the legal constraints facing municipalities in Canada when it comes to setting user charges. As interpreted by the courts, provincial legislation on user fees in British Columbia and Alberta, as in other provinces, requires that revenues from fees be earmarked for the service for which they were levied and that the magnitude of the fee has to be supported by the actual costs incurred. In other words, no surpluses are permitted. On the other hand, so-called "regulatory fees" (such as development charges), which are imposed in relation to rights or privileges awarded by the government, must be used for the stated purpose but may, unlike user fees, also be used solely to alter individual behaviour.

Tedds finds that as a share of municipal revenues municipal user fees are 40 per cent higher in British Columbia than in Alberta although regulatory charges do not account for a significant portion of municipal revenues in either province. She suggests that one possible reason for the difference in the importance of user fees between the two provinces may be that regional districts in BC are required to provide goods and services on a cost-recovery basis, which has led them to opt for fees over taxes. In terms of road pricing, the major cities in the two provinces – Metro Vancouver, Calgary, and Edmonton – do not levy tolls, although the BC provincial government does collect tolls on two local bridges. User fees are levied for public transit in both provinces, but, unlike in Alberta, transit is a provincial responsibility in British Columbia.

The next two chapters look at some relevant experience outside Canada. Chapter 6 by Robert Ebel and Yameng Wang reviews user charges in the United States with respect not only to hard physical infrastructure such as roads and transit but also to social infrastructure such as education and hospitals, which are not covered in the Canadian chapters. User charges as a proportion of municipal revenues in the US have clearly increased over the last twenty years both at the state and local levels. Current charges have increased markedly in relation to current expenditures for higher education and even more so for hospitals, which (like highways) are largely state government responsibilities. They have also increased in air transportation, sea and inland waterways, sewerage, solid waste management, and parking, which are either local or joint state–local in nature. States with higher per capita incomes and higher revenue capacity rely less on user charges to finance infrastructure.

Ebel and Wang expect user charges to continue to rise in the future in part because of the decline in revenue productivity of the major tax sources of local governments – property, income, and sales – as well as the growing anti-tax movement and improvements in technology (particularly in the areas of road use and parking) that make it easier to implement charging. These factors are also relevant in Canada, although in addition to the different statistical universe reported in the US, which has much more comparable data on revenues and expenditures for each of the more than 89,000 local governments, the conceptual framework is different. For example, since water services are almost always supplied by separately reported public utilities, information on water revenues and expenditures is largely excluded from the US story told in chapter 6. Another important difference is that US local governments are permitted to charge more than is required to meet current expenditures and can allocate surplus funds to other purposes; neither practice is permitted in Canada.

In contrast, chapter 7 by Bernard Dafflon again focuses in particular on water pricing and describes in some detail how user charges for water, wastewater, and solid waste are designed in Switzerland. Responsibility for water, wastewater, and solid waste is shared among all three levels of government – federal, cantons (similar to provinces), and communes (local governments). The objectives, implementation, and financing of these systems are set out in the federal constitution (a very "top-down" approach) and other – often very detailed – federal and cantonal legislation. Each communal tariff has to include a connection charge, access charge, annual charge (difference between historical and current replacement value of existing investment plus future investments to improve services), and annual operating charge (fixed and variable operating costs). As in Canada, but unlike the US, cross-subsidies between services are not permitted in Switzerland. Unlike these two countries, however, Swiss local governments are also required to include in their water tariffs a "charge for the future," which is related to future investments and paid in advance through capitalization.

The methodology for pricing of water, wastewater, and solid waste in place in Switzerland comes much closer to full-cost pricing than that in most other countries. For this tightly constructed system to work properly, Dafflon emphasizes, requires a clear legal framework with strong coordination among the three levels of government, an accurate accounting system that relates the costs to the benefits, and a judicial system that permits users, beneficiaries, and payers to be heard when the benefit principle (linking those who benefit with those who pay) is violated. As Dafflon discusses, it took considerable effort over a fairly long period to develop this system and put it into place, generally without serious problems, in almost all of the country. At present, Dafflon reports, user charges cover over 80 per cent of the full-cost price of water and wastewater services on average (and over 90 per cent in most large cities) as well as over 60 per cent of the cost of dealing with solid waste (over 80 per cent in most large cities).

In chapter 8, Matti Siemiatycki examines the role user fees have played in urban transportation public–private partnerships (PPPs) over the last twenty years. Although discussed by economists primarily in terms of the efficiency effects of pricing, in reality much of the initial interest in user fees in Canada arose from the perceived political desirability of shifting infrastructure costs from away from taxpayers and on to users. Much of the current interest in PPPs seems similarly to have been driven by the desire to shift costs – or so many think – to the private sector. User fees have often played a direct, although often contentious, role in PPPs around the world. In Canada, where the first wave of PPPs in the 1990s and early 2000s were mainly for roads and bridges and where PPPs were seen as a way for cash-strapped governments to deliver infrastructure without taking on public debt, user fees were often part of the package. However, once PPPs were up and running, considerable opposition developed, with the public perceiving that they too often put private interests ahead of the public interest.

In the second wave of transportation projects over the last decade less emphasis was therefore put on PPPs as a way to generate revenue through user fees. Instead, they were seen as a way to spur innovation, encourage life-cycle asset management, and allocate risks to those best able to manage them. Indeed, only six of the twenty-three urban highway and bridge projects in Canada include road tolls. Even where tolls are applied, the demand and revenue risk has been retained predominantly by the public sector. In terms of transit, PPPs are delivering far more projects than in the first wave but transfer very little demand risk to the private sector. This structure has the advantage of making it easier to seamlessly integrate these projects into the wider transportation network. But it has the disadvantage of loading more of the cost onto taxpayers in general and less on the users benefiting most directly from the improved infrastructure. Although the implementation of user fees has been increasing in Canada overall, user fees for roads are much less prevalent in Canada than in other countries.

Economists, like most of the authors in this volume, are often puzzled about why so little attention has been paid to the pricing of infrastructure by policy makers and what might be done to change matters. In chapter 9, Richard Bird first recaps the arguments why users should pay for infrastructure and then presents a number of technical, economic, and especially political reasons why so little attention has been paid to user fees in Canada or elsewhere. He concludes by suggesting some ways in which one might be able to sell more and better user charges to the skeptical and resistant public. Since, as noted earlier, an important effect of poor pricing is to inflate artificially the apparent need for more investment in infrastructure, the current move around the world to expand infrastructure investment suggests that this may be a good time to think more about these issues.

How might people who are not paying for services now (or who are paying prices that are below marginal social cost) be convinced that they should pay more – the right price – for services? As Bird suggests, since people are less likely to resist paying for a service that they did not have before than to pay more for services they already receive, the time to determine how to charge is before a project begins, not least because the size and shape of any infrastructure project depends in part in the expected demand, and demand is sensitive to price. In addition, those who wish to move to more charging need not only to address any significant distributional problems with explicit offsets through direct transfers (for example, income-related tax credits), but also to spend much effort before building a project in building a supporting coalition of support from users who know they will have to pay for what they get. Most basically, considerable effort is generally needed to move the public narrative away from the notion that a "public service" means something that should be provided freely to all to the idea that when people receive identifiable benefits from the provision of public services they should – in the absence of important distributional arguments to the contrary – expect to pay for them. Unless one has a good answer to the question "If users do not pay, who should?" and an even better reason why users should not pay, the presumption should be that they should. Too many involved in the debate about infrastructure finance seem to assume simply that "someone else" should pay: why should they? This book argues that there is seldom a persuasive answer to this question.

NOTES

1   Although usually referred to as the "federal gas tax," the source of federal funds is actually a lump-sum amount (originally $2 billion, but now indexed annually by the rate of inflation).

2   For a look at this problem from an explicitly international perspective, see Frank and Martinez-Vazquez (2016).

3   We thus do not discuss some important categories of local public infrastructure, notably "point" (rather than "network") investment in schools, hospitals, and other social services or in administrative buildings.

4   If markets functioned perfectly, these costs would sum up to social opportunity costs. If, as is likely, there are known market imperfections,

there is a huge literature on how cost-benefit analysis of new investment projects should be corrected to account for such problems, and of course similar corrections should be made to pricing if necessary (Bird 2005).

5   There are potential problems with excessive earmarking: for a fuller discussion; see Bird and Jun (2007).

2

Financing Urban Infrastructure in Canada: Overview, Trends, and Issues

ENID SLACK AND ALMOS T. TASSONYI

The poor state of municipal infrastructure in Canada – defined to include transportation (transit, highways, roads, bridges, street lighting, etc.), water and wastewater, solid waste collection and disposal, public libraries, and public recreation centres – is the subject of frequent news stories.[1] Roads are congested, transit systems need major investments, bridges are crumbling, water treatment plants need to be replaced, and the list goes on. Local governments, staggered by what they perceive to be a growing problem, have turned to the federal and provincial governments to help them out, and, to some extent, these governments have responded favourably with increased funding.[2] But, are transfers from other governments really the best way to pay for municipal infrastructure?

Economists argue that proper pricing, where prices are set at marginal cost (the additional cost of producing one more unit of output), would be better because it rations the use of existing facilities and gives appropriate capital investment signals. Underpricing a service, on the other hand, results in overconsumption and greater demand for more of the unpriced infrastructure, which leads to more expensive infrastructure investment than is economically efficient (Kitchen and Lindsey 2013; Bazel and Mintz 2014). Transfers generally mean that access to infrastructure is not being priced correctly so the tendency is to overuse it. Although Canadian local governments can and do levy user fees mainly for public transit, water, and waste collection, few have embraced road or bridge tolls and few are applying marginal-cost pricing principles.[3]

This chapter provides an overview of how municipal infrastructure is funded in Canada with a particular emphasis on the role of user fees. The chapter begins with a brief discussion of the infrastructure deficit and how it is measured. The second section sets out a rationale for user fees on the basis that they are the best way to link revenues to expenditures. The third section provides an overview of capital expenditures and the sources of capital financing used by municipalities in one province – Ontario. The fourth section provides a more detailed discussion of the different sources of revenue to pay for infrastructure in Canadian municipalities. The final section suggests that user fees are increasing in Canadian municipalities but better pricing is needed to link those who benefit with those who pay for municipal infrastructure.

IS THERE AN INFRASTRUCTURE DEFICIT?

Increasing concern has been expressed about the large and growing municipal infrastructure deficit in Canada. Perhaps the most often-cited estimate of that infrastructure deficit is $123 billion, which was put forward by the Federation of Canadian Municipalities (FCM) in 2007. More recently, FCM has produced the Canadian Infrastructure Report Card, which is based on a survey of municipalities across the country. In it, they estimated that the replacement value of all assets in 2009–10 (including municipal roads, drinking water, and wastewater and stormwater infrastructure) was $538.1 billion, of which the replacement value of assets in very poor condition was almost $51 billion and those in fair condition, $121 billion (Federation of Canadian Municipalities 2012).

Although the public discourse appears to have adopted these and similar numbers put out by other organizations, Fenn and Kitchen (2016) caution against taking these numbers at face value. For example, they argue that many of these estimates are based on surveys conducted by associations with a vested interest in making the number significant enough to attract federal and provincial funding. Similarly, some estimates are based on a benchmark or standard of identified needs, but, again, those standards are often set by associations with an incentive to inflate the size of the deficit. Moreover, benchmarks are generally based on engineering standards and do not take account of economics – is there an asset management problem or is it a pricing problem? They also raise issues around the lack of information on the quantity and quality of the capital stock, resulting in some questionable estimates.

The starting point has an important influence on the measure of the deficit – does the starting point necessarily reflect the right level of investment? Where deficits have been estimated, it is assumed that existing taxing and pricing policies for the services delivered by the assets will continue; there is no estimate of infrastructure needs if more effective demand management or conservation-based pricing policies were adopted, for example. Efficient prices for services such as road use, water, and wastewater would reveal the true demand for infrastructure because people know the cost of providing those services and they would give an indication of the efficient supply.

Notwithstanding the criticisms of the estimates of the infrastructure deficit, there is little doubt that municipal governments, on average, have underinvested in infrastructure. One indication of that underinvestment is the comparison of the net book value of assets (current value less depreciation) as a proportion of the costs of those assets. To preserve the value of capital assets, municipalities would have to invest at least the same amount of money as the amount of depreciation, but they are generally not doing that (Tassonyi and Conger 2015). In 2013, for example, the net book value of municipal capital assets in Ontario was over $128 billion and the value of the assets at cost was almost $196 billion. In other words, municipal capital assets were worth only 66 per cent of their original cost.[4] Investment has not kept pace with depreciation – municipal assets are losing value. Similarly, in Alberta in 2013, net book value was almost $53 billion, or 67 per cent of the cost of $78 billion (Tassonyi and Conger 2015). Although there is no defined threshold to determine if a municipality's ongoing infrastructure investment is adequate, it is interesting that the average for Ontario and Alberta municipalities is similar. In both provinces, however, there is considerable variability across municipalities in the proportion of book value relative to capital cost. In Ontario, for example, Toronto is below the average (at 59 per cent), as are many northern municipalities, but rapidly growing municipalities such as the City of Vaughan are at 90 per cent (Slack, Tassonyi, and Grad 2015). In Alberta, Edmonton was close to the provincial average at almost 70 per cent in 2013, while Wood Buffalo (Fort McMurray) was at almost 99 per cent in the same year (Tassonyi and Conger 2015).

A FRAMEWORK FOR SELECTING REVENUE SOURCES:
LINKING REVENUES TO EXPENDITURES

For governments to operate efficiently, it is important to establish a clear link between expenditure and revenue decisions. Simply stated, those who make expenditure decisions should also make revenue decisions and the type of revenue should match the type of expenditure being funded. Sometimes referred to as the Wicksellian connection, this linkage should result in more accountable government with taxpayers being less averse to paying taxes as long as they know where their tax dollars are being spent.[5]

From this perspective, the optimal way to design a local tax system would be to determine what local services to deliver and how much, and then put in place the revenue system (a combination of user fees, taxes, and transfers) that faces local decision makers with incentives that will lead them to choose to finance precisely that package of expenditures. To be efficient in allocating scarce investment resources, governments should allocate costs associated with a given benefit as much as possible to those individuals, firms, neighbourhoods, and groups that enjoy the benefit (Bazel and Mintz 2014).

Figure 2.1 illustrates that different fiscal tools are appropriate to pay for different types of infrastructure. User fees play an important role for those services with private good characteristics (such as water, sewers, garbage collection and disposal, transit, and some recreation). The first rule of local public finance is to charge a user fee. Good user charges not only produce revenue for local governments, they also promote economic efficiency. When people are not explicitly charged for consuming a service, the implied value they will rationally attach to the last unit they use is approximately zero. Consequently, more is consumed (and demanded) than people would be willing to pay for if they were faced with the real costs of providing the service (Bird and Slack 2014). Underpricing, or providing services for free, results in overconsumption and often in subsequent ill-advised investment.[6] For example, when subsidized roads become crowded, the political pressure to expand them becomes greater. Overinvestment in underpriced facilities leads to inefficient use of scarce public resources. Good user charges can avoid such waste.

Where user fees cannot be charged, local revenues to finance services and infrastructure should be collected only from local residents, preferably in relation to the perceived benefits they receive from local

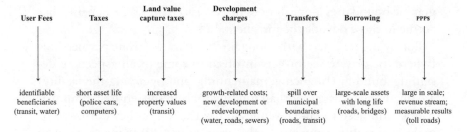

User Fees	Taxes	Land value capture taxes	Development charges	Transfers	Borrowing	PPPs
identifiable beneficiaries (transit, water)	short asset life (police cars, computers)	increased property values (transit)	growth-related costs; new development or redevelopment (water, roads, sewers)	spill over municipal boundaries (roads, transit)	large-scale assets with long life (roads, bridges)	large in scale; revenue stream; measurable results (toll roads)

Figure 2.1   Matching fiscal tools to infrastructure type

services. Revenues from other sources (including local business activities) should similarly match the benefits they receive from local services.

Services with public good characteristics (for example, fire protection, neighbourhood parks, local streets, and street lighting) generate collective benefits that are enjoyed by local residents. Benefits from these services cannot easily be assigned to individual beneficiaries, and therefore it is difficult to levy specific fees or charges. In lieu of fees or charges, then, some form of local benefit-based taxation such as the property tax should be adopted. This type of tax permits individuals to express their collective demand for services. In this respect, the property tax is considered to be a generalized, or non-specific, user charge and is appropriate for infrastructure that has a short life (Kneebone and McKenzie 2003).[7] Property taxes (or pay-as-you-go financing methods more generally) are less appropriate for large infrastructure that lasts for thirty or forty years because there would be a large spike in property taxes in the year of the investment. Land value capture taxes are a refinement of local taxes where infrastructure increases land values; development charges are appropriate for growth-related capital costs associated with new development or redevelopment.

For services where the benefits (or costs) spill over municipal boundaries but where local provision is still desirable, a federal or provincial transfer may be appropriate. Positive spillovers (externalities) occur if residents of neighbouring jurisdictions receive a service for free or at less than the cost of providing the service. For example, major roads constructed in one jurisdiction may be used by residents of another jurisdiction without any charge to the latter. The result is an underallocation of resources for that service because the providing jurisdiction bases its expenditure decisions on the benefits captured within its geographic boundaries alone. It does not take account of the benefits that accrue to those outside the jurisdiction.[8]

Borrowing for assets with a long life and public–private partnerships (where the private sector gets involved in some or all aspects of designing, building, financing, maintaining, and operating the facility) are financing tools rather than funding tools in the sense that municipalities still need to raise revenues to pay back what they borrowed or make availability payments to the private sector (if there are no user fees). Each of these fiscal tools will be discussed more fully in the fourth section, with the exception of public–private partnerships, which are discussed in chapter 8.

BRIEF OVERVIEW OF INFRASTRUCTURE EXPENDITURES AND REVENUES

Information on annual capital expenditures and the revenues used to finance those expenditures is not available on a uniform basis for municipalities across Canada. Statistics Canada does not provide information on capital expenditures and sources of capital finance, and each province provides municipal financial information in a different format. In particular, capital expenditures are often not separated from operating expenditures.[9]

For these reasons, table 2.1 shows municipal capital expenditures for only one province – Ontario. In 2014, Ontario municipalities spent almost $9.5 billion on capital expenditures (also referred to as the acquisition of tangible capital assets). Forty per cent of these expenditures were for transportation, and of these expenditures 25 per cent were for transit (or 10 per cent of total capital expenditures). Environmental expenditures (water, sewers, and solid waste collection and disposal) were the next largest expenditures at 33 per cent of total capital expenditures. Based on the earlier discussion of how to pay for services, user fees would be most appropriate to pay for transportation and environmental expenditures, which account for almost three-quarters of total capital expenditures in Ontario municipalities.

In terms of sources of capital financing (table 2.2), user fees and charges account for less than 3 per cent of the total and property taxes for just over 5 per cent.[10] The largest component of own-source revenues (that is, revenues excluding transfers) is reserves and reserve funds. Reserves include user fees and property taxes that were collected in previous years as well as development charges that were previously levied

Table 2.1
Distribution of capital expenditures, Ontario municipalities, 2014

General government	5.4
Protection (fire and police)	3.8
Transportation (roads and transit)	40.0
Environmental (water, sewers, solid waste)	33.0
Health and social services	1.8
Social housing	2.9
Recreation and culture	11.8
Planning and development	0.5
Other	0.8
Total	100.0

Source: Ontario Ministry of Municipal Affairs, Financial Information Returns.

Table 2.2
Sources of capital financing, Ontario municipalities, 2014

Municipal user fees and service charges	2.6
Municipal property tax	5.2
Development charges and other contributions	22.5
Other sources	0.5
Transfers:	
Federal capital grants	4.0
Canada gas tax transfer	6.9
Provincial capital grants	5.4
Provincial gas tax transfer	1.0
Transfers from other municipalities	0.9
Total transfers	18.2
Borrowing	13.8
Reserves and reserve funds	37.2
Total	100.0

Source: Ontario Ministry of Municipal Affairs, Financial Information Returns.

and placed in (dedicated) reserve funds. Development charges are a significant source of revenue to pay for growth-related capital costs in new developments. Transfers from the federal and provincial governments accounted for over 18 per cent of total revenues for capital purposes. Municipal borrowing also represents a significant proportion of the sources of capital financing.

SOURCES OF REVENUE TO PAY FOR INFRASTRUCTURE

The following discussion describes the use of different revenue sources to pay for infrastructure and suggests that few Canadian municipalities apply the Wicksellian connection, although some funding options do link those who benefit with those who pay.

User Fees

User fees are levied by local governments in Canada to pay for at least part of the costs of a number of services. Fees range from fixed charges that are unrelated to consumption to charges that vary with the quantity consumed or a combination of the two. Decisions related to pricing depend on a number of considerations – local tradition, the type of service, the tastes and preferences of residents, and the willingness (or lack thereof) of local politicians and bureaucrats to substitute prices for local taxes (Kitchen and Tassonyi 2012).

Economists have been making the case for pricing municipal infrastructure for a long time and yet few Canadian municipal governments price services correctly.[11] Current practice in setting user fees in Canada almost always deviates from what is fair, efficient, and accountable (Kitchen and Tassonyi 2012; Fenn and Kitchen 2016). The tendency is to set fees to generate revenue rather than to allocate resources to their most efficient use. By not pricing municipal services correctly (i.e., setting prices equal to marginal cost), unintended subsidies can occur. For example, lower fares for seniors on the transit system could result in a single mother on social assistance subsidizing an older, wealthier lawyer going to the office (Kitchen 2015). If these types of subsidies were made explicit, they would surely be unacceptable. Some examples of pricing services in Canadian municipalities follow.[12]

WATER AND WASTEWATER
User fees for water in Canadian municipalities tend to take one of four structures (Kitchen and Tassonyi 2012; Fenn and Kitchen 2016): a fixed charge that does not vary with consumption but may vary by type of property (residential, commercial, industrial) or by characteristics of the property (number of rooms, number of water-producing fixtures, etc.); constant unit rates; declining block rates; and increasing block rates. The latter three structures are all based on volume. As Kitchen notes in his chapter in this volume, the majority of municipalities across

Canada use constant unit rates; the use of a fixed charge has declined significantly over the last twenty years. Sewage collection and treatment are generally recovered through surcharges on the water bill and are not based on sewage flow. Flat-rate sewage charges are the most common not only in municipalities with flat-rate water charges but also in municipalities with metered water (Kitchen and Tassonyi 2012). For other municipalities, the sewage charge is calculated as a percentage of the water bill.

As a share of disposable income, Canadians pay one of the lowest water supply and sanitation rates among twenty-two OECD countries – 1.2 per cent of disposal income compared to 2.3 per cent average for the OECD countries (OECD 2010 as reported in Elgie et al. 2016). In Ontario, wastewater pricing is based largely on volumes of water used rather than on volume discharged. Some municipalities (for example, Ottawa, Toronto, and Durham Region) levy over strength discharge fees that are intended to recover the additional costs of treating substances at higher concentrations than allowed by sewer bylaws.

By not charging marginal cost for water and sewage, considerable inefficiencies result. In particular, the consumption of water is higher because there is no incentive to restrict water use or to use the service efficiently. The result is overinvestment in water and sewage treatment facilities relative to what the level of investment would be with a more efficient pricing policy. Underpricing has also been said to discourage innovation in alternative water and sewer technologies.

Although there are many efficiency advantages to using marginal-cost pricing for water and sewers, Canadian municipalities rarely use it. Kitchen and Tassonyi (2012) list a number of reasons they do not: marginal-cost pricing is complex and not always able to match revenues with costs resulting in revenue instability, and a history of reliance on capital grants (often at 85 per cent of replacement costs) has meant that there is no incentive to include replacement costs in prices. Moreover, municipalities cannot implement marginal-cost pricing properly if they do not include the opportunity cost of using water, if they do not set rates that capture differences in distance from the source of supply and differences in use by time of day, and if they do not include asset replacement costs in annual operating costs. However, better metering as well as pricing methodology could go some way to correcting the most glaring deficiencies in this area of municipal service provision. Furthermore, better inclusion of costs using life-cycle costing, which includes the total cost of constructing, maintaining, renewing, and operating the infrastructure asset throughout its service life, would be appropriate.[13]

STORMWATER MANAGEMENT

Stormwater is one area where a few Canadian municipalities have introduced better pricing mechanisms. For example, the City of Kitchener, Ontario, applies a tiered flat-fee stormwater rate to properties based on their impervious area.[14] In Alberta, the City of Edmonton levies a monthly stormwater utility charge calculated on the basis of the area of the property, development intensity (proportion of the lot that is used for intended development), and a runoff coefficient that is related to the permeability of the surface of the lot (Henstra and Thistlethwaite 2017).

In 2016, Mississauga introduced a stormwater levy that is based on the impervious area of the property (which correlates with the property's contribution of runoff volume to the collection system).[15] Different assessment methods are used for residential and non-residential properties. For single residential properties, the rate is based on the remote sensing of each property. The roofprint area (total surface area covered by the rooftops of all buildings on the property) is used to predict the total impervious area of the property and to assign a property to one of five tiers (smallest, small, medium, large, or largest). A fixed number of billing units is then assigned to each tier. For multi-residential and non-residential properties, the rate is based on an individual assessment of the total impervious area on each property using aerial imagery. The number of stormwater billing units assigned to each property is calculated by dividing the total impervious area by the area of one billing unit (267 m²). To calculate the charge for each property, the number of billing units for each property is multiplied by a universal rate ($100). A credit program for multi-residential and non-residential properties rewards those property owners who reduce stormwater runoff volumes or peak flow rates or improve the quality of the runoff before it enters the municipal system.

User fees for stormwater management are fair because they are based on runoff contribution rather than property values and are thus more closely related to benefits received than is a property tax: owners of properties (residential or commercial/industrial) with a large impervious area pay higher user charges than those who do not burden the drainage system to the same degree (Aquije 2016).

SOLID WASTE COLLECTION AND DISPOSAL

User fees require customers to pay for waste pickup on the basis of volume or weight, whereas tax revenues are unrelated to how much waste is put out on the curb. When waste collection is paid from taxes, the price per kilogram of waste discarded is zero, which certainly does not reflect the marginal cost of the service (Dewees 2002). Marginal-cost pricing would result in efficient waste management.

User fees provide not only a source of revenue to local governments but also a financial incentive to reduce, reuse, and recycle. User fees are generally charged in areas where there is a recycling program so that residents have an alternative to putting out waste. In some jurisdictions, customers are required to purchase special tags to be attached to each garbage bag – in some cases, each bag carries the same price; in other cases, customers receive one free tag per week per household and can purchase additional tags. A second method is to require customers to place all garbage in a special container and pay a fee for each container. The price may vary with the size of the container (as in Toronto, for example). In a third method the municipality weighs the waste as it is picked up and bills the customer according to the actual weight of the garbage.

A number of studies have examined the effects of user-pay systems in municipalities in Canada and the US – most compared property-tax-supported garbage pickup with a per-bag fee. In general, they reported reductions in solid waste tonnage because consumers increased recycling, generated less waste, and increased the use of other options such as composting (for a summary of these studies, see Kelleher, Robins, and Dixie 2005). Moreover, the resulting lower costs for cities freed up property taxes for other services.[16]

In cases where municipalities operate a landfill site, the cost per cubic metre of waste needs to reflect the operating cost plus all amortized capital costs including closure and post-closure costs, the opportunity cost of the space, and the value of the environmental harm caused by the waste and its disposal (Kitchen and Tassonyi 2012). Government-operated landfills tend not to charge tipping fees that reflect future scarcity of landfill sites, however. Many charge only per-tonne fees to private haulers. The tipping fee for waste from municipal operators is more often paid by local taxes than by tonnage charges.

TRANSIT

Transit is funded, at least in part, from user fees in cities across Canada. In the Greater Toronto and Hamilton Area, transit fare revenues cover between 70 and 80 per cent of operating costs (one of the highest proportions in North America) but a smaller fraction of total costs when infrastructure investment is included (Kitchen and Lindsay 2013). Although it is generally believed that some of the costs of running the transit system should be covered by fares and the rest should be subsidized, the exact amount of subsidy is difficult to determine. Part of the problem is that roads are not priced on a user fee basis (see discussion of road pricing below). If road use were priced according to marginal cost (including pollution, congestion, and so on), public transit might not require a subsidy to be competitive with road use or at least not the amount of subsidy it currently enjoys in some cities.

The efficiency of transit fares depends not only on the amount of the fare but also on its structure (Kitchen and Lindsay 2013). For example, fares should vary by distance since the social cost of transit trips increases with the distance travelled. By charging a uniform fare, riders who travel short distances subsidize riders who travel long distances. Thus, flat fares do not meet the benefits-received principle and can encourage sprawl. Fares should also reflect the time of day that a trip is taken. Failure to charge higher fees during peak hours creates an incentive to overinvest in public transit infrastructure (Kitchen and Lindsay 2013).

PARKING

Parking in large cities includes a mix of residential and non-residential spaces on private land, streets, surface lots, and parking garages. Parking is often inefficiently priced, encouraging more people to drive.[17] On-street parking in high-demand areas is often priced well below its scarcity value. As a consequence, drivers spend considerable time looking for a vacant spot (Shoup 2006). Excessive cruising leads to considerable traffic congestion and pollution, as well as inefficiencies and lost productivity (Grush 2013). Meanwhile, privately owned garage parking tends to be overpriced because operators possess a degree of monopoly power owing to their unique locations. Overpricing of garage parking contributes further to the stock of cars cruising for parking (Arnott and Rowse 2009), thus increasing traffic-related costs.

Local governments in Canada can and do charge for car parking on local roads, but do they charge efficiently? Efficient parking levies/taxes could help reduce the volume of traffic and lead to less congestion, faster trips, fewer traffic enforcement costs, and reduced demand for new and expanded roads and highways (Kitchen and Lindsey 2013).

Parking levies could also generate much-needed revenue for improving and expanding public transit. Indeed, it has been argued that "underpriced parking does more to promote automobile use than good transit does to discourage it" (Grush 2013, 132). To overcome these concerns, three policies could be considered: a commercial parking sales tax which is a special tax imposed on parking transactions and is used by Translink in Vancouver;[18] a parking levy which is a special property tax applied to non-residential parking spaces, which is used in Montreal;[19] and changes in on-street and off-street parking practices (user fees).[20]

ROADS

Efficient road prices are widely recognized as an effective travel demand management tool because they influence all aspects of travel choice: trip frequency, destination, travel mode, time of day or week, route, and so on. To the extent that traffic demand is managed, cost pressure on local budgets is lowered because traffic-related costs should be reduced and infrastructure demands lowered. Furthermore, if revenues are dedicated to public transit and roads, they are more likely to gain public acceptance. Without proper road pricing, drivers lack incentives to make efficient decisions about how often to use the road, where to live and work, and other economic decisions. The lack of efficient pricing has been a primary cause of excessive highway congestion, environmental degradation, lost productivity, and reduced economic activity in many large cities and urban areas in Canada (Kitchen and Lindsey 2013).

High occupancy toll (HOT) lanes is a pricing scheme that is used in some metropolitan areas in the US and was recently introduced as a pilot project on some highways in Ontario.[21] Tolling is applied only to vehicles that are below a minimum occupancy requirement – typically two or three people. Tolls can vary by time of day and location in order to maintain high speeds in the HOT lanes. The tolled infrastructure would be new, and it would offer drivers a choice of paying for a quicker trip or using the existing toll-free lanes. HOT lanes could also be constructed on some major local and arterial roads and highways that enter into or pass through large cities.[22] Tolling can now technically (if not often politically) be feasibly imposed through electronic registration of vehicle use.

A second, larger-scale mechanism is to toll major highways and possibly some major arterial roads and highways that run into or through cities. Tolls may be set as a flat charge or may vary by time of day (as is done on Highway 407 in the Greater Toronto Area and the Autoroute 25 in Montreal). Tolling all lanes at different rates is more efficient than tolling only some lanes because it is easier to control the total number of vehicles using the road as well as the distribution of traffic across lanes on the road. Advances in technology have made it much easier for local governments to impose road tolls, but there is still much debate about whether to do so. For example, Toronto City Council approved a proposal to levy tolls on the Gardiner Expressway and the Don Valley Parkway in December 2016. However, the provincial government refused to approve the City's request.

Of course, road pricing addresses congestion only on major roads, not in the downtown core. The congestion charge in London (UK), introduced in 2003, is a daily fee charged to most motor vehicles that drive into Central London on weekdays between 7:00 a.m. and 6:00 p.m. Although congestion charges have also been used in other locations such as Singapore and Stockholm, they have not been tried in Canadian cities. Nevertheless, Althaus, Tedds, and McAvoy (2011) have explored some of the technical and administrative issues that would need to be addressed to implement a congestion charge in the Halifax Regional Municipality.

Property Taxes

Municipalities often use current operating revenues (property taxes, in particular) for assets with a short life expectancy (such as police cars and sometimes fire engines) or recurrent expenditures (such as the maintenance and upgrading of sidewalks, roads, street lighting, and parks). For non-recurrent expenditures (such as expenditures for libraries, museums, and other large fixed assets) or assets with a long life expectancy (such as sewer lines and waterworks), annual operating revenues are inappropriate, however, because current taxpayers fund projects that benefit future users. Using operating revenues to pay for capital expenditures breaks the link between revenues and expenditures over time.

Land Value Capture

Land value capture as a way to finance major infrastructure projects is currently very popular in the media and in policy circles in Canada and around the world. The idea behind land value capture is to recoup some or all of the unearned increment in private land values arising from two sources – public investment or a change in regulations.

LAND VALUE CAPTURE TO RECOUP UNEARNED INCREMENT
ARISING FROM PUBLIC INVESTMENT

With respect to a public investment, the tax is levied on those property owners who benefit (indirectly) from roads, transit, water and sewerage systems, and other major infrastructure through increased land values. One way to capture land value increases arising from a public investment is through a special assessment, which is a specific charge or levy added to the existing property tax on residential and/or commercial/industrial properties to pay for additional or improved capital facilities that border on those properties.[23] The charge is based on a specific capital expenditure in a particular year, but the costs may be spread over a number of years (Tassonyi 1997). Examples of capital projects financed in this way include the construction or reconstruction of sidewalks, the initial paving or repaving of streets, and the installation or replacement of water mains or sewers. In each instance, the abutting property is presumed to benefit from the local improvement and is expected to bear at least some of the capital costs. Where special assessments are used, there is a link between those who benefit and those who pay for infrastructure.

Special assessments do not generally contribute large sums of revenue to local budgets, but they are an important way to fund local improvement projects. It is possible to design them so that the costs of the project are allocated according to some measure of benefits received. For example, the most common method is front footage, which is appropriate for financing projects where the cost per property increases with the width of the lot. For projects such as neighbourhood parks, whose benefits largely accrue to particular areas or blocks within a community, the best approach to apportioning costs may be zone assessment, under which all properties in the serviced area pay the same share of total costs.[24]

Tax increment financing (TIF) is another way to capture the increase in land value arising from a public investment.[25] Under a TIF, property tax revenue from the designated area is divided into two categories for a specific period of time (long enough to recover all costs of public funds used to redevelop the property, usually between fifteen and thirty years). Taxes based on pre-developed assessed property values are retained by the municipality for general use. Taxes on increased assessed values arising from redevelopment (the tax increment) are deposited in a special fund to repay bonds that have been issued to finance public improvements in the redeveloped area. In other words, increases in property tax revenue from the redevelopment of an area are dedicated to financing public improvements in that area.[26]

Although TIFs are widely used in the United States, they are not as common in Canada. In Manitoba, cities are permitted to use TIFs, and the Municipal Government Act in Alberta permits municipalities to use a form of TIF known as the "community revitalization levy." This levy allows a municipality to redirect a portion of provincial tax revenues (the provincial education share of property taxes) from a designated revitalization area towards approved municipal expenditures in the specified area. Any increase in provincial education property tax revenues over the benchmark year is provided to the municipality for a twenty-year period. The City of Edmonton uses this levy to help fund revitalization in two areas – the Capital City Downtown Plan and the Quarters; the City of Calgary is using the levy to invest in infrastructure improvements in the Rivers District.

Ontario municipalities may use tax increment equivalent grants (TIEGs), but these are not the same as TIFs because they involve a subsidy component.[27] Under this program, municipalities can designate an area or the entire municipality as a community improvement project area. They can then implement a community improvement plan (CIP) with grants and/or loans that can, if the municipality chooses, be calculated on a tax increment basis. Under this scheme, the municipality can offer developers a grant or loan that is based on the higher property tax that is generated from development. In other words, part or all of the annual tax increase arising from the development over a specified period (usually ten years) is returned to the new business as a grant.[28]

Tax increment financing does link those who benefit from public infrastructure (albeit indirectly through an increase in property values) with those who pay. One of the major questions around TIFs, however, is the extent to which they can be used to pay for major infrastructure projects such as transit lines. Although there are a few examples of TIFs to pay for transit, Haider and Donaldson (2016) suggest that TIFs in North America are generally used for projects in the millions of dollars, not in the billions of dollars. Although they might be used to pay part of the cost of new transit lines, they probably cannot cover the entire cost. TIFs may be useful to pay for transit stations, as they are in Hong Kong, where land value capture at transit stations brings in significant revenues for the mass transit system. Of course, the high density and corresponding high land values in Hong Kong contribute to making this model a success. It is not clear how replicable this model would be in other locations.

Two recent studies in the Greater Toronto Area looked at the potential use of TIFs for major transit investments. One study concluded that if TIFs had been used to finance the Sheppard subway line in 2006, they would not have been able to cover all of the capital costs (Haider and Donaldson 2016). This result is perhaps not all that surprising given the low ridership on that subway line. Another study of the proposed SmartTrack proposal for the city of Toronto suggested that there would be sufficient commercial development in the city to fund the proposed $2.6 billion investment (Found 2016). It seems that the jury is out on the viability of using TIFs to finance major infrastructure.

LAND VALUE CAPTURE TO RECOUP UNEARNED INCREMENT
ARISING FROM A CHANGE IN REGULATIONS
The sale of building rights, commonly known as density bonusing, is a method of capturing land value resulting from a change in land use regulations. In Ontario, for example, section 37 of the Planning Act allows local governments in the province to secure "facilities, services or matters" (benefits) from developers in return for heights and densities that would otherwise exceed existing zoning bylaw restrictions (Moore 2013). Section 45(9) of the Planning Act refers to Committee of Adjustment or OMB approvals of minor variances with conditions attached that may include community benefits. Similarly, the City of Vancouver exchanges density for benefits through Community Amenity Contributions agreements (CACs). In both cities, the local government negotiates the amount of density and the value of a variety of benefits secured on a case-by-case basis (Moore 2013).

Although there is no consistent reporting of the amount of revenues from section 37 (and section 45[9]) of the Planning Act, the City of Toronto reported that it secured over $112 million in future cash contributions in 2013 and 2014 (City of Toronto 2015) and almost $52 million in in-kind contributions.[29] Since 1998, the city has secured over $482 million in section 37 and section 45(9) community benefits plus substantial (but unspecified) in-kind, non-cash benefits. Estimates for the City of Vancouver show that approvals for additional density in 2015 secured public benefits of approximately $103 million. Contributions can vary from year to year depending on the number of approvals. In Vancouver, for example, over the period from 2010 to 2014, the total value of public benefits secured was as high as $234 million in 2014 and as low as $27 million in 2010 (City of Vancouver 2016).

According to Moore (2013), there are at least three justifications for density bonusing: to cover the cost of infrastructure necessary to support the increased density, to share the windfall profit when local governments grant developers higher densities, or to compensate local residents negatively affected by the increased density (e.g., shadows or increased congestion created by the new development). Regardless of the justification, the value of the uplift generated by the additional density has to be determined and the resulting benefits negotiated. Calculating the uplift can be complicated and difficult for the public to understand – transparency has become a serious issue with these mechanisms.

Development Charges and Contributions

A development charge (known as development cost charges in BC and off-site levies in Alberta) is a one-time levy on developers to finance the off-site, growth-related capital costs associated with new development or, sometimes, redevelopment. Charges are levied for works constructed by the municipality, and the funds collected have to be used to pay for the infrastructure made necessary by the development. Development charges are appropriate to finance infrastructure in areas experiencing new growth; they are not used to pay for the maintenance and replacement of existing services.

The rationale for charging developers for growth-related capital costs is that "growth should pay for itself" and not be a burden on existing taxpayers (Slack 2002). "Growth-related" costs have traditionally included "hard" costs for roads and water and sewage systems, and, in some jurisdictions, also include "soft" costs for services such as libraries, recreation centres, and schools.

An economically efficient development charge should cover the full cost of the infrastructure and vary by the type of property (residential, commercial, or industrial), the density of the development (single versus multi-unit buildings), and the distance from existing services (Kitchen and Tassonyi 2012). Marginal-cost pricing, or a reasonable approximation, is better at linking revenues and expenditures for specific developments than average cost pricing, which charges every unit the same amount regardless of the type of unit, location, or density.

Most Canadian municipalities, however, do not use marginal-cost pricing but rather impose the same charge regardless of whether a property is located close to existing facilities or farther away. Developments close to existing infrastructure pay the same charge as developments far away even though the costs are higher for the more distant developments. Although uniform charges are easier to calculate than variable charges, uniform charges also mean that municipalities levy the same charge on residential dwellings in low-density neighbourhoods as on those in high-density neighbourhoods even though the marginal cost per property of infrastructure projects in low-density areas is higher (Blais 2010). The consequence of uniform pricing can be urban sprawl (Slack 2002). Although it may be difficult to calculate the growth-related infrastructure costs for each individual property, it would be possible to calculate costs by neighbourhood as a way to discourage inefficient development patterns (Kitchen and Tassonyi 2012; Slack 2002).

Intergovernmental Transfers

As noted earlier, the federal government has responded to the calls for funding infrastructure with a wide array of programs and transfers, starting in 2002 and continuing into the present (see table 2.3). The largest contributions are for major infrastructure and strategic infrastructure; the gas tax fund transfer is by far the largest transfer and is ongoing.[30] Provincial governments also provide (conditional) transfers to municipalities to pay for infrastructure. In some cases, federal programs require contributions from both the provinces and municipalities.

Grants from senior levels of government (federal or provincial) for capital infrastructure can be justified on economic grounds if the projects for which funds are provided generate spillovers or if they are projects in which the donor government has a specific interest or need. For these purposes, conditional grants are appropriate with the funding rate set to match the proportion of benefits deemed to be in the form of spillovers, or the rate could be set to match the proportionate interest of the donor government. Dahlby and Jackson (2015) make a case for federal transfers in the national interest for productivity-enhancing infrastructure that generates nation-wide benefits (as opposed to infrastructure that improves the quality of life).[31] Even if it does not generate spillover benefits to individuals in other communities, federal funding can be justified because the increase in federal tax revenues

Table 2.3
Infrastructure Canada contribution and transfer programs, 2002–2016.

Program	Description	Approved (*$millions*)
Public Transit Infrastructure Fund	Up to 50% of eligible costs allocated on the basis of ridership	1,417
Canada Strategic Infrastructure Fund (closed)	Up to 50% for projects of regional and national significance	362
New Building Canada Fund – National and Regional Projects	Base amount plus per capita allocation for medium and large-scale projects	1,565
New Building Canada Fund – National Infra-structure Component	Federal cost matching up to 50% for projects of national significance	1,110
Building Canada Fund – Major Infrastructure Component	Large infrastructure projects of national or regional significance	6,031
New Building Canada Fund – Small Communities Fund	Generally costs shared one-third by each level of government; for smaller communities	713
Green Infrastructure Fund	Federal cost matching up to 50% for environmental infrastructure	628
Building Canada Fund – Communities Component	Funding for small communities on a one-third basis for three levels of government	1,024
Building Canada Fund – Large Urban Communities Component (Quebec only)	Infrastructure projects in large communities in Quebec	194
Building Canada Fund – Research and Planning Component (Quebec only)	Funding for research and planning	3
Tuktoyaktuk to Inuvik Highway (NWT only)	Construction of road	200

Program	Description	
Canada Strategic Infrastructure Fund	Federal cost matching up to 50%	4,622
Municipal Rural Infrastructure Fund	Funding for small-scale infrastructure projects on a one-third basis for three levels of government	981
Border Infrastructure Fund	Federal cost matching up to 50% for Canada–US border crossings	591
Infrastructure Stimulus Fund (closed)	Up to 50% federal cost matching for short-term stimulus	3,612
Building Canada Fund – Top Up to Communities Component (closed)	Short-term economic stimulus funding	463
G8 Legacy Fund (closed)	Funding to support hosting of G8 Summit	45
Building Canada Fund – National Infrastructure Knowledge Component (closed)	Merit-based application program for projects of national significance	0
Total contribution programs		**23,545**
Gas Tax Fund (statutory payment with ongoing commitments)	$2 billion annually indexed at 2% per year	18,770
Provincial-Territorial Base Fund	Up to 50% for provinces (75% for territories) to address core infrastructure priorities; used to build or renew infrastructure in most Building Canada Fund eligible priorities	2,301
Public Transit Fund (closed)	Funding allocated on a per capita basis	400
Total transfer programs		**21,471**

Source: Infrastructure Canada, http://www.infrastructure.gc.ca/prog/table-tableau-eng.php; and Dahlby and Jackson (2015).

from the productivity improvement benefits citizens across the country through reduced tax rates or increased expenditures.[32]

Although the distinction between productivity-enhancing infrastructure and quality-of-life infrastructure appears, at first, to be intuitively appealing as a way to justify federal funding, it is difficult to apply it in practice. For example, clean water is considered to be quality-of-life infrastructure but is it not also essential for productivity? Moreover, since there is little or no information on the benefits of productivity-enhancing infrastructure, we have no idea what share of benefits generated are assumed to be collective rather than strictly local or, by extension, how much should be funded by the federal government. To design a transfer on this basis, it is necessary to estimate the relative share of the total benefits that are enjoyed across the country, but most transfer programs appear to assume (without much evidence) that this share is very large because we see that the federal matching rate tends to range between a third to a half of the cost of the infrastructure. In the case of a road, for example, there may be a national benefit, but it is likely to be much less than 50 per cent of the cost of the road.

If grants fund more than the collective benefits, they can create problems (Slack 2010, 2015). In particular, grants can distort local decision making by lowering the price of some services, and often require municipalities to spend the funds they receive according to the guidelines of senior governments and not according to their own interests.[33] They often require matching funds on the part of the recipient municipality, and some municipalities do not have the capacity to match funds.[34] Funding from senior governments can lead to inefficient local revenue decisions. In particular, there may be little incentive to use proper pricing policies for services where grants cover a large proportion of capital costs. For this reason, infrastructure grants, where they are given, should require local governments to implement efficient pricing and taxation policies (Boadway and Kitchen 2014). Historically, transfers have also removed the incentive to set up carefully thought-out asset management and asset cost recovery programs, but this is changing in many parts of the country.[35]

Transfers reduce accountability. When the level of government making spending decisions (cities, for example) is not the same as the level of government that raises the revenues to pay for them (a senior level of government), accountability is blurred. There is also little incentive to be efficient when someone else is responsible for funding. In terms of linking expenditures and revenues, federal grants can be justified

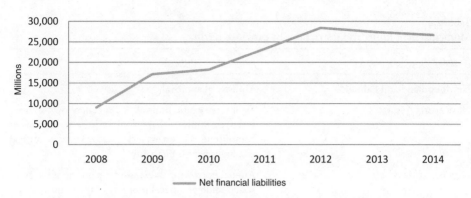

Figure 2.2   Net financial liabilities, municipalities, Canada, 2008–2014
Source: Statistics Canada, CANSIM table 385-0037

only if the benefits from the resulting expenditures are at least partially enjoyed by Canadians across the country (a point discussed earlier).
Finally, grants are rarely a stable and predictable source of revenues. If
capital grants are unexpectedly reduced, local governments have to borrow or increase taxes or delay infrastructure investment.

Borrowing

For infrastructure projects that benefit future residents, fairness, efficiency, and accountability are enhanced if the projects are financed by
borrowing. Annual interest charges and repayment of the borrowed
funds should be paid from local tax revenues (for capital assets that benefit the municipality in general but for which specific beneficiaries cannot be identified) and user fees (for capital assets that benefit specific
users) imposed on future beneficiaries (Kitchen and Tassonyi 2012). Examples of capital expenditures for which borrowing is appropriate include fire and police infrastructure, recreational facilities, libraries,
roads and streets, public transit, solid waste facilities, and water and
sewer systems (these do not include growth-related capital infrastructure, which, as was suggested above, should be financed from development charges).[36]

   Figure 2.2 shows the extent of municipal borrowing in Canada from
2008 to 2014.[37] Net financial liabilities (financial liabilities minus financial assets) show a steady increase for most of the period but then
begin to decline starting after 2012.

Table 2.4
Municipal debt limits and restrictions by province/territory

Province	Borrowing restrictions
Newfoundland and Labrador	Ministerial approval
Nova Scotia	Debt service ratio limit of 30 per cent of own-source revenues. Ministerial approval for lease agreements or commitments in excess of $100,000; $500,000 for Halifax Regional Municipality
New Brunswick	Annual borrowing in excess of 2 per cent of the assessed value of the real property of the municipality.
Quebec	Ministerial approval
Ontario (excluding the City of Toronto)	Debt service limit of 25 per cent of own-source revenue adjusted by debt service payments to other governments; City of Toronto sets own policy.
Manitoba	Total debt, maximum 7 per cent of municipal assessment, annual debt service not to exceed 20 per cent of annual revenue – guideline set by Manitoba Municipal Board
Saskatchewan	Established by Saskatchewan Municipal Board upon application
Alberta	Cities of Edmonton, Calgary, Medicine Hat, and R.M. of Wood Buffalo: debt limit of 2.0 times of total revenue excluding capital transfers; debt service limit of 35 per cent of revenue; debt limit of 1.5 times of total revenue excluding capital transfers; debt service limit of 25 per cent of revenue.
British Columbia	City of Vancouver: aggregate debt not to exceed 20 per cent of assessed value based on average assessment of previous two years; own policy limit of 10 per cent of operating expenditures. Debt service limit of 25 per cent of consolidated reoccurring own-source revenues and municipalities "whose economies are not well-diversified may face a lower limit," administered by the Municipal Finance Authority of BC.
Yukon	Three per cent of the current assessed value of all property.
Northwest Territories	Debt service not to exceed 25 per cent of own-purpose revenues
Nunavut	Ministerial regulation (federal)

Source: Based on Tassonyi and Conger (2015).

Municipalities in Canada are restricted in terms of how much they can borrow by provincial/territorial governments. Table 2.4 summarizes the rules in each province/territory. In most provinces, a formula-based approach is used; in others, restrictions are based on an approval process. Notwithstanding provincial restrictions on borrowing, Tassonyi and Conger (2015) suggest that Canadian municipalities have considerable unrealized borrowing capacity. Using data for 2013, table 2.5 estimates aggregate municipal borrowing capacity for municipalities in three provinces – Alberta, British Columbia, and Ontario – based on provincial guidelines. Column 3 shows that the percentage share of net debt charges in net revenue is well below provincial guidelines in each province and is much lower for Ontario municipalities, on average, than for municipalities in BC or those municipalities in Alberta that have more generous borrowing limits. Column 5 provides an estimate of the unused borrowing capacity in each province, calculated as the difference between how much municipalities are permitted to borrow (the regulated percentage of net revenues allowable for debt service) and how much they actually borrow (measured by their actual net debt charges). Overall, the table suggests there is capacity to increase levels of municipal borrowing in all three provinces.[38]

Efforts have been made in different provinces to encourage municipal borrowing by lowering the cost through pooling municipal debt. Municipal finance authorities have been established in most provinces (such as the Municipal Finance Authority of British Columbia, the Municipal Capital Borrowing Board in New Brunswick, Nova Scotia Municipal Finance Corporation, and the Newfoundland and Labrador Municipal Financing Corporation).[39] In Ontario, Infrastructure Ontario (IO), a crown corporation with a mandate to manage large infrastructure projects, operates like an infrastructure bank. It offers short-term and long-term loans for eligible public-sector infrastructure projects at affordable rates and provides access to capital market financing without fees or commissions.

Municipal financing authorities are able to gain greater access to national and international capital markets and to benefit from higher credit ratings. The credit risk of all local governments combined is almost always less than that for each individual local government. Pooling local government debt reduces borrowing costs both by reducing the cost of capital and by lowering the administration costs to issue debt. A municipal finance authority substitutes one contract with an underwriter for separate contracts between each borrower and debt

Table 2.5
Municipal borrowing capacity in Alberta, British Columbia, and Ontario

	Net debt charges ($millions)	Net revenues ($millions)	Net debt charges/ net revenue (%)	Maximum permissible debt service – 30%/25% of net revenues ($millions)	Aggregate municipal borrowing capacity ($millions)
	(1)	(2)	(3) = (1/2)	(4)	(5) = (4)−(1)
Alberta – higher limit	1,189	7,026	16.9	2,108	918
Alberta – municipalities	201	4,927	4.1	1,357	1,156
Alberta – Total	1,391	11,952	11.6	3,465	2,074
British Columbia	1,216	7,086	17.2	1,772	1,216
Ontario	1,983	30,969	6.4	7,742	5,760

Source: Based on Tassonyi and Conger (2015). Authors' calculations are based on provincial sources of municipal statistics using provincial definitions of appropriate debt charges and revenue.

issuer. It should be able to economize on transactions costs because it issues debentures more frequently than most individual municipal borrowers and it operates in a volatile capital market that is subject to a large amount of uncertainty. It can exercise a greater degree of flexibility over issue terms and costs to municipal clients. The federal government has also made a commitment to introduce a Canadian infrastructure bank to pass on its lower borrowing rates to municipalities (for details, see Siemiatycki 2016).

Reserves and Reserve Funds

Financing capital projects with reserves (funds that are set aside in a separate fund for capital spending) is essentially the reverse of financing through borrowing. In place of borrowing to finance capital expenditures and repaying this debt in the future, reserves or reserve funds reverse that timetable.[40] Another way of thinking about the use of the reserves in contrast to using debt is to think in terms of the contrast between a debit card that reduces savings and a credit card that creates indebtedness (liabilities). A portion of current revenue is set aside annually in a special account(s) and allowed to accumulate until it is eventually withdrawn and used to finance or partially finance a specific capital project or projects. These reserves, while they are accumulating, are deposited in interest-earning accounts. Capital reserves are created for future acquisitions. Most cities have moved towards greater reliance on reserves for replacing assets such as buildings, facilities, vehicles, and equipment, as is evident from the share of these funds in total sources of capital finance (see table 2.2). Nevertheless, the use of reserves breaks the link between expenditures and revenues over time, depending on the method of calculation.

FINAL COMMENTS

Municipalities across Canada have welcomed recent announcements by the federal government that it will increase its investment in municipal infrastructure. This funding is surely needed to maintain existing infrastructure in a state of good repair as well as to invest in new infrastructure. Although some federal funding can be justified on the grounds of externalities and national interest, there are pitfalls in municipalities relying too heavily on these transfers. They are rarely stable and predictable – the next government may have different ideas about federal transfers for municipal infrastructure, for example. Transfers do not encourage municipalities to be efficient or price services correctly, and they reduce accountability. Those making decisions about how to spend the money and are not the same as those making decisions about how to raise it.

A more Wicksellian approach to paying for municipal infrastructure would require better use of user fees. Although the application of user fees by municipalities has increased, especially for water and wastewater, as we look across the country we see very few cases of municipalities pricing roads and bridges, and, where user fees are levied, municipalities generally do not use zone pricing or peak-time pricing that would reflect marginal cost. Parking is rarely priced correctly. Yet, advances in technology have made it much easier for cities to impose road tolls, transit fares, and parking charges. In Singapore, for example, in-vehicle units affixed to car windshields allow drivers on toll roads to be charged according to location and time of day. In San Francisco, new technology permits the use of marginal-cost pricing for parking: the city uses smart meters that allow it to charge variable rates, record parking use and duration through sensors, and transmit the data to a central collection system.

The underlying problem with adopting a more Wicksellian approach to infrastructure funding is that political leaders do not want to tell users that they should pay for what they receive or that redistribution through setting the wrong prices for local public services is a bad idea. Moreover, when governments establish an inefficient pricing scheme, it is very difficult to change it. Going back to the example of lower transit fares for seniors, it would be difficult to remove that subsidy because the losers (seniors) will protest and the winners (everyone else) are unlikely to notice any gains. Nevertheless, if local governments are to adopt better user fees, someone has to persuade people that it is a good idea.

NOTES

The authors would like to thank Richard Bird, Harry Kitchen, Mel McMillan, and the participants at the "Financing Infrastructure: Who Should Pay?" conference held in October 2016 for helpful comments on an earlier draft. Any errors or omissions are the responsibility of the authors.

 1 As an example, see Oliver Moore, Oliver Sachgou Les Perreaux, and Gary Mason, "Canadian Cities Caught between Crumbling Infrastructure and Growing Calls for Transit," in *Globe and Mail*, 9 June 2015.

2 Since 2002, the federal government has provided about $45 billion in municipal infrastructure grants. See table 2.3 for more details.

3 In 2012, with the exception of international crossings, Canada had only eight tolled bridges, and less than 0.25 per cent of paved roads were tolled (Bazel and Mintz 2014).

4 This percentage has been steadily declining from almost 68 per cent in 2009.

5 The term Wicksellian connection was used by Breton (1996) in honour of the Swedish economist Knut Wicksell, who first set out this argument in 1896. For more on its application to financing local public services, see Bird and Slack (2014) and Slack and Bird (2015).

6 Another perspective suggests that the absence of pricing will lead to underinvestment in infrastructure because, when infrastructure is paid for out of taxes, there is a tendency to want to ease the burden on taxpayers. This underinvestment results in deferred maintenance and construction (Bazel and Mintz 2015).

7 A local sales tax or personal income tax could also play a role in paying for services with public-good characteristics (see Kitchen and Slack 2016).

8 Another way to internalize externalities would be to provide the service at a metropolitan or regional level or have it provided by a provincial government.

9 This differentiation has been particularly problematic since 2009, when municipalities moved to accrual accounting as the basis for financial reporting. This move was accomplished with significant effort, difficulty, and controversy. Municipal budgeting and rate decisions for taxes and fees still reflect rules based on the modified accrual and fund accounting concepts. On balance, the introduction of the accrual framework is a positive development but the gaps created in published and retrievable data suggest a need for a stronger effort by both provinces and municipalities to provide information that can be readily understood. For more on cash versus accrual accounting, see Dachis and Robson (2015), Boothe (2007), and Dahlby and Smart (2015).

10 On the operating side (not shown in table 2.2), approximately $9.1 billion was collected in user fees and service charges by Ontario municipalities in 2014 – 21.5 per cent was used to finance transportation operations and capital, of which nearly 90 per cent went to transit; 53.9 per cent was used to fund environmental services, split almost equally between water and wastewater; and 7.1 per cent was spent on recreation. These estimates are based on the authors' calculations from information in On-

tario Ministry of Municipal Affairs, Financial Information Returns (Schedule 10).

11 See, for example, the classic work by Bird (1976) on charging for public services.

12 The discussion of user fees in this paper is not meant to be exhaustive. For example, user fees are also used by libraries, recreation centres, and other facilities. See Kitchen and Tassonyi (2012) for a discussion of some of these other user fees.

13 Two methods are generally used to calculate the cost of using an asset and to generate revenue to fund its replacement. The depreciation method (using the straight-line method or reducing-balance method) recognizes the reduction in the value of the asset through wear and tear and aging. The cost of a tangible capital asset with a limited life less any residual value is amortized over the asset's useful life. The second method is the sinking fund method, whereby the municipality estimates the future value of the asset at the time of replacement, using an appropriate rate of inflation, and calculates the appropriate annual contribution, including an allowance for growth with interest. This annual contribution forms a part of the annual estimate of necessary revenues. For a more detailed description of lifecycle costing, see Watson and Associates and Dillon Consulting (2012, 4.1–4.3).

14 In Ontario, Mississauga, Waterloo, and Richmond Hill also levy stormwater levies.

15 Historically, funding the stormwater program was based on development charges and property taxes. Since Mississauga is largely built out (which means development charge revenues are declining) and because the costs associated with the operation, maintenance, or replacement of existing infrastructure cannot be covered by development charges, the city needed to find other ways to pay for stormwater infrastructure.

16 One of the downsides of charging for waste collection is littering and illegal dumping, but these problems have largely been controlled in jurisdictions using pricing (Dewees 2002).

17 Furthermore, in some property tax systems, the assessment of land used for parking receives special treatment as either excess land or in the tax treatment of parking lots. See Bird, Slack, and Tassonyi (2012).

18 The parking tax is paid on the sale of a parking right and is calculated on the purchase price of parking rights with the Translink service region. It includes parking rights sold by the hour, month, year, or any other basis. See http://www.translink.ca/en/About-Us/Taxes/Parking-Tax/About-the-Parking-Tax.aspx.

19 In Montreal, a parking lot tax is levied on indoor and outdoor parking spots located in non-residential buildings. Rates apply to the taxable area of the parking lots and vary by location and whether the parking spot is indoors or outdoors. See http://ville.montreal.qc.ca/portal/page?_pageid=44,57217573&_dad=portal&_schema=PORTAL.

20 See Kitchen and Lindsey (2013) for a more detailed discussion of parking practices and changes that could be made to improve them.

21 HOT lanes may have become more politically feasible in the Greater Toronto and Hamilton Area because of general public acceptance of the temporary implementation of HOV (high-occupancy vehicle) lanes during the Pan Am Games. During the Pan Am Games, vehicles travelling with three or more passengers were permitted to access the HOV lanes for a one-month period. For three weeks in August, vehicles travelling with two or more passengers could access the HOV lanes. Electric and hybrid vehicles could also access HOV lanes regardless of the number of passengers. Under the pilot HOT scheme, drivers can apply for HOT lane permits that cost $180 for a three-month period.

22 Road pricing charges tend to be most effective if they are applied at a metropolitan or regional scale where there is a greater likelihood of managing inter-municipal traffic and a greater opportunity to minimize distortions that often arise from taxes or charges that are restricted to smaller geographic areas.

23 Special assessments are included under total property taxes dedicated to capital finance in table 2.2.

24 A sensible approach and one that cities tend to follow is to split the cost of improvements that benefit an abutting property and the public at large by charging the bordering properties, for example, 40–60 per cent of the total construction costs, with the municipality raising the balance. The challenge, of course, is to match the share assigned to abutting properties with the marginal benefit to those properties (Kitchen and Tassonyi 2012).

25 Unlike special assessments, TIFs capture both the presumed increases in land values arising from a public investment in infrastructure and value changes resulting from regulatory changes.

26 TIFs in the US have generated a fair amount of criticism. Although originally intended for "blighted" areas in urban cores where development would not take place "but for" the incentive, the requirement that the area be "blighted" has often been ignored. More recently, TIFs have been used in more affluent neighbourhoods and open spaces (including farmlands) where there is greater potential for property value increases and

higher tax revenues (Youngman 2011). The "but for" test has also been compromised because many developments would have occurred anyway (Youngman 2011). Finally, TIFs target funds to a designated area and this targeting may be at the expense of areas on the periphery of the TIF district or at the expense of overall municipal growth.

27 The Province of Ontario passed TIF legislation in 2006 but never enacted regulations.

28 TIEGs are often used to provide incentives for brownfield developments. Of the forty-four Ontario municipalities that have CIPS, 93 per cent are using tax increment equivalent grants and 77 per cent are using tax assistance measures (Ministry of Municipal Affairs and Housing 2010). In 2015, $840 million was spent on grants, loans, and tax assistance under this legislation. There are commitments for $33 million in 2016 and total commitments to 2020 and beyond of $356 million (Schedule 79 of the Financial Information Returns).

29 "Secured" means that there is an agreement that the applicant will provide the funds at a future date, generally at the time of application for a building permit.

30 The federal gas tax transfer was originally a tax-sharing scheme calculated on the basis of 1.5 cents per litre in 2005 and increasing to 5 cents per litre by 2009–10. In 2013, it was converted to an annual fund of $2 billion indexed at 2 per cent per year.

31 Infrastructure that improves quality of life is said to include, for example, parks and recreational facilities, and water and sewage treatment facilities. Infrastructure that is productivity enhancing includes roads, bridges, transit, and educational facilities (Dahlby and Jackson 2015).

32 Dahlby and Jackson (2015) provide two other justifications for federal infrastructure transfers – when fiscal stimulus is needed during an economic recession, such measures are more effectively instituted at the federal level and spending on public infrastructure is a useful fiscal instrument. Furthermore, federal infrastructure investment is justified where it fulfills international trade or environmental agreements.

33 For a time, the federal government required that all projects over $100 million go through a screening process for suitability for public–private partnerships administered by P3 Canada (a federal agency). The tying of grant financing to the use of public–private partnerships, which is no longer in effect, was controversial (Conger and Tassonyi 2016). This chapter does not discuss the use of PPPs to finance infrastructure; see Matti Siemiatycki's chapter in this volume for more on this topic.

34 Of course, inter-municipal (and interpersonal) distributive adjustments

should be part of a benefit-based financing system (Bird and Slack, 2014). A provincial–municipal equalization transfer system, for example, would presumably address insufficient fiscal capacity (or higher expenditure needs) for some local governments. In Canada, provincial–municipal equalization transfers can be found in seven provinces.

35 The publication of detailed asset management plans has become part of the requirements that municipalities must meet to obtain provincial conditional capital transfers in some provinces. Asset management considers how to finance a facility's costs over the entire lifecycle of maintenance, rehabilitation, and replacement (Elgie et al. 2016). Asset management planning includes accounting for costs and depreciation, financing of acquisitions, and maintaining a state of good repair. See Watson and Associates (2016) and Ontario Ministry of Infrastructure (2016).

36 Monies in development charge reserve funds can be used to fund the growth-related portion of the debt service for projects that have been debenture financed. Large projects often serve both existing and growth communities.

37 Because Statistics Canada moved from the Financial Management System (FMS) to Government Finance Statistics (GFS) in 2008, comparable data are not provided before that year. The increase in net financial liabilities from 2008 onward may reflect the post-2008 recession and federal stimulus transfers that required municipalities to match federal (and provincial) funds for infrastructure.

38 While limits differ by province, a systematic examination of the rationale for these limits other than being rooted in history and any potential discernible impact on borrowing levels, does not exist. See Hanniman (2015) for a recent re-examination of municipal credit conditions and Bird and Tassonyi (2001) for a review of the history of these rules.

39 In some provinces, such as Nova Scotia and New Brunswick, all municipalities have to borrow through the provincial authority. In other provinces, larger cities are not required to borrow through the provincial authority. For example, the cities of Winnipeg, Regina, Saskatoon, Edmonton, Calgary, and Vancouver issue their own debt rather than using the provincial agencies.

40 Reserves (budgetary appropriations) stem from an annual decision, whereas reserve funds are formally created by bylaw and work as savings accounts.

3

Paying for Water in Ontario's Cities: Where Have We Come from and Where Should We Go?

HARRY KITCHEN

For much of the 1900s, especially the period prior to the 1990s, a city's water pricing structure was seldom deemed to be an important public policy issue. Water was generally viewed as being plentiful, the provincial government doled out grants to cover up to 85 per cent of water and sewer infrastructure costs, capital costs were not amortized over the life of the infrastructure, asset management programs were basically non-existent, and water rates or pricing structures were generally set without consideration for efficiency criteria and conservation goals.

Since 1990, however, a number of changes have emerged in water pricing. Water, for the most part, is now treated as a relatively scarce good; meters are in place almost everywhere; full-cost recovery is widespread, although there is considerable discrepancy about what full-cost recovery means; ongoing annual provincial grants have largely disappeared; amortization of capital costs is now required; asset management programs are now mandatory although funding them adequately remains a budgetary challenge for some municipal authorities; and financing new and rehabilitated infrastructure has moved to the forefront as a policy concern.

Despite these advancements, there remains much to do. At the forefront, water is becoming an increasingly scarce resource. In some parts of the United States and many other countries, it has already become very scarce. Recognizing this, it is imperative that pricing structures be designed or redesigned, with efficiency criteria and conservation goals playing an important role. Increased attention must be directed to pricing of sewage and stormwater runoff. Infrastructure financing is a hot issue, especially given concerns over reducing the alleged infrastructure deficit gap. Concerns over the capacity of some municipalities or local utilities to adopt efficient pricing and be sustainable brings out the need to reconsider the way in which smaller and remote municipalities provide water and wastewater. Have we moved to the point where we need a provincial water regulator? These are some of the issues discussed in this chapter. The chapter is organized in the following way. The first section comments on where we have come from; the second part considers where we should go; the final section provides a summary and offers some observations on the future.

WHERE HAVE WE COME FROM?

It could be argued that the first comprehensive report on water pricing and water sustainability in Ontario was published in 1990 (Fortin and Mitchell). This report argued that municipalities must raise the price of water to reflect its true cost; they must charge for water according to volume consumed; revenues received from water must be reserved and spent only for operating and maintaining water and sewage systems; and senior governments must commit or arrange for special funding for catch-up where municipalities are unable to do so by themselves. Much has happened in the water and wastewater field since then, most notably the events surrounding and responding to the Walkerton tragedy in 2000.[1]

In May 2000, the municipal water system in Walkerton was tainted with the dangerous 0157:H7 strain of E. coli bacteria, affecting more than 2,500 water consumers, of whom five died and many others endured long-term health effects. Because of that crisis, the Ontario government appointed Justice Dennis O'Connor to review the circumstances of the Walkerton tragedy, with a mandate to recommend measures to prevent a repetition (O'Connor 2002). The O'Connor Inquiry offered a number of constructive suggestions in its 121 recommendations. Among the most relevant was its advocacy for fiscal sustainability of water services by implementing full-cost accounting and full-cost pricing. That report also argued that water systems should take advantage of economies of scale by organizing on a regional, watershed, or commercial basis, where they could benefit from both operational and financial benefits, including overcoming the political reluctance to embrace full-cost pricing at the local level. Despite the fiscal constraints of the period, Justice O'Connor challenged the conventional and accepted view among municipalities, utilities, and local water consumers that water and wastewater services should continue to receive ongoing provincial subsidies.

The report also made it clear that full-cost pricing included more than just the cost of ongoing operations and repairs. It extended to all aspects of waterworks system sustainability, including depreciation, replacement, upgrading, expansion, and technological improvement. In an era before widespread public concerns about climate-change impacts and prudent water use, it employed conservation arguments. By taking a full-system approach, the inquiry recognized that high and wasteful consumption inevitably leads to demands for very expensive capital expansions and the costly consequences of unaddressed issues around system leakage (O'Connor 2002).

After five years of activity by the Ontario government, its agencies, and municipal water utilities in response to the O'Connor Inquiry, the government took stock of Ontario's water services. This culminated in the appointment of the Water Strategy Expert Panel that, in May of 2005, produced a report entitled *Watertight: The Case for Change in Ontario's Water and Waste Water Sector* (Swain, Lazar, and Pine 2005). Recommendations in this report mirrored many of those in the O'Connor report. Despite reasoned and well-researched findings, both the Swain and O'Connor recommendations met strong headwinds. While the recommendations called for increasing investments in water systems, and by implication, higher water rates to sustain those investments, there was strong, local resistance to increasing rates and provincial officials were sensitive to cost increases and public backlash. The result was, by and large, tight budgets that rationed investment in refurbishment and improvements to existing water, wastewater, and stormwater infrastructure.

These reports highlighted a number of issues that were relevant then and are still relevant today. Of particular note is progress on water, sewer, and stormwater pricing and changes in these pricing practices since 1990. Before we discuss this progress, readers are referred to figure 3.1, where a plea is made for improved data collection and analysis.

Water Pricing

Over the past two to three decades, water rates in Ontario have been characterized by two general structures: flat rates that do not vary with

Figure 3.1: An aside on data availability

Given the rising importance of water services in the twenty-first century, one might assume that the resources devoted to data collection and analysis by federal and provincial agencies and water-related associations would be sustained and expanded, and the outputs would progressively improve in quality, reliability, and usefulness. Unfortunately, that has not been the case.

Somewhat surprisingly, researchers and policy makers will find that the traditional source of survey and analysis on water and wastewater services in Canada, Environment Canada, discontinued publishing its work with the 2009 survey (reported in 2010 and 2011). For their part, the Ontario Ministry of the Environment and Climate Change or other provincial ministries and agencies (which routinely collect all manner of municipal data and plan documents) do not have publicly available information on comparative water rates, water consumption, and full-cost pricing. Given the considerable (and encouraging) efforts that have gone into ensuring that municipalities develop plans for both asset management and water system planning over the past fifteen years, it would appear logical to make public those results on a comparative basis (e.g., progress towards full-cost pricing, cataloguing of rate structures, expansion of water metering, reductions in water consumption and energy consumption, and so on).

In the absence of such information, one can only use samples from disparate municipal data sources and projections based on anecdotal evidence, supplemented with interviews and inquiries. While it makes comparison to past, more comprehensive, data sets less consistent and reliable, this approach may be sufficient for the time being. Furthermore, from this miscellaneous collection of material and information, it is apparent that the statistical pattern noted in the data from 1991 to 2009 has continued since 2009. As an example, the City of Peterborough was not metered in 2009 but is now metered. Actions such as this support the trends noted in this paper.

The issues addressed in this paper are important, and so are the data necessary to understand them. Federal and provincial governments are best positioned, both in vantage point and resources, to restore this important basis for making evidence-based policy decisions, especially with the federal government's renewed interest in investing in infrastructure and addressing climate-change impacts. Municipalities and utilities often complain about intrusion in their affairs by other orders of government and their agencies. In this area, a return of federal involvement should be encouraged and welcomed.

Source: This plea was also made in Fenn and Kitchen (2016).

consumption and a variety of volume-based charges. Regardless of the pricing structure and changes in their relative importance, however, it should be noted that municipalities in Ontario are no longer permitted to fund municipal water systems from the general property tax – funds must come from charges on users (LAC and Associates 2015, 3). Even though municipalities or utilities cannot overtly cross-subsidize, decisions about what constitutes full-cost recovery might have the effect of shifting some operating costs from the utility rates to the property tax base. This is unlike Quebec, however, where municipalities may overtly fund water and wastewater systems from the general property tax base. This practice is far from efficient and fair because there is no incentive for managing water in an efficient and conservation-oriented manner and it provides no incentive for municipalities to control leakage losses in potable water.

FLAT RATES

Flat rates are the simplest structures to understand and administer. Flat rates are fixed payments per billing period, unrelated to volume consumed but varying by customer class (residential vs commercial) and property type, such as the number and types of rooms, size of lot, the number of water-using fixtures, whether or not there is a swimming pool, and so on. For flat-rate charges, meters are not required because the water price is not related to consumption.

In municipalities where flat rates have been used over the past twenty-five years, average daily residential consumption per capita has been considerably higher than in municipalities where volume-based charges have been used (table 3.1). In fact, as reported in column 4 of table 3.1, the average daily residential consumption per capita under flat-rate systems exceeded volume-based consumption by something between 37 per cent and 133 per cent, depending on the year. Regardless of the rate structure, however, water consumption per household in most Canadian cities has declined over the past two decades, largely because of two initiatives: higher water rates and a variety of water-conservation initiatives.

Flat-rate charges have virtually disappeared in Ontario. In 1991, 18.6 per cent of the residential population with water systems was served by flat-rate pricing structures (column 2 of table 3.2). By 2009,[2] only 2.1 per cent of the residential population faced flat-rate charges, a considerable decline over the twenty-five-year period. Since then, this percentage has declined even further. A similar trend has emerged in other OECD countries (OECD 2010).

Table 3.1
Residential flat rate vs volume-based rate average daily flow (ADF), Ontario,
1991–2009

Year (1)	Flat ADF in litres per capita (2)	Volume ADF in litres per capita (3)	Percentage by which flat-rate use exceeds volume-based use (4)
1991	392	234	67.5
1994	412	230	79.1
1996	416	239	74.1
1999	428	254	68.5
2001	425	258	64.7
2004	573	246	132.9
2006	495	249	98.8
2009	302	221	36.7

Source: *Municipal Water and Wastewater Survey*, Environment Canada, Ottawa, selected years. Reported in the table called "Residential Flat versus Volumetric Rate Average Daily Water Use Per Capita."

VOLUME-BASED RATES

Volume-based rates link the amount paid for water to the amount of water consumed. They require the use of meters, which are now largely universal. These rates take a variety of forms including constant unit charges, decreasing block rates, increasing block rates, or some combination of these. As noted in column 7 of table 3.2, the use of volume-based charges and, hence, meters covered about 98 per cent of the residential population served by water utilities/departments in 2009, up from a little over 81 per cent in 1991.

Constant unit charges (CUCs) are by far the most common volume-based charge (column 3 of table 3.2). It served almost 53 per cent of the population in 1991, rising to more than 60 per cent through the remainder of the 1990s before falling to about 45 per cent in 2001 and then rebounding to almost 80 per cent by 2009.

Declining block rate (DBR) structures generally include a basic or fixed service charge per period combined with a volumetric charge that decreases in blocks (discrete steps) as the volume consumed increases (the more you use, the less you pay per unit). Typically, one or two initial blocks cover residential and light commercial water use, with subsequent blocks levied on heavy commercial and industrial uses. The fixed component of the charge often varies with the size of the service connection. Minimum charges that correspond to a minimum amount

Table 3.2
Residential water rate structure: percentage of population served by each rate structure,
Ontario, 1991–2009[1]

| Year (1) | Flat rate (2) | Volumetric rates | | | | Total volume (7) |
		CUC[2] (3)	DBR[3] (4)	IBR[4] (5)	Complex[5] (6)	
1991	18.6	52.7	23.3	4.1	1.0	81.4
1994	16.8	61.5	11.9	4.9	5.0	83.2
1996	15.8	62.8	11.2	5.1	5.0	84.2
1999	15.3	63.1	11.7	4.8	5.0	84.7
2001	12.6	45.6	1.2	39.0	1.5	87.4
2004	3.6	55.8	3.8	36.8	–	96.4
2006	2.6	51.8	9.8	35.8	–	97.4
2009	2.1	79.6	8.7	9.6	–	97.9

[1] Prior to 2009, municipalities that had more than one pricing scheme (for different water-distribution systems or different areas of the municipality) reported only the one that applied to the largest number of people. For 2009, all of the pricing schemes and their associated populations were reported. 2009 is the last year for which data were collected.
[2] CUC is constant unit charge.
[3] DBR is declining unit rate.
[4] IBR is increasing unit rate.
[5] Complex systems have decreased in popularity and are no longer reported as a separate category. They may combine two different DBRs (one for residential and one for commercial) onto one schedule or they may arise if sewer charges are calculated on the basis of block limits that differ from block limits used for the water-rate schedule.

Source: Municipal Water and Wastewater Survey, Environment Canada, Ottawa, selected years. Reported in the table called "Residential Population Served Water by Rate Type, by Province."

of water consumption in each billing period are common in systems of this kind.

DBRs were more common in the 1990s than they are now. Their use declined from servicing more than 20 per cent of the population in 1991 to serving less than 5 per cent in the early 2000s before rising to around 8 to 10 per cent by 2006 and 2009 (column 4 of table 3.2).

Increasing block rate (IBR) structures are the opposite of DBRs in that the more you use, the more you pay per unit. The first block for a given class of customer is generally designed to cover the normal water use of an average customer in that class. IBRs were not prominent in the 1990s, accounting for 5 per cent or less of all water systems (column 5 of table 3.2). In the early 2000s, their reported usage increased dramatically, ris-

ing to between 35 and 40 per cent of all systems. By 2009, their reported use had decreased to less than 10 per cent. It is not clear why this dramatic decline came about, but it may have been partially triggered by
a change in reporting methodology (see note to table 3.2).

Seasonal-rate systems and peak-load demand rates are used in some
municipalities. As well, municipalities often use variations or combi-
nations of the different pricing structures. Two-part pricing schemes,
for example, are fairly common in any pricing structure. They consist
of a fixed charge designed to cover meter reading, billing, customer accounting, and capital and maintenance costs of meters plus a constant
commodity charge applied to all consumption. Another variant is the
lifeline rate, which is an artificially reduced price for a minimum
amount of water that is deemed to be required for essential water consumption. It is introduced to assist low-income households. Lifeline
pricing is most common in cities with a fixed charge as all customers
must pay the fixed charge regardless of consumption. Other variants
include vintage rates, which distinguish between new and existing
customers, or seasonal or peak-demand rates to reflect increased cost
of delivery or a desire to reduce consumption during certain seasons
or times of the day. A few municipalities have combined components
of residential and commercial pricing systems into one schedule. For
example, some impose declining block rates to "subsidize" major employers that depend on high volumes of low-cost water; others impose progressively more expensive increasing block rates to promote
conservation or to reflect the marginal cost of infrastructure to meet
peak demands.

Sewer Pricing

For residential, small commercial and small industrial users, sewage collection and treatment expenses are almost always recovered through
surcharges on water bills, not on sewage discharge. This is largely for administrative simplicity. In most cities, the surcharge is a percentage of
the water bill but in some cities, it might be a fixed charge or a flat rate.

Large industrial and commercial users are metered in some cities. As
well, many of these cities have adopted sewer use bylaws limiting the
concentration of contaminants allowed in wastewater. Some bylaws
also have over-strength discharge fees with the fee based on the differential between the actual and permitted level of contamination (Elgie
et al., 2016).

Stormwater Pricing

Traditionally, stormwater infrastructure has been funded by property taxes and development charges. More recently, however, the impact of climate change (severe storms and flooding) has created a demand for more robust and resilient systems and increased funding for stormwater infrastructure (sewers, spillways, retention and detention ponds, etc.) and, where it exists, for separation of sanitary sewers from storm sewers. These developments have given rise to a desire by some municipalities to convert stormwater facilities to a utility model, supported by "user" charges.

The following two examples will serve to illustrate the type of change that is emerging in Ontario. The City of Kitchener's stormwater user rate is based on the contribution of stormwater runoff as calculated by the impervious surface area of the property. The city uses a 13-tiered flat fee rate schedule to calculate the rate for each property which is administered on monthly utility bills. The tiers are based on property type (residential, multi-residential, and non-residential) and impervious ("smallest" to "largest") or number of residential units. For example, the average single-dwelling homeowner is currently charged approximately $11.44/per month for stormwater management. The city also offers incentives to all ratepayers who demonstrate best practices for managing stormwater runoff.

In 2016, the City of Mississauga started funding stormwater management through a stormwater charge. The city previously funded this service through property taxes and reserves. Mississauga's stormwater charge is based on the amount of impervious area of a property. Residential properties are categorized into five tiers based on the size of their rooftop ("smallest" to "largest") as an indicator of total impervious area, with charges ranging from $50 to $170 per year. The charge for multi-residential and non-residential properties is determined by dividing the property's total impervious area by a single billing unit (267 m²) and then multiplying it by the stormwater rate ($100). To make it easy for property owners to determine their charge, the city created an online "stormwater charge estimator" where property owners can enter an address to determine what their charge might be.

Tracking Pricing Practices and Spending since 1990

There are a number of ways in which one might track the change in water/sewer prices and spending over time. Table 3.3 records the

Table 3.3
Residential price per cubic metre for water and sewers, Ontario, 1991–2009

Year	Constant unit charge[1]				First block prices[1]				Last block prices[1]			
	Mean	Med.	10th per.	90th per.	Mean	Med.	10th per.	90th per.	Mean	Med.	10th per.	90th per.
	$	$	$	$	$	$	$	$	$	$	$	$
1991	0.81	0.76	0.48	1.21	0.70	0.72	0.41	0.92	0.54	0.56	0.29	0.80
1994	0.92	0.87	0.62	1.39	0.85	0.92	0.40	1.00	0.66	0.65	0.36	1.11
1996	0.94	0.93	0.74	1.36	0.97	0.92	0.50	1.47	0.76	0.65	0.36	1.58
1999	0.98	0.98	0.68	1.32	0.98	0.93	.057	1.47	0.79	0.70	0.36	1.58
2001	1.17	1.17	0.82	1.49	1.16	1.18	0.90	1.47	1.22	1.22	0.90	1.58
2004	1.16	1.00	0.73	1.56	1.23	1.23	0.90	1.69	1.24	1.27	0.72	1.99
2006	1.35	1.25	0.85	1.98	1.28	1.42	0.91	1.42	1.24	1.47	0.67	1.47
2009	1.98	1.89	1.33	2.53	1.43	1.50	0.53	1.89	1.34	1.43	0.75	1.65

[1] All prices include the costs for both water and sewer services where available.

Notes: Mean is the average of all water and sewer operations. Med. is the median or mid-value for all water and sewer operations. 10th per. is the value at the tenth percentile. 90th per. is the value at the ninetieth percentile.

Source: Municipal Water and Wastewater Survey, Environment Canada, Ottawa, selected years. Reported in the table called "Residential Population Served Water by Rate Type, by Province."

Table 3.4
Average water rates for 20 cubic metres per month in selected Ontario cities, 2011–2015

Year	Ottawa Fixed water rate	Ottawa Variable cubic metre	Markham Fixed water rate	Markham Variable cubic metre	Hamilton[1] Fixed water rate	Hamilton[1] Variable cubic metre	London[2] Fixed water rate	London[2] Variable cubic metre	Toronto Fixed water rate	Toronto Variable cubic metre
	$	$	$	$	$	$	$	$	$	$
2011	2.63	2.8644	n.a.	2.2129	16.16	1.7127	12.24	3.0422	n.a.	2.2842
2012	2.73	3.038	n.a.	2.4164	16.84	1.7856	13.11	3.2701	n.a.	2.4897
2013	2.93	3.2507	n.a.	3.6277	17.56	1.86	14.03	3.515	n.a.	2.7137
2014	3.14	3.4785	n.a.	3.0649	17.64	1.96	38.01	2.54	n.a.	2.9579
2015	3.33	3.6868	n.a.	3.3154	18.25	2.05	42.11	2.72472	n.a.	3.195

Year	Peel Region (Mississauga, Brampton) Fixed water rate	Peel Region (Mississauga, Brampton) Variable cubic metre	Vaughan[3] Fixed water rate	Vaughan[3] Variable cubic metre	Thunder Bay Fixed water rate	Thunder Bay Variable cubic metre	Sarnia Fixed water rate	Sarnia Variable cubic metre	Windsor Fixed water rate	Windsor Variable cubic metre
	$	$	$	$	$	$	$	$	$	$
2011	n.a	1.52517	n.a.	2.4084	29.335	2.1105	67.77	0.4248	–	–
2012	n.a.	1.64987	n.a.	2.624	31.3	2.2523	67.77	0.4248	–	–
2013	n.a.	1.7577	n.a.	2.8347	33.51	2.4115	67.77	0.4248	–	–
2014	n.a.	1.64987	n.a.	3.0856	35.53	2.5568	71.23	0.4473	–	0.429
2015	n.a.	2.02817	n.a.	3.391	39.76	2.8595	72.96	0.4582	–	0.477

[1] Hamilton has a tiered rate. The rate in this table is a blended rate. For 2015, the rate on the first 10 cubic metres was $1.37 per cubic metre and on subsequent cubic metres it was $2.73.

[2] London has a tiered rate; however, the first 7 cubic metres per month are free – referred to as a lifeline rate.

[3] A minimum monthly charge of $16.

n.a. – fixed charges do not apply.

Source: City of Ottawa – Water and Wastewater Rate Review Study, LAC and Associates Consulting, Ottawa, October 2015, Annex 2.

monthly residential water rate per cubic metre for Ontario for the period from 1991 to 2009. Here, it is noted that the price per cubic metre more than doubled under almost all measures.

Table 3.4 considers more recent data (2011 to 2015) on water pricing for a handful of Ontario municipalities. Here, one may observe, prices vary widely. Some municipalities use only variable charges (Toronto, Mississauga, Brampton, Markham, and Vaughan). Some have both a fixed charge and a volumetric charge. Where fixed monthly charges are high – Sarnia for example – volumetric charges are low. London, as with some other cities, has a lifeline rate (first seven cubic metres per month are free) to assist low-income users.

Table 3.5 is another way in which one might compare residential spending on water. In particular, it records mean (average) and median monthly residential spending at specific consumption levels (10, 25, and 35 cubic metres) along with expenditures at the tenth and ninetieth percentiles for the same years. Like table 3.3, mean and median expenditures more than doubled over this period.

For commercial water rates (table 3.6), prices increased modestly for 10 cubic metres, more than doubled for 35 cubic metres, and in some cases tripled for 100 cubic metres. In every scenario, water rates increased and spending rose over the two decades – some might even say significantly.

This is not surprising because increased prices and spending have been driven by a number of factors, not the least of which is the higher cost of labour and materials, increased emphasis on improved treatment especially from large industrial consumers, greater monitoring and reporting requirements to meet tougher legislative requirements, and a reduced reliance on provincial grants for capital purposes, which has forced municipalities to carry a higher proportion of rehabilitation costs and to recover them through higher water rates.

Whether this increase in price is significant is a debatable question. To shed light on this, let's cast this pricing and spending pattern another way. Take the average monthly spending on water at each cell in table 3.5 and multiply it by 12 to obtain an estimate of yearly spending for 10, 25, and 35 cubic metres respectively. Next, take the yearly expenditures for each cubic measure as a percentage of after-tax economic family income. This is a definition of a family unit that is used by Statistics Canada. These percentages are reported in table 3.7 for three different consumption levels. Depending on the measure and the year, spending on water seldom exceeded 1 per cent of after-tax family in-

Table 3.5
Residential water prices for selected volumes of service in Ontario, 1991–2009

Year	10 cubic metres per month				25 cubic metres per month				35 cubic metres per month			
	Mean	Med.	10th per.	90th per.	Mean	Med.	10th per.	90th per.	Mean	Med.	10th per.	90th per.
	$	$	$	$	$	$	$	$	$	$	$	$
1991	11.92	12.20	6.53	15.80	23.82	23.33	14.40	34.00	31.91	30.93	20.60	46.60
1994	14.42	15.00	8.20	22.00	27.65	27.14	20.50	40.13	36.58	34.67	26.23	53.20
1996	15.18	16.00	8.00	20.00	29.04	30.00	20.00	40.00	38.51	39.00	28.00	51.00
1999	15.59	15.52	7.50	21.31	30.00	30.45	18.75	39.96	39.83	39.15	26.25	54.45
2001	18.97	19.27	10.03	23.74	34.52	38.63	20.46	42.16	45.19	50.80	28.64	56.91
2004	23.46	15.56	8.86	40.17	41.11	32.74	22.15	63.79	53.50	43.65	31.01	77.77
2006	23.28	14.91	10.58	62.13	43.07	35.75	26.46	74.90	56.55	50.44	37.04	83.41
2009	25.31	20.02	13.32	43.32	53.52	47.29	33.31	75.04	72.41	66.20	46.63	103.95

Notes: Mean is the average of all water operations. Med. is the mid-value for all water operations. 10th per. is the value at the tenth percentile. 90th per. is the value at the ninetieth percentile.

Source: Municipal Water and Wastewater Survey, Environment Canada, Ottawa, selected years. Reported in the table called "Residential Prices ($ per month) for Volume Based."

Table 3.6
Commercial water prices for selected volumes of service in Ontario, 1991–2009

Year	10 cubic metres per month				35 cubic metres per month				100 cubic metres per month			
	Mean	Med.	10th per.	90th per.	Mean	Med.	10th per.	90th per.	Mean	Med.	10th per.	90th per.
	$	$	$	$	$	$	$	$	$	$	$	$
1991	23	20	9	41	36	32	16	56	71	68	20	129
1994	26	24	10	44	40	38	17	61	82	84	24	138
1996	27	24	11	48	42	41	19	67	84	87	24	141
1999	29	26	13	49	45	43	20	74	91	90	28	149
2001	37	28	12	58	54	46	22	80	101	91	28	162
2004	38	28	10	63	58	50	22	97	110	101	28	207
2006	40	36	9	70	62	52	24	99	124	115	32	216
2009	26	20	13	42	74	66	47	105	200	189	133	263

Notes: Figures are rounded to the nearest dollar. Mean is the average of all water operations. Med. is the mid-value for all water operations. 10th per. is the value at the tenth percentile. 90th per. is the value at the ninetieth percentile.

Source: Municipal Water and Wastewater Survey, Environment Canada, Ottawa, selected years. Reported in the table called "Commercial Water Prices ($ per month) for Volume Based."

Table 3.7
Estimated total residential water payments per year as a percentage of after-tax economic family income in Ontario, 1991–2009[1]

Year	10 cubic metres per month				25 cubic metres per month				35 cubic metres per month			
	Mean	Med.	10th per.	90th per.	Mean	Med.	10th per.	90th per.	Mean	Med.	10th per.	90th per.
	%	%	%	%	%	%	%	%	%	%	%	%
1991	0.2	0.2	0.1	0.3	0.4	0.4	0.3	0.6	0.6	0.6	0.4	0.8
1994	0.3	0.3	0.1	0.4	0.5	0.5	0.4	0.6	0.7	0.6	0.5	1.0
1996	0.3	0.3	0.1	0.4	0.5	0.5	0.4	0.7	0.7	0.7	0.5	0.9
1999	0.3	0.3	0.1	0.3	0.5	0.5	0.3	0.6	0.6	0.6	0.4	0.9
2001	0.3	0.3	0.2	0.4	0.5	0.6	0.3	0.6	0.6	0.8	0.4	0.9
2004	0.4	0.2	0.1	0.6	0.6	0.5	0.3	1.0	0.8	0.7	0.5	1.2
2006	0.4	0.2	0.2	0.9	0.6	0.5	0.4	1.1	0.9	0.8	0.6	1.3
2009	0.4	0.3	0.2	0.6	0.8	0.7	0.5	1.1	1.1	1.0	0.7	1.5

[1] Total yearly residential payments obtained by multiplying average monthly payments from table 3.5 by 12 months and taking this total as a percentage of after-tax economic family income.

Source: Same as table 3.5 with after-tax income data from Statistics Canada, CANSIM table 202-0802.

come. More specifically, it only exceeded 1 per cent for the 90th decile of users at 25 and 35 cubic metres and only since 2004. And it amounted to 1 per cent of after-tax family income for the mean and median user at 35 cubic metres per month. In none of these cases does spending on water appear to have reached critical levels when it comes to affordability. For those where it might be a problem, and as mentioned earlier, there are income relief programs that may be accessed.

WHERE SHOULD WE GO?

Historically, pricing and managing water and sewer systems have been viewed as an engineering issue rather than an economic issue. Local politicians and administrators, reluctant to use water prices to promote efficiency and conservation, have relied on technological improvements and non-price demand management tools such as restrictions on use – for example, forbidding lawn watering during periods of low rainfall or limiting residential construction until water/sewer infrastructure capacity expands. These may be useful but they are not as effective as properly set prices and pricing structures in generating efficient outcomes and proper levels of infrastructure investment. Fortunately, improvements have recently been made in the way in which prices are structured. Through the Public Sector Accounting Board (PSAB) requirements and asset management programs,[3] capital costs are recorded and recovered through these prices. There remain, however, a number of issues around costs to be recovered, pricing structures and efficiency, infrastructure financing, production and delivery, and the possibility of regulating water rates. These are discussed next.

Full-Cost Pricing

While there is a growing consensus on the merit of imposing "full-cost pricing" for water and wastewater services, there is no consensus on what is meant by full-cost pricing and what it should include. Many practitioners argue that full-cost pricing is achieved if revenues from water and wastewater systems cover all production and maintenance costs. Most medium-sized and large municipalities in Ontario are doing this now, although some municipalities are phasing in full-cost recovery programs over a ten- to fifteen-year period. Others, mainly the smaller systems, are concerned that they may not be able to achieve full-cost recovery because of the impact of water rates on their customer's ability to pay (Watson and Associates with Dillon, 2012).

Others take a more expansive view of the costs of a water system, in part as a response to contemporary utility accounting practices. They recognize that replacement costs may be greater than anticipated, due to more demanding technical specifications, greater system resilience to deal with climate change, and enhanced environmental provisions, such as those separating stormwater runoff from sanitary sewers. These calculations of "full-cost" add full valuation of water-related assets and liabilities, the use of depreciation and provision for replacement, and life-cycle capital planning.

Still others argue that the current approach ignores additional costs that should be included. They suggest that the definition of annual operating and capital costs is too narrow, because it ignores the opportunity cost of water withdrawn from the natural environment including the commercial exploitation of aquifers such as is being witnessed in the controversy with Nestlé's bottled-water plant in Aberfoyle, Ontario, and its potential impact on regional wells; the opportunity cost of land holdings; the opportunity cost of invested capital; and the harm caused by pollution (Renzetti 2009). Here, it must be noted, these costs are significant (Dupont, Renzetti, et al. 2013).

From an economics perspective, opportunity costs are a complete and accurate way of measuring all costs. They capture the return that would be generated if the resources were put into their next best alternative. One study on one municipality in Ontario in the late 1990s highlighted the magnitude of these costs. The study concluded that the wholesale price for water would have to increase by at least 15 per cent and possibly by as much as 45 per cent if all of these costs were to be recovered (Renzetti and Kushner 2001). On this basis, one may infer that most Ontario municipalities are far from full-cost pricing if all financial and social costs are to be included (Environment Canada 2011, 14). We are, however, closer to full-cost pricing than we were in 1990 largely because of the advances in accounting rules[4] and provincially mandated asset management programs. As well, the elimination of the provincial capital grant program in 1992[5] forced municipalities to raise their prices annually to recover an annualized portion of capital costs.

Much of the opposition to the implementation of full-cost pricing has come, in part, from a desire to retain existing rate structures to preserve and possibly increase revenues. Many system operators and municipal officials have argued that moving to efficiency-based prices will discourage consumption, thereby reducing total revenues, making it difficult to cover costs. In response, there are at least two comments that should be made. First, it is suggested that the existing plant capacity may be too big and there is evidence that some municipalities, in the past, overbuilt largely because of inefficient prices (Strategic Alternatives et al. 2001, 39; Swain, Lazar, and Pine 2005, 53–4). Second, because the demand for water is inelastic (Kitchen 2007, table 3.3), an increase in price will be accompanied by a much smaller percentage reduction in quantity, leading to an overall increase in total revenue, not a decrease.

Pricing Structures

In principle, water and sewer rates should be set so that the charge per litre equals the extra cost of supplying and treating the last unit; that is, price should equal marginal cost (OECD 2010; Kitchen and Tassonyi, 2012). The efficiency advantages of marginal-cost pricing are well documented, but municipalities seldom implement marginal-cost pricing as usually proposed by economists. One study on seventy-seven water utilities in Ontario (Renzetti 1999) from a few years ago estimated that the marginal cost of supplying water exceeded the price for water in every municipality studied. Specifically, the average price for residential customers was calculated to be $0.32 per cubic metre while the estimated marginal cost was $0.87 per cubic metre. By comparison, the average price for the non-residential sector was $0.734 per cubic metre and the estimated marginal cost was $1.492 per cubic metre. At the same time, the average marginal cost of sewage treatment was $0.521 per cubic metre while the average price was $0.128 per cubic metre. Another study estimated that Ontario municipalities recovered only 64 per cent of the full costs of water and wastewater services from water revenues. This shortfall, the study argued, led to "rust-out, less reliable service, more leaks, increasing risk to public health and convenience, environmental damage and demand for subsidies" (Swain, Lazar, and Pine 2005, 53). Failure to include all costs leads to overconsumption, overinvestment, and larger facilities (and obviously more costs) than would exist if more efficient pricing practices were in place (Clayton 2014).

Not only have Canadian studies found that the price level affects demand (Kitchen 2007 and 2010), there is some evidence suggesting that households respond to the structure of water prices as well. For example, Reynaud, Renzetti, and Villeneuve (2005) found that the sensitivity of Canadian residential water demand to a 1 per cent increase in price differed according to the pricing scheme used. For flat rates, demand increased by .02 per cent; for constant, decreasing and increasing block rates, demand decreased by 0.16 per cent, 0.10 per cent, and 0.25 per cent respectively. An earlier study on the manufacturing sector concluded that firms also respond to water prices; specifically, water intake fell by 0.8 per cent for each 1 per cent increase in price (Dupont and Renzetti 2001).

VOLUMETRIC WATER PRICING STRUCTURES
AND EFFICIENCY EFFECTS

The range of water pricing structures was outlined earlier. Each has its own set of incentives or disincentives, as discussed below, in meeting efficiency objectives.[6] A *constant unit charge*, which is a prominent structure, is an efficient pricing policy only if the marginal cost of water is constant (in which case, the average cost will be constant). We know, however, that the marginal cost is not constant – it either rises or falls with quantity consumed. Since price must equal marginal cost for efficient use, this pricing structure is inefficient and is not effective in encouraging water conservation.

A *declining block rate* (DBR) is efficient if the marginal cost of water provision is falling, such as may exist if economies of scale are present when servicing large-volume customers. Critics argue, however, that DBRs do not promote water conservation since the price of water declines as more water is used, and hence there may be little incentive to economize on water use.

An *increasing block rate* may be appropriate for residential customers who as a customer class are the main cause of peak demand, and for industrial customers if limitations on the availability of water justify shifting the cost burden to the largest users. Here, it is these users that have the largest impact on water system planning and sizing since systems are built to meet the largest demands. Of particular interest to policy makers interested in promoting conservation, price differences from block to block could be set in a way that would give the customer a clear and strong incentive to conserve water.

A *humpback block rate* system of water charges combines increasing and decreasing block rates to produce the rate structure, shaped like an inverted "U." Under this approach, the municipality applies its highest rate to the consumption block that captures the peak seasonal demand of residential customers. The intention is to encourage water conservation by residential customers by encompassing residential use within increasing block rates while offering large industrial users block rates that decline as use increases and thereby benefit from the economies of scale associated with providing water to customers of this kind.

This structure is sometimes used in municipalities that are promoting economic development. Unlike the 1990s, when manufacturing had just begun its decline in Ontario, many municipalities today are eager to leverage any competitive advantage that they may enjoy, with a view to retaining and attracting industries and jobs. Despite some implicit cross-subsidization among classes of users, the ready availability of clean water at a reasonable price can be a distinct advantage in sectors like food processing or beverage manufacturing. For example, the City of London is quite explicit in characterizing a lower block rate for major users as being for "economic development" purposes (Canadian Municipal Water Consortium 2015, 19).

A *seasonal-rate or time-of-day* system applies a high volumetric rate during the peak water-demand season or time of day and a lower rate during the remainder of the year or day. By targeting peak demand, higher rates can promote water conservation. The economic rationale for a peak-demand system is that in order to meet this demand, the municipality must maintain supply facilities that are larger than they need to be to meet demand for most of the year or most of the day. A peak charge recovers the extra costs of this excess capacity directly from the component of demand that causes those costs.

An *excess-use rate* is a high volumetric rate that applies to all consumption during the peak water-consumption season in excess of a threshold amount. The amount is set equal to the average off-peak-season consumption or a modest multiple of this consumption – for example, 1.3 times winter consumption. The municipality applies a base charge to all of a customer's off-peak-season consumption and to the portion of peak-season consumption that is below the threshold.

SEWER PRICING

Sewage charges for residential users are based on water consumed, not sewage discharged. This is also true for small commercial and industrial users. In a few cities, however, large industrial and commercial users[7] are metered with rates or prices varying by volume of discharge but often not by quality. In addition, some larger cities have sewer by-laws that limit the concentration of contaminants entering the sewer system. If actual levels of contamination exceed the permitted limit, over-strength fees or charges based on the difference between the actual level of concentration and the permitted limit come into effect with the fee varying by the differential. These additional fees are intended to cover the extra treatment costs (Elgie et al. 2016) or to provide an incentive for users to treat their own sewage or to minimize its impact on municipal treatment systems.

In practice, pricing schemes for sewage collection and treatment are far from optimal. Charges prorated on the basis of the water bill are inefficient because they fail to reflect accurately the marginal cost of sewage disposal. The assumption that residential water consumption is directly and positively correlated with sewage generation is often inaccurate. For example, a large component of water consumption may be attributed to lawn sprinkling, car washing, swimming pools, and many other household uses, almost all of which are unrelated to sewage generation; that is, the runoff generally goes into the stormwater system, not the sanitary system, unless the two sewers are combined, which is common in older, more densified areas of many cities.

Like the underpricing of water, the underpricing of sewage (collection and treatment) is allocatively inefficient because there is no incentive to restrict use. Underpricing has also led to investment in sewage treatment facilities that are larger than they would be under a more efficient pricing policy (Renzetti 1999). One empirical study on pricing of sewage by Norwegian local governments (Borge and Rattso 2003) showed that sound user-charge financing of sewer services significantly reduced the cost of providing sewer services. Finally, it has been observed that underpricing of both water supply and sewage treatment has discouraged the development of alternative water and sewage treatment technologies (Gardner 1997).

For commercial and industrial properties, efficiency objectives and conservation goals could be improved through the efficient use of meters with sewer rates based on both the volume and quality of the discharge (Elgie et al. 2016). Pricing based on quality is currently used in some places in Ontario, but much more could be done. In fact, it is quite possible that metering of sewage discharge would help in identifying unauthorized sewage discharges such as is observed when smaller, older industries like auto body shops, paint shops, and metal fabricators dump high levels of waste into both sanitary and storm systems.

STORMWATER PRICING

Surface water is a direct source of potable water for some water systems, and its impact on the recharging of aquifers affects the groundwater sources of many municipal and private drinking water systems. Many older waterworks systems are still working to separate stormwater and sanitary sewage carried in the same pipes, either routinely, or during peak flows.[8] These combined flows must, of course, be treated as sanitary sewage when they reach the end of the pipe, creating significantly higher demands on sewage treatment plants and overflow cisterns. The majority of municipal water departments and utility corporations in cities and towns in Ontario do not have a separate charge for stormwater. It is generally lumped in with the wastewater charge and calculated as part of water consumption. This aggregation, however, means that consumers don't know how much they are paying for stormwater management.

Since 1990, with the increasing impact of climate change (severe storms and flooding), there have been notable design requirements for more robust and resilient systems, and, correspondingly, increased funding required for stormwater infrastructure (sewers, spillways, retention and detention ponds, etc.) and, where they persist, for separation of sanitary sewers from storm sewers. These developments have given rise to a desire by some municipalities to convert stormwater facilities to a utility model, supported by "user" charges. User fees make considerable sense because benefiting properties are those that add runoff or are served by the provision of stormwater services and they can be identified. As such, fees paid by stormwater generators can be based on the estimated amount of water that leaves their property or in relation to the services that the property receives. Those who live or have businesses on properties whose impervious area is large will pay higher user charges than owners of properties that do not burden the drainage system to the same degree. As long as user charges are based on the property's burden on the stormwater infrastructure, an incentive is provided for property owners to reduce that burden by reducing the amount of runoff discharged into the municipal system (Aquije 2016).

Infrastructure Financing

For financing purposes, a distinction may be made between financing infrastructure for growth-related projects and infrastructure for renewal or rehabilitation purposes. In either case, however, the underlying principle is the same as the criteria for financing the operating costs of water and sewer systems; that is, those who use the system should be those who pay for it. In particular, payments should be in the form of user fees that reflect usage levels (Ontario Institute for Competitiveness and Prosperity 2015; Clayton 2014).

GROWTH-RELATED INFRASTRUCTURE

Development charges (DCs) are used by all large and medium-sized Ontario municipalities to finance the off-site capital cost[9] of new development that requires water, sewer, and stormwater infrastructure. In the early 1990s, DCs were used mainly by larger municipalities and a few medium-sized cities and towns. Since then, their use (in coverage and dollar value) has expanded to include more services and all cities, towns, and municipalities that are trying to cope with the cost of providing infrastructure to service new growth.

An efficient development charge must cover the full cost of delivering the service. This should include a capacity component that covers the capital cost of constructing the facility, plus a location or distance/density charge that reflects the capital cost of extending the service to properties or neighbourhoods (Kitchen and Tassonyi 2012). The most efficient development charges vary by type of property (residential, commercial, or industrial), neighbourhood, and distance from source of supply, so that each charge captures the extra cost of the infrastructure required to service the new growth.

However, most Ontario municipalities do not use variable charges to capture cost variations. Instead, they impose identical charges on all properties of a particular type, regardless of location. The same charge, then, is levied on residential dwellings in low-density neighbourhoods as on residential dwellings in high-density neighbourhoods. This occurs even though the marginal cost per property of infrastructure projects in low-density areas is higher, which can lead to urban sprawl (Slack 2002). Developments close to existing infrastructure are charged the same as developments farther away. As well, similar charges are often levied on properties that absorb different amounts of resources, due to factors such as terrain or soil type. Practices such as these encourage development in the wrong places. While it may be naive to expect municipal officials to calculate the infrastructure cost for each new property, costs could and should be calculated for each new development area or neighbourhood, to discourage inefficient patterns of development (Kitchen and Tassonyi 2012).

A recent study, however, has taken a contrasting view. It opposes development charges for water and sewers (Clayton 2014). In particular, it argues that development charges for these services should be terminated and replaced by user fees that are high enough to cover the costs of new infrastructure (which could be financed initially by borrowing). The argument continues that development charges are not used for other similar monopolistic-type community utility businesses such as natural gas. This change, the study continued, would lead to increased efficiency and conservation because each litre consumed would be priced more efficiently. At the moment, the development charge is a lump-sum up-front payment, and, as such, there is no reason to recover this cost through annual water prices. Consequently, prices are lower than they would be if they captured all annualized costs on a per unit basis. As noted earlier and repeated here, lower prices lead to overconsumption and overinvestment in infrastructure. As well, the report continues, it would be fairer because new users, through existing water rates, pay a share of the costs of providing water to existing customers while new customers are not being supported likewise by existing users. It could also increase housing affordability, the study maintains.

RENEWING OR REHABILITATING INFRASTRUCTURE

Renewing or rehabilitating existing infrastructure has become a major concern at the municipal level. In fact, it has led to a number of estimates on the size of the infrastructure deficit and what should be done to eliminate it. Before considering financing tools, I must express caution about buying into the existing estimates of the size of the municipal infrastructure deficit, primarily because of the way in which these estimates have been made (Fenn and Kitchen 2016, box 4). In short, it is difficult to find a clear-cut definition of what is meant by the infrastructure deficit. In general, one may argue it exists if the level of government responsible for spending on a physical asset to meet some desired or acceptable standard is deemed to have insufficient revenue or a lack of revenue capacity to pay for the asset. Such a definition, however, begs the question of what is insufficient revenue or lack of revenue capacity or, for that matter, are the desired standards appropriate?

Municipal governments, by and large, have the capacity to pay for their infrastructure, but quite often not the political will to do so if it means raising taxes or user fees. As such, it is politically more expedient and acceptable to constituents if elected officials simply claim that they have an infrastructure deficit and require funding from a more senior level of government. Indeed, this is the scenario that plays out annually at the municipal level in Canada (Curry 2015). Municipalities through their respective municipal associations claim that there is a revenue imbalance in the Canadian political system and that they deserve/need additional revenue from senior governments, generally in the form of more grants to finance their alleged infrastructure deficit.

The bulk of the empirical evidence on the size of the deficit appeared more than a decade ago (for a summary, see Kitchen 2003), although there have been occasional updates replicating the methodology of the earlier studies. The most recent estimate for Canada has been provided by the Federation of Canadian Municipalities, where it was noted that $39 billion is needed for improving wastewater systems; $25.9 billion for drinking water, and $5.8 billion for stormwater systems (FCM 2012). All studies have a similar conclusion – a municipal infrastructure deficit exists, although its size varies from study to study.

In summary, methodological and data problems associated with existing studies lead one to wonder if discussions around the so-called infrastructure deficit aren't largely driven by political objectives to achieve grant funding. At the same time, one could argue that it is more important to know whether current practices should be changed to assist in correcting the alleged shortfall rather than knowing whether or not a deficit or need exists and its size. An important start here would be a requirement that municipalities set efficiently designed prices for water, sewers and stormwater. Here, it may be important to remind the reader that efficiently structured fees (prices) play an important role as a mechanism for revealing the true demand for – and therefore, indicating the efficient supply of – water related infrastructure.

Which Financing Instrument?

There are three main instruments that are often used for financing existing infrastructure: reserves, borrowing, and grants.

RESERVES
Reserves[10] are created when a portion of current water rates (for example, one, two, or three cents per litre) are set aside annually in a special account accumulating interest until funds are eventually withdrawn and used to finance or partially finance water and sewer infrastructure. Financing through reserves is essentially the reverse of financing through borrowing.

Reserves have grown in popularity over the past few years. However, their application is not without problems. In particular, asking current users to pay for infrastructure that will benefit future users creates intergenerational inequities and has the potential for leading to a level of capital spending that may not be allocatively or economically efficient.

BORROWING

Borrowing makes considerable sense for water and sewer systems because the benefits from this infrastructure accrue to future users. As such, this form of financing is fair, efficient, and accountable. At the moment, many cities and regions have the capacity for more borrowing (Kitchen 2013) but are reluctant to do so. This reluctance may be somewhat short-sighted given recent evidence on the productivity-enhancing and quality-of-life benefits of investing in water and sewer infrastructure. For example, a number of studies have illustrated the extent to which spending on infrastructure is very much an investment, not just an expense. The Conference Board of Canada has suggested that infrastructure spending produces a $1.11 increase in gross provincial product for every infrastructure dollar invested and accounted for fully 12 per cent of provincial labour productivity gains in the 1980–2008 period (Antunes, Beckman, and Johnson 2010; Brodhead, Darling, and Mullin 2014). A more recent independent research study commissioned by the Residential and Civil Construction Alliance of Ontario (RCCAO) used an alternative economic modelling technique (agent-based) to make the case that investing in infrastructure pays net fiscal dividends to Canadian taxpayers that are much higher than reported in previously completed studies (Smetanin et al. 2014).

GRANTS

From 1974 to 1992, provincial grants funded 85 per cent of the capital costs of community water systems. Increasing strains on provincial finances and an expanding demand for funds to finance a larger range of services demanded by a growing urbanized population in the late 1980s and early 1990s led to the program's elimination. Since 1992, grants for water and sewer infrastructure have declined substantially. Over the past twenty-five years or so, they have mainly consisted of occasional one-off grants to accommodate specific requests from municipalities with financial problems or to stimulate economic growth in recessionary periods.

Most recently, grants have surfaced as a revenue source, especially through federal stimulus grant programs. These grants, by and large, have concentrated on shovel-ready projects because of the difficulty in meeting the short timeline for project approval and spending commitments, a timeline that municipalities generally could not meet for large costly projects requiring extensive planning and often time-consuming environmental assessments (Kitchen 2013). Very recently, the federal government announced a multi-billion-dollar infrastructure investment program targeting water and wastewater infrastructure through a two-phase capital grant program beginning with near-term repair and refurbishment, to be followed by a more substantial tranche of capital grants to rebuild water, wastewater, and stormwater infrastructure in municipalities and First Nations communities across Canada.

As well, there are capital grants from the federal and provincial gas tax fund. The federal Gas Tax Fund (GTF), in particular, is a per capita grant awarded to provinces that, in turn, allocate grants to municipalities. The latter are able to use these for seventeen different types of infrastructure; 90 per cent is spent on water, sewer, wastewater, local roads, and public transit.

In general, commentary at the municipal level over water and sewer infrastructure has had little to do with reforming existing water rates to achieve more efficient consumption levels and much to do with the need for more money. Is there a case for grants for water and sewers? In response, water and sewer systems provide goods that economists would classify as private goods – that is, specific beneficiaries can be identified and charged for the service and non-users can be excluded. As well, levels of consumption can be measured easily and per unit costs calculated readily. This suggests that those who use the service should be those who pay for it. Indeed, this was a recommendation of Ontario's Drummond Commission, which stated that user fees should cover all costs of water and sewer systems (recommendation number 12.2). This, Drummond continued, would lead to stable investment in infrastructure and efficient levels of consumption, would be fair on an intergenerational basis, and would promote conservation (Drummond 2012, 45). In short, setting user fees to cover full costs is efficient, fair, accountable and transparent.

Economic arguments for capital grants are not strong. Their use, where they are prevalent, should be conditional on recipient governments setting efficient water rates. As well, recipients should have proper asset management programs along with a requirement that asset replacement costs be included in the charge or price for water consumed. This seems to be progressing, and is in place in some municipalities but still has a way to go in a number of municipalities. To go even further, it may be time that the opportunity cost of water and sewer services be used as the base for formulating pricing structures and price levels. In simple terms, if we are going to use capital grants to restore our water, wastewater, and stormwater infrastructure over the next decade to compensate for past neglect and the absence of full-cost pricing, it should be the last time we do it. Once rebuilt, our infrastructure's users should pay the full cost of the service, including capital replacement costs.

Governance of Water-Related Services:
Who Should Be Responsible?

There is a historic, dynamic tension in the organization and delivery of water services in Ontario. On the one hand, natural forces create conditions where regional factors determine the availability of water – watersheds, aquifers, marshlands, freshwater lakes, and rivers. On the other hand, municipal waterworks have evolved historically from the efforts of several hundred local communities to provide safe drinking water, sewage treatment, and the channelling of stormwater in urban areas and agricultural drainage works in rural areas. As a result, water and wastewater systems and flood control have been municipal government responsibilities since the earliest days of Ontario's urban development.

Where these localized arrangements proved inadequate in scale and resources, beginning after the Second World War, mandates were shifted to regional entities, such as conservation authorities after 1946 and, in the late 1960s and early '70s, to regional municipalities and their amalgamated successors. In a few places where regional governance does not exist, municipalities have co-operated in developing major water and wastewater facilities, or contracted for sharing unused capacity. An example here is the cities of London and St Thomas, where they have a jointly operated facility to draw water from Lake Huron and Lake Erie to serve their communities. As well, the City of Hamilton and the County of Haldimand have contracted to share Hamilton's surplus potable water supply. For much of the rest of Ontario, however, the situation remains: local authorities manage water-related functions that often transcend their political boundaries and, in smaller communities, test their technical and financial capacity. It is here where there continue to be concerns over the municipality's ability to ensure water quality, to implement proper pricing structures to achieve full-cost recovery, and implement sustainable asset management programs.

For these places, the need may exist for widespread consolidation and integration of small, local waterworks and sewage collection and treatment facilities (Manahan 2010a), or local systems may need to be contracted to an operator with technical depth and financial resources beyond that typically available to a local municipality on its own (Swain, Lazar, and Pine 2005). The Ontario Clean Water Agency (OCWA) is a government agency whose original mandate was to build and operate water and wastewater infrastructure for the Ontario government. Over time, its mandate has expanded to allow OCWA to take over municipal facilities or to operate those facilities on a long-term contract. While it has the scale, depth, and technical knowledge needed to operate contemporary water systems, OCWA remains a government agency closely circumscribed by the policies and political sensitivities of the government of the day.

Another example of a viable approach for Ontario may be drawn from Alberta, where a small-scale "regional" model has been implemented in the Grande Prairie region. Facing many of the same issues as rural and small urban municipalities within Ontario counties, municipalities in this region of Alberta have created a municipally owned "private" utility company, Aquatera. Initially providing water and wastewater services management, it has since expanded into solid waste management and offers a range of "utility" services to other municipalities and, through a subsidiary, to industries. Aquatera appears to bring commercial discipline to utility services while generating local economic activity and yielding dividends for taxpayers through its municipal ownership (Aquatera 2014).

In other parts of the world, water services are often organized quite differently. In many parts of the US, autonomous water and sewer districts manage their systems on a regional basis, using a utility model similar to electricity distribution. In the UK, the essential watershed linkages between water, wastewater and stormwater produce entities that are integrated and organized regionally on a very large scale and frequently with private management or ownership (introduced to ensure more adequate investment and efficiency than was the case in its decaying infrastructure before 1989). In Europe, public ownership of water utilities is less common, with national and even transnational utility companies providing water services on contract or by franchise, much as Ontario does with natural gas distribution. The features that all of these arrangements share are: (a) a watershed-wide approach to the sourcing, treating, and managing of water resources; and (b) an in-depth capacity to deal with the many engineering, financial, water quality, environmental, and customer service issues that arise over time.

Some might argue the case for a greater degree of private operation, ownership, and investment in Ontario's municipal water or wastewater utilities. At the moment, it is largely restricted to contracted service management by major providers, like American Water Canada or Veolia Canada. Regulated private ownership is a route that was followed by the United Kingdom to overcome chronic problems with its water and wastewater utilities, which came to a head in the 1980s. It appears to be a model that works safely, efficiently, and economically in many developed countries. In an era where infrastructure investment is a priority but government tax resources are constrained, it is a model that is favoured by major public-sector pension funds and other investment funds with an interest in public infrastructure as a class of assets.

Others might argue that we do not need to move to a full-scale privatization or contracting-out model, provided we can introduce the efficiency and operational sustainability disciplines of commercial practices while retaining public ownership or at least strong regulatory control (Swain, Lazar, and Pine 2005). At the moment, there is no clear-cut direction as to where Ontario should go, but there would be real merit in exploring the potential for reorganizing and integrating water, wastewater, and stormwater services on a regional or watershed basis. The alternative would be to transfer these responsibilities by contract or franchise to a public or private organization with deep resources and/or regional scope that could deliver these services on behalf of the participating municipalities (Fenn and Kitchen 2016).

Regulating Water Rates?

For decades now, water and wastewater rates have been set by municipal councils or utility commissions. On the surface, this is how it should be. Water is a local service, users can be identified, production and delivery costs can be calculated, and rates can be set. If the rates are perceived to be too high, those elected to the decision-making body may be voted out at the next election. Water rates like property taxes, however, are highly visible and increases are often subject to severe criticism. Unfortunately, this has led to widespread reluctance to raise water rates in many municipalities. As such, it may be unrealistic in the current political environment to expect a local governing body to make efficient decisions about the structure and level of water rates without guidelines and support from an established province-wide regulatory body. While there may be a desire to use reduced water rates for economic development purposes, for example, or to cushion the impact on the vulnerable, system sustainability considerations should be paramount. At a minimum, the regulatory framework could be developed and used by municipal councils to approve rates and financial plans that ensure that rates attain a level sufficient to sustain the water-related systems into the future. If compliance with such a framework cannot be achieved through voluntary co-operation, there may be a need to impose some form of administrative tribunal process on those unable or unwilling to comply. This concept was unsuccessfully espoused by MPP David Caplan's Private Member's bills 13/10 and 237/10, which contained a number of other "full-cost" provisions (Manahan 2010b), but it may deserve a revisit.

SUMMARY AND OBSERVATIONS

Water, for the most part, is increasingly recognized as a scarce resource; meters are in place almost everywhere and volumetric prices of one sort or another have largely replaced fixed-rate charges; full-cost recovery is widespread, although there is considerable discrepancy as to what full-cost recovery means; ongoing annual provincial grants have disappeared and been replaced with one-off infrastructure grants at infrequent and unpredictable intervals; amortization of capital costs is now required; asset management programs have either occurred or are in the process of being implemented; and financing new and rehabilitated infrastructure has moved to the forefront as a policy concern.

Despite these advancements, shortfalls and inefficiencies remain, most of which have to do with prices and pricing structures that do not adhere to efficiently set and conservation-oriented principles. When this happens, we overconsume, which leads, in turn, to a larger-than-necessary demand for very expensive infrastructure.

What should municipalities do and what should senior levels of government do? Municipalities should concentrate on setting efficient prices for water, sewer, and stormwater runoff. For water consumption, this includes multi-part pricing to accommodate such things as capacity constraints, economies of scale, periods where peak-load demand differs from regular demand; greater use of meters and volumetric pricing for residential and commercial sewer usage; and the implementation of user fees based on volume of water runoff for stormwater systems. Concerns over the capacity of some municipalities or local utilities to adopt efficient pricing and maintain sustainability suggests that we should reconsider the way in which smaller and remote municipalities provide water and wastewater. This might include the amalgamation or regionalization of a number of smaller systems into one relatively large utility. It might include, as is done in a number of countries, the privatization of water and sewer systems for all municipal providers regardless of cost.

What should the province do? In essence, it should set water safety standards and serve as coordinator-planner for water utility systems. An additional responsibility and one that is almost certain to be important in the near future is that of regulator. Political repercussions from setting higher water rates at the municipal level suggest that many local councils or utilities will be reluctant to set prices at levels needed for funding annual operating and capital costs without a provincial regulatory framework to approve and support these increases. Another area in which the province could require change is around the provision of grants for water and sewer systems. Although the economic arguments are not strong, their use should be conditional on recipient governments setting efficient water and sewer rates.

NOTES

I would like to thank Enid Slack, Richard Bird, Michael Fenn, and Adam Found for helpful comments on an earlier draft. Any errors, omissions, or misinterpretations, however, are the responsibility of the author.

1 For a more detailed discussion of this and other parts of this paper, see Fenn and Kitchen (2016).
2 This is the last year for which data were collected.
3 An asset management plan is a strategic document that states how a group of assets is to be managed over a period of time. The plan describes the characteristics and condition of the infrastructure, the levels of service expected from it, planned actions to ensure that assets are providing the expected level of service, and financing strategies to implement the planned actions.
4 Public Service Accounting Board (PSAB) accounting rules (launched in 2001 and largely implemented in the 2009 municipal fiscal year). See Tassonyi (2002) and Altus Group Limited (2008) for a discussion of these.

5 From 1974 to 1992, the Ontario government provided grants to municipalities that covered up to 85 per cent of all capital costs for municipal
water systems.

6 For a more detailed discussion, see Kitchen (2007), Renzetti (2009),
Kitchen and Tassonyi (2012).

7 Examples include food and beverage establishments and laundries with
business revenues exceeding a threshold limit.

8 Newly developed areas in most cities now require the separation of
stormwater runoff from the sewer system.

9 On-site services are the responsibility of the developer in most municipalities and are included in subdivision approval plans.

10 This discussion of reserves differs from the discussion of development
charges, which also go into designated and legally circumscribed reserve
funds.

4

Financing Urban Infrastructure in Quebec: Use of Fees in the Water and Transportation Sectors

JEAN-PHILIPPE MELOCHE
AND FRANÇOIS VAILLANCOURT

INTRODUCTION

The purpose of this chapter is to examine the financing of urban infrastructure in Quebec. This is of interest given the various statements as to the existence of an urban infrastructure deficit. The chapter is divided into four sections. The first examines the nature of urban infrastructure, the level of government that provides infrastructure – both in some OECD countries and Canadian provinces – and the nature of municipal infrastructure in Quebec. The second section examines the role of taxes and charges (including user charges) in financing infrastructure in various Canadian provinces and American states and in Quebec municipalities, singling out Montreal for particular attention. The third contrasts the use of water charges in Canadian provinces and attempts to explain differences in their use by Quebec municipalities. In the fourth section, we examine the financing of public transit, comparing the cases of Montreal, Toronto, Vancouver, and nine transit authorities outside Canada. We also look at the complementary case of road tolling for eight foreign experiences as well as practices in greater Montreal and Vancouver. A conclusion follows.

URBAN INFRASTRUCTURE IN QUEBEC

On the Nature of Infrastructure

Various authors have examined the definition of infrastructure in the economic literature. Baldwin and Dixon (2008) and Torrisi (2009), in particular, offer interesting insights to guide the production of indicators on the subject. The first observation that one gleans from their work is that there is no clear consensus around a common and precise definition of the concept. Through their literature review, they identify elements generally regarded as infrastructure in the literature. These elements usually include assets related to the areas of transport, communications, and utilities including water, sewage, and electricity. Schools and hospitals are sometimes added to the list, as are courthouses and prisons.

The public nature of the assets is central to the definition of infrastructure. Baldwin and Dixon (2008) refer mostly to "public infrastructure." According to them, the public dimension refers not only to the ownership of assets, but also to their nature and use. If the infrastructure assets are not always public property, they have a public utility dimension. They therefore require some involvement of the state, be it by regulation. This role of the state is justified by the fact that infrastructure provision often occurs in the context of market failures. Some authors suggest a connection between the infrastructure and the concept of public goods (Torrisi 2009), but it is mostly externalities and the natural monopoly nature of infrastructure that make government intervention necessary for their effective provision.

The question of whether to include environmental, institutional, social, and cultural capital in the definition of infrastructure is raised by Baldwin and Dixon (2008) and Torrisi (2009). They recognize that natural or intangible assets may be substitutes for tangible infrastructure. The presence of marshy areas in a territory, for example, can control floods in the same way as the construction of dams and channels (Baldwin and Dixon 2008). In this case, the preservation of wetlands is expected to reach, in terms of future value, the same value as the built physical assets that generate the same benefit. The lack of a specific definition of what constitutes the stock of these natural and intangible assets, however, greatly restricts their use in infrastructure measures. For the sake of pragmatism, the definition is then generally limited to measuring what Baldwin and Dixon (2008) call a "subset" of infrastructure that consists of built physical assets.

According to Torrisi (2009), infrastructures are defined by their attributes and functions. In terms of attributes, for lack of a better approach, infrastructure is considered to be built physical assets that have a long life and are subject to market failures. Functionally, these assets provide support for the creation or development of other economic activities. They play a fundamental role as structural underpinnings of the economy. Following the same reasoning, Baldwin and Dixon (2008) highlight five key elements of the definition of infrastructure. According to them, infrastructure includes works (1) that have a long useful life; (2) whose construction is carried out over a long period; (3) for which there are few short-term alternatives; (4) that provide a flow of goods and services that are difficult to inventory; and (5) that are complementary to other goods, services, or factors of production.

These elements are interesting but their use raises questions. The first – long life – is clearly a characteristic of infrastructure, but it is not clear what constitutes "long." The authors in their discussion note that machinery may not qualify as long-lived, but in terms of producing publicly provided outputs, a long-lived garage for snow removal equipment is fairly useless in clearing streets unless it is filled with shorter-lived rolling stock. The second – long construction period – is odd as it is a characteristic of how the infrastructure is produced and not of the infrastructure as such. Improved productivity that would shorten construction time does not change the output characteristics of a given infrastructure. One could raise queries about the other three elements, such as what does "difficult to inventory" mean – list of physical assets, value of physical assets, or both? Our point is that the definition of infrastructure is not obvious. In practice we will use infrastructure as it is defined by producers of the data we use: the Department of Municipal Affairs in Quebec and Statistics Canada.

Following Baldwin and Dixon (2008), we consider as infrastructures all public buildings and engineering structures. Engineering structures are defined by Statistics Canada as civil engineering constructions used for the transportation of persons, merchandise, resources, equipment, gas, or electrical signals. Such structures may include bridges, roads, pipes, dams, lighting, rails, and so forth. Since the focus of our chapter is in part on transportation we also include vehicles in our definition of infrastructure. We acknowledge that vehicles do not fit in the definition of Baldwin and Dixon (2008), but they are important capital expenditures used in providing public transportation.

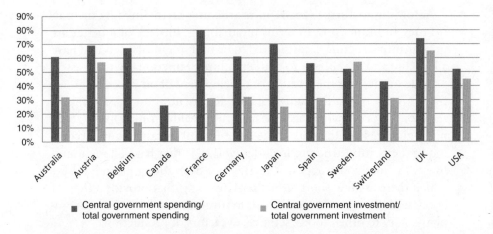

■ Central government spending/
    total government spending

■ Central government investment/
    total government investment

Figure 4.1   Importance of central governments in public spending and investment, twelve OECD countries, 2007–2014, average

Source: Dafflon and Vaillancourt (2017, figure 8.3)

Urban Infrastructure

The provision of infrastructure is usually shared between government and private firms. In Canada, telecommunication infrastructures, for instance, are mainly provided by private firms, under federal regulations, while governments provide infrastructure for the justice, health, and education sectors, as well as major engineering structures such as road and water systems and, in some cases, electricity and gas. In a multi-tier governance system, the responsibility for the provision of publicly owned infrastructure is divided between different levels of government. As Dafflon and Vaillancourt (2017) point out, central governments usually play a smaller role in the provision of public infrastructure than their share of public revenues (see figure 4.1). In Canada, where the federal government plays a small role in public spending, its share of infrastructure financing is particularly low, nearly 10 per cent. This means that the major contributors to public infrastructure financing are provincial and local governments (about 90 per cent).

The "urban" in urban infrastructure usually refers to the specific infrastructure owned and operated by local governments of a municipal nature. Since municipalities are not endowed with the same responsibilities in all jurisdictions, the nature of urban infrastructure may vary

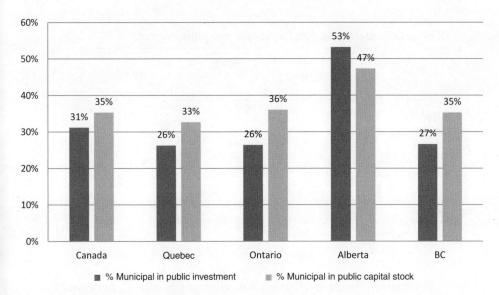

Figure 4.2   Municipal share of public capital stock and investment, Canada and four provinces, 2014

Note: Statistics Canada includes under "fixed non-residential capital" the following four items: non-residential building, engineering construction, machinery and equipment, and intellectual property products. We remove the last item from the data used in this paper. The denominator is "Government sector" and the numerator "Other municipal government services." Capital stock is valued using linear depreciation – year-end value.

Source: Authors, with data from CANSIM table 031-0005.

between these jurisdictions. Indeed in countries with a French public-sector tradition, one may find that primary and secondary schools are built and owned by regional and municipal general governments. In the case of Canada, municipalities do not own primary or secondary school buildings; more or less autonomous school boards or provinces do. Figure 4.2 shows the share of municipalities in the net stock of public capital for Canada as a whole and for the four most populous provinces. If municipalities account for similar shares of public assets in British Columbia, Ontario, and Quebec, that share is significantly higher in Alberta. This is due, in part, to the fact that some Alberta municipalities own assets like natural gas networks that are not owned by municipalities in other provinces. Although these assets are owned by a small number of municipalities, they account for a significant part of local assets where they are located.

Table 4.1
Municipal capital stock by type, Canada and four provinces, 2014

	Non-residential buildings (%)	Engineering/ construction (%)	Machinery/ equipment (%)
Canada	24	71	4
Quebec	**19**	**75**	**5**
Ontario	26	69	3
Alberta	23	72	4
British Columbia	27	72	1

Note: Percentages do not sum to 100 as intellectual capital has been left out.

Source: CANSIM table 031-0005, "Flows and Stocks of Fixed Non-Residential Capital, by Industry and Asset, Canada, Provinces and Territories."

As shown in figure 4.2, Quebec's municipalities own 33 per cent of all public infrastructure in the province, while all other public bodies (federal government, provincial government, education and health bodies, and aboriginal governments) own more than 60 per cent. Most of this non-municipal infrastructure is made up of health care, education, and other government buildings. Focusing only on engineering structures, we observe that municipalities own over 50 per cent of these assets in Quebec (Meloche 2017). Thus, municipalities play a major role in providing and maintaining public infrastructure in Quebec, accounting for 26 per cent of public investments in 2014.

Table 4.1 indicates the importance of engineering structures in municipal infrastructure for municipalities of Canada as a whole and for four provinces. These structures account for more than 69 per cent of municipal assets. We notice that municipal buildings in Quebec account for a lower share of municipal infrastructure than in other provinces. One possible explanation may be the different mix of provincial and municipal services in the various provinces. The lower value of real estate in Quebec may also explain a lower value for municipal buildings there. The share of machinery and equipment is also significantly higher in Quebec, particularly when compared to British Columbia. This may be partly explained by the fact that transit is a municipal responsibility in Quebec, while it is considered a provincial service in British Columbia. Thus rolling stock used for public transportation appears as a municipal asset in Quebec, but not necessarily in British Columbia.

Table 4.2
Net value of municipal capital assets and capital expenditures for Quebec municipalities, 2014

	Net value of municipal infrastructures		Capital expenditures	
	(M$)	(%)	(M$)	(%)
Buildings	6,700	15.5	589	13.9
Network infrastructures	34,619	79.9	3,302	78.1
– Water/sewage	15,164	35.0	1,043	24.7
– Roads	13,033	30.1	969	22.9
– Others	6,422	14.8	1,289	30.5
Vehicles	2,021	4.7	338	8.0
Total	43,340	100.0	4,229	100.0

Note: Assets like furniture, machinery, equipment, and land are not included in this table.

Source: Summary of Municipal Financial reports. Ministry of Municipal Affairs
(Sommaire des rapports financiers des municipalités, MAMOT), p. S22-7,
http://www.mamrot.gouv.qc.ca/fileadmin/publications/finances_indicateurs_fiscalite/information
_financiere/publications_electroniques/2014/rapports_org_muni/C1_Munloc_RF2014_Sommation.pdf.

Municipal Infrastructure in Quebec

Municipal responsibilities in Quebec can be grouped under five large categories: public security (fire and police), environment (water, sewage, and waste), transport (transit and roads), urban planning (including economic development), and leisure (sports and cultural activities). Among these responsibilities, most infrastructure needs come from the provision of environmental and transport-related public outputs. Table 4.2 shows the net value of municipal capital assets and capital expenditures for buildings, engineering structures (total and three types), and rolling stock for 2014 for Quebec municipalities. According to these municipal data, engineering structures represent nearly 80 per cent of all municipal capital assets (infrastructure) in Quebec, with roads and water infrastructure accounting respectively for 30 per cent and 35 per cent of the total value of municipal infrastructure. Municipal buildings account for 16 per cent, vehicles for 5 per cent, and all other infrastructure for 15 per cent; they are mainly waste management assets and electricity facilities. This last item is of importance in only nine municipalities that own electrical facilities in Quebec. Transit facilities like bus terminals also appear in this "other" category.

Turning to the share of each type of infrastructure in capital expenditures of Quebec's municipalities in 2014, we can see that water and sewage represent the most important shares of capital spending for these municipalities, followed by roads. The share of capital assets owned as vehicles and used for public transportation is unknown. Public security, road maintenance, and waste collection also use vehicles. It appears clear however that the discussion about urban infrastructure financing should focus mainly on water and transportation in Quebec, where transportation includes roads and all rolling stock used in road maintenance and public transportation as well as other transit facilities sunk in the "other" engineering infrastructure category.

FUNDING URBAN INFRASTRUCTURE IN QUEBEC: THE ROLE OF CHARGES

There are three main sources of revenues to fund urban infrastructures: taxes, user charges, and transfers from other levels of government. However, since transfers from federal and provincial governments are paid for by collecting taxes and user charges from taxpayers, including those who pay local taxes and charges, there are thus only two ways to fund local infrastructures: through taxes or user charges collected directly by local governments or received as transfers from other levels of governments. The distinction between fund (real source of revenue) and finance (channels through which funds flow) should be noted.

Funding Urban Infrastructure with Taxes

The share of municipal capital spending covered by transfers in Quebec is about 24 per cent ($1.0 billion out of capital spending of $4.2 billion in 2014). The federal government contributes to infrastructure funding (60–65 per cent of federal transfers every year over the 2010–15 period) mainly through a transfer of a share of the federal excise tax on gasoline. These funds are paid to a provincial agency, the SOFIL (Société de Financement des Infrastructures Locales), which distributes them, and are mostly (over 90 per cent) spent on water and roads infrastructure (Meloche, Vaillancourt, and Boulenger 2016). Other federal funds come from various infrastructure programs such as the Strategic Investment Fund. The federal government also contributes through transfers (equalization, CHT CST mainly) to the financing of 17 per cent of provincial expenditures and thus to some of the provincial transfers to municipalities dedicated to urban infrastructure. However, the major portion of transfers for urban infrastructure from the government of Quebec comes from tax revenues. Tax revenues collected by the government of Quebec are made up mainly of personal income tax (47 per cent), corporate income tax (10 per cent), and consumption and excise taxes (30 per cent) (as shown in the Comptes publics 2013–14, Government of Quebec). These are the main revenues that underpin the 24 per cent portion of municipal capital expenditures financed with transfers from the provincial government.

Municipal capital expenditures in Quebec are financed in large part by the issuing of local debt. In 2014, municipalities financed more than 60 per cent of their capital expenditures by borrowing ($2.6 billion of bonds issued). Ultimately, these bonds will have to be repaid using revenue from local taxes and user charges, or transfers from other levels of government. In Quebec, local tax refers mainly to the property tax. It is the only major tax levied by municipalities. Most of the revenue from the property tax comes from a tax based on property assessment (85 per cent of tax revenues in 2014). Other taxes are levied on different properties' features like the number of housing units or the frontage, but they are all grouped on the same tax bill as the property value tax. Altogether, these tax revenues account for 58 per cent of all municipal revenues in Quebec for the year 2014. The other major own-revenue source is the sale of goods and services.

Financing Urban Infrastructure with Charges

Own revenue from the sale of goods and services is said to be coming from "charges." We should first clarify the definition of charges. In Quebec charges are considered as revenue generated by a process where the municipality receives money for a service provided. It is not always paid by individuals as "user charges." Some of the services are paid by other municipalities, other levels of government, or corporations. In municipal accounting, municipal services provided to other municipalities are clearly identified. There is no distinction however between services paid for by individual or corporate users and those paid for by the provincial government. Parking fees or fees charged by a municipality for the maintenance of a provincial road will both appear as "Transportation charges." That is why we use the term charges and not user fees or user charges, since we do not know what proportion is really borne by users.

The amount of charges levied by all municipalities in the province of Quebec in 2014 was $3.5 billion, which represents around 17 per cent of their total revenues. These numbers include an amount of $2.2 billion considered as municipal revenues coming from the sale of goods and services, as well as "fiscal charges" associated with water, sewage, and waste, which account for more than $1.2 billion. Although many of these fiscal charges are flat rates unrelated to the consumption of goods and services, others are linked to volumetric or weighting measurement of household consumption. This generates confusion when analyzing local charges, since these fiscal charges are considered as taxes in municipal accounting. In order to produce numbers that allow comparison with water charges elsewhere in Canada (and specifically data presented in the chapter by Kitchen in this volume), we consider these fiscal charges as the product of the sale of water, sewage, and waste services.

It is not clear what part of charges are dedicated to the operating costs of specific urban services let alone to the funding of urban infrastructure. Are some charges earmarked as revenues for specific spending? In general such earmarking is not done in Quebec, at least not formally. Informally, councils may take into account specific revenues when determining specific spending. Another practice is to provide some services (like swimming pools) through local NGOs, which keep the relevant fee revenue and also receive transfers from the municipality. Some revenue from charges are clearly devoted to current expenditures.

We observe that the proportion of charges in municipal revenues is lower in Quebec than in most other jurisdictions where local governments have similar (but not the exact same) responsibilities. Table 4.3 reports information from Meloche, Vaillancourt, and Boulenger (2016). This study compares the share of revenue sources in municipal finances for four Canadian provinces and six American states. It presents a comparison of local governments' charges as a share of local government revenues per capita and a share of their province's or state's GDP. The amount of local charges paid by residents in Quebec is lower than in the other nine jurisdictions included in the analysis. It is lower in spending per capita and lower as a percentage of GDP. With the exception of New Jersey and Massachusetts, the amound of local charges is also lower as a proportion of municipal revenues. Compared to Alberta, residents of Quebec's municipalities pay nearly half the charges. In Florida, residents pay four times the amount of charges in Quebec for local services.

Table 4.3
Share of local government revenue coming from charges in six American states and four
Canadian provinces, 2013

	Charges as share of municipal revenues (%)	Local governments' charges per capita ($Can)	Local governments' charges as % of GDP
Quebec	17.4	428	0.9
Ontario	21.7	678	1.3
Alberta	22.2	849	1.0
British Columbia	31.1	726	1.5
New York	18.0	604	0.9
New Jersey	16.0	700	1.1
Massachusetts	14.8	803	1.2
Pennsylvania	19.6	559	1.1
Florida	36.2	1,671	4.0
California	41.5	1,565	2.6

Note: Municipal revenues refers to local municipalities only, while local governments include top-tier or regional authorities (metropolitan bodies and counties), school boards, and special-purpose districts. Exchange rate is 1$US=1.03$Can

Source: Meloche, Vaillancourt, and Boulenger (2016, tables 3.5 and 3.7). Numbers for Quebec are different since we have added fiscal charges for water, sewage, and waste.

As noted in the discussion of urban infrastructure, what falls under the definition of municipal responsibilities may vary from one jurisdiction to another. In the US, for instance, many local governments (often special-purpose districts) own electrical facilities or provide some health and social services. These services are usually financed through user charges. The fact that very few municipalities own electrical facilities in Quebec and that all health and social services are provided by the provincial government may explain in part the lack of importance of charges in Quebec. When we take a closer look at local charges in Quebec and elsewhere, however, we see that water charges are significant in all other jurisdictions, but of relatively less importance in Quebec. That may be a peculiarity of Quebec's local government financing.

Charges as a Municipal Revenue in Quebec

For a better understanding of what constitutes a local charge in Quebec, table 4.4 examines the amount of revenues collected as charges by municipalities and the share of each type of charge in total charges, including fiscal charges for water, sewage, and waste. What we observe in

Table 4.4
Amount of revenues from charges and the share of each charge in total charges for all Quebec municipalities and the City of Montreal, 2014

Types of services	Quebec's municipalities		City of Montreal		Montreal as % of Quebec
	Millions $	%	Millions $	%	
General administration	68	2.0	17	1.8	24.5
Public security	52	1.5	23	2.4	43.3
Roads	130	3.8	67	7.0	51.6
Transit	788	22.8	537	56.2	68.1
Other transport	118	3.4	81	8.5	68.7
Water	486	14.1	23	2.4	4.8
Sewage	146	4.2	0	0.0	0.0
Wastewater	113	3.3	0	0.0	0.0
Waste	468	13.5	14	1.4	3.0
Other water, sewage and waste	73	2.1	7	0.7	9.1
Housing	83	2.4	80	8.4	97.0
Urban planning	136	3.9	99	10.4	73.2
Leisure and culture	293	8.5	45	4.7	15.2
Electricity	336	9.7	0	0.0	0.0
Intermunicipal charges	168	4.9	0	0.0	0.2
Total	3,458	100.0	993	100.0	28.7
Population (000)	8,070		1,698		21.0
Total municipal revenues (millions $)	19,851		6,281		31.6
Charges as % of revenues	17.4		15.8		

Source: Municipal financial reports, Ministry of Municipal Affairs (Rapports financiers des municipalités, MAMROT), Analyse des revenus consolidés et non consolidés, pp. S27-1, S27-6, and S27-7,
http://www.mamrot.gouv.qc.ca/finances-indicateurs-de-gestion-et-fiscalite/information-financiere/profil-financier-et-autres-publications/rapport-financier-des-organismes-municipaux/exercice-financier-2014/#c628.

this table is that transit is the major source of municipal charges, representing 23 per cent of all revenue from charges in Quebec. Water provision, including sewage and wastewater treatment, accounts for 21 per cent of charges, which is also important. The other two types of services where charges are important as a source of revenue are solid waste collection (13.5 per cent), and electricity (10 per cent).

The City of Montreal is the largest city in Quebec, with 21 per cent of the population. Table 4.4 shows that charges in Montreal come mainly from transit. Montreal accounts for 29 per cent of all charges levied in Quebec, but for 68 per cent of all transit charges. Transit charges represent nearly 57 per cent of all revenue from charges in Montreal. On the other hand, water, sewage, and waste charges are relatively low in the city. Charges for water account for 2.4 per cent of charges revenues in Montreal and solid waste collection for 1.4 per cent. These lower charges for water, sewage, and waste are unique to Montreal. Given the importance of the City of Montreal in Quebec, this also affects the municipal data for the whole province.

Transit is the most important source of charges, but few municipalities have access to these charges in Quebec. In fact, only 79 municipalities out of 1,122 (7.0 per cent) have access to revenues from transit charges in Quebec. This is also the case with electricity. Only nine municipalities (0.8 per cent of all municipalities) receive revenue from the provision of electricity (power distribution services, with four producing some electricity). While cities with public transit are major cities – they encompass 65.4 per cent of Quebec's population and account for 71.4 per cent of total municipal revenues – municipalities with electrical power services are smaller – they only account for 5.6 per cent of Quebec's population and 6.3 per cent of total municipal revenues. Since charges for the provision of electricity account for nearly 10 per cent of all charges in the province, these charges are major revenue sources in the few cities where they are collected. On the other hand, fiscal charges related to water are widely used, as are charges for leisure and cultural activities. Fiscal charges for solid waste are also common, but not charges for sewage or wastewater treatment.

As we have shown in the first part of this chapter, urban infrastructure in Quebec is mainly made up of roads (and other transport infrastructure) and water facilities (including sewage and wastewater treatment plants). Roads in Quebec are subject to direct charges only in exceptional circumstances – specifically, two bridges (A25 and A30) and part of one expressway (A30), all owned by private firms and the provincial government in public–private partnerships. However, some uses of the roads' network are more commonly subject to charges. Such is the case with public parking spaces and public transit (buses) implicitly associated with the use of roads. These charges are not necessarily channelled to the financing of public infrastructures, but they at least appear to fund services that make intensive use of some urban infrastructure.

In the case of water, the use of charges is not always linked to consumption, since fiscal charges are often lump-sum taxes. Even if the use of these charges is common among Quebec's municipalities, their relative importance in a major city like Montreal makes this source of financing a marginal one in comparison with other major cities in

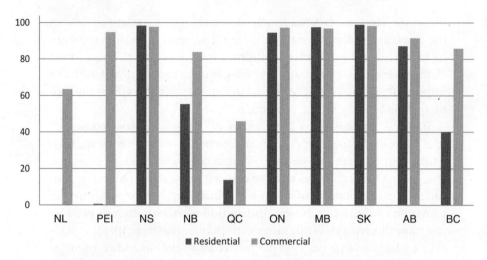

Figure 4.3   Proportion of properties with water meters in Canadian provinces, 2009

Source: Environment Canada, *2011 Municipal Water Use Report. Municipal Water Use 2009 Statistics.*

Canada. Following the most recent Quebec-wide policy on potable water (Government of Quebec 2011), things are changing, at least for industrial, commercial, and institutional use of potable water. In the case of residential use, the debate is still ongoing. The next section digs into water charges in Quebec.

WATER CHARGES

Use of Water Charges and Water Production Costs

As shown in figure 4.3, the proportion of residential and commercial properties equipped with water meters and subject to volume charges for the provision of water varies across provinces in Canada. In 2009, Quebec had the third-lowest share of residential properties and the lowest share of commercial properties with metered water.[1] With an estimated 14 per cent of houses subject to volume charges, Quebec relies more on water charges than Newfoundland and Labrador and Prince Edward Island, where there are usually no charges at all for residential use. On the other hand, with only 46 per cent of commercial properties subject to charges for water, the province of Quebec was far behind the

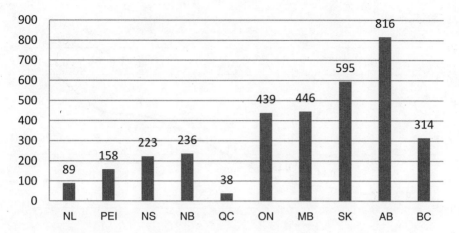

Figure 4.4 Mean household spending ($), water and sewerage, ten provinces, 2014

Source: CANSIM table 203-0021, "Survey of Household Spending (SHS), Household Spending, Canada, Regions and Provinces"

other provinces in 2009 (63 per cent in Newfoundland and Labrador and over 80 per cent in all other provinces).

The most recent numbers produced by the government of Quebec show that the sources of municipal revenues devoted to the provision of potable water (including wastewater treatment) are 50 per cent from general property tax, 40 per cent from lump-sum fiscal charges, and 10 per cent from volumetric charges (Government of Quebec 2015). The annual report on the implementation of Quebec's Water Strategy indicates that 39 per cent of industrial, commercial, and institutional buildings were equipped with water meters in 2014 – a situation similar to that observed by Environment Canada five years earlier (figure 4.3). Water meters are found in 66 per cent of Quebec's municipalities and cover 100 per cent of water consumed by industrial, commercial, and institutional users in 20 per cent of them in 2014 (Government of Quebec 2016). Montreal lags behind, with 29 per cent of industrial, commercial, and institutional buildings equipped with meters in 2014 (City of Montreal 2015). The objective of Quebec's water policy is to have 90 per cent of the province's non-residential potable water consumption metered by September 2018.[2]

Quebec's policy does not target residential consumption. In 2014, only 13 per cent of housing units were equipped with water meters in Quebec, a situation similar to the one shown in the survey of Environment Canada in 2009 (figure 4.3). The proportion of households mak-

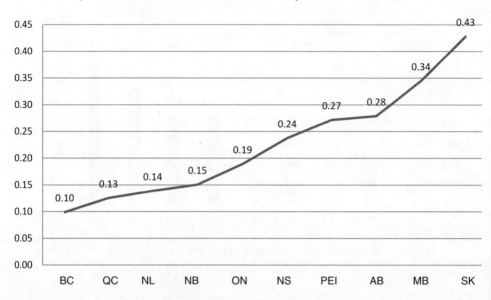

Figure 4.5   Operation and maintenance cost of water treatment plants for the ten provinces of Canada, by increasing cost, 2011

Source: Calculations by authors using tables 1.1 and 6.1. Data taken from *Survey of Drinking Water Plants*, Statistics Canada 16-403-X, http://www.statcan.gc.ca/pub/16-403-x/16-403-x2013001-eng.pdf.

ing water bills payments in Quebec is thus relatively low. That is why average spending on water and sewage by household in Quebec is the lowest in Canada in 2014, as shown in figure 4.4.

One explanation for Quebec's unique situation may come from the production cost of water. Data presented in figure 4.5 show that the Province of Quebec had the second-lowest operation and maintenance costs of water treatment plants in 2011. Treatment plants, however, account for only a small part of water production costs. The lack of data about full production costs of potable water on a provincial basis in Canada makes any comparison difficult.

Another explanation for the lower costs may be that that wastewater treatment standards are lower in Quebec. According to Environment Canada (2011, 12), "primary treatment is prominent in Newfoundland and Labrador, Nova Scotia, Quebec, and, to a lesser extent, New Brunswick and British Columbia. Ontario and Manitoba's populations are almost entirely served by secondary-mechanical treatment, while 78 per cent of Alberta's population is served by tertiary-level wastewater treatment."

As noted by both Kitchen and Dafflon in this volume, the cost of water should not only refer to the operating costs of water and wastewater treatment plants, it should also include amortization of the water distribution and wastewater collection infrastructures. Full cost should also include future costs or at least a form of maintenance provision. The government of Quebec has recently revised its method to calculate the full cost of potable water. This cost is estimated with actual operating costs of municipalities, on top of which is added the cost of investment needs. Investment needs refers to the replacement cost of actual infrastructures divided by their remaining lifetime. Most recent data collected from a sample of municipalities allow us to estimate a full production cost of $2.26/m^3$ of potable water in Quebec in 2012 (Government of Quebec 2015). Operating cost, including debt financing, is estimated to be $1.02/m^3$ for the same year. In Montreal, the full production cost is estimated to be $1.76/m^3$. We observe scale economies in the production of potable water in Quebec.

According to the Government of Quebec (2015) estimate, revenues allocated to water production by municipalities cover only 35 per cent of the full cost of water production. Based on municipal data, we estimate that fiscal charges linked to water, sewage, and wastewater cover less than 50 per cent of the costs associated with these items by municipalities (operating costs only) in 2014.[3] For the City of Montreal, charges don't even recover 10 per cent of the operating costs. This is by far less than what is observed for Ontario by Kitchen in this volume.

Path Dependency or Distinct Behaviour

Another explanation for Montreal's and Quebec's lesser use of water charges may lie in historical considerations. From 1801 to 1845, water provision in Montreal was carried out by a private company, the Compagnie des Propriétaires de l'Aqueduc de Montréal (CPAM). Faced with growing urban development in 1845, the City of Montreal bought the company's infrastructure to ensure a development of the network coherent with its needs (Fougère 2004). According to the census of 1851, the City of Montreal had a population of nearly 60,000 at that time. It was the largest city in Canada, slightly ahead of Quebec City (with nearly 50,000 residents), and twice as big as Toronto (with a population of around 30,000). Nearly 20 per cent of all of Canada's urban population was living in Montreal. The choice of municipalizing water provision at that time was driven by the need to harmonize water infrastructure with urban development. But it was also influenced by difficulties with the financing of infrastructures. Water meters were not common at that time. Water charges were based on household and housing characteristics or on the type of use and the dimension of buildings. Taxing was considered to be more efficient for ensuring the financial viability of the network.

Since Montreal was the biggest water network in Quebec and in Canada, and was providing water free of charge (fully financed by taxes), it developed as a model for water provision in Quebec. In 1891, a private company, the Montreal Water and Power was providing water to municipalities on the island of Montreal such as Westmount, Outremont, Saint-Henri, and Villeray. After many disputes with municipal authorities served by its network, the company was bought by the City of Montreal in 1927 (Lauzon, Patenaude, and Poirier 1997). As Hirsch (1959) points out, water and sewage infrastructure networks are subject to important economies of scale. Growing fast, the water network of the City of Montreal was also producing water efficiently and at lower cost than in many other cities. Montreal still ranks among the cities with the lowest production costs in Quebec, since we still observe scale economies in the production of water today (Government of Quebec 2015).

It seems plausible that the development of water and sewage infrastructure in other municipalities in Quebec was inspired by the experience of Montreal. Since Montreal made the choice of using taxes instead of charges to finance its water facilities, many other municipalities did so. At the end of the 1990s, there was some discussion about privatization of water production in Quebec (Lauzon, Patenaude, and Poirier 1997). The debate at that time was driven mainly by the need to reduce public debts. The economic benefit from using charges was not necessarily at the centre of the discussion. Adopting Quebec's Water Policy in 2002, the government set targets aimed at reducing the use of drinkable water by municipalities. In 2011, the government was even more explicit by mentioning in its Water Strategy the need to use water charges in order to reduce water consumption. The use of consumption charges was targeted only towards industrial, commercial, and institutional sectors. The argument put forward by the government at that time was not linked to fiscal health or the size of the public debt, but to environmental concerns.

Some empirical studies support the Quebec Water Strategy. According to Olmstead and Stavins (2009), the price elasticity of water consumption is higher for industrial, commercial, and institutional use than it is for residential. Moreover, the cost of metering water is mainly linked to meter installation and maintenance and the administrative costs of billing (Cowan 2010). Since the province of Quebec has 120,000 industrial, commercial, and institutional buildings and 1.8 million residential units, the emphasis on industrial, commercial, and institutional water metering is cost effective (Government of Quebec 2016). In the City of Montreal, the industrial, commercial, and institutional sectors also account for the major part (58 per cent) of water consumption (City of Montreal 2015). The smaller size of households in Montreal also reduces the use of water per unit, which lowers the potential net benefit of water metering.[4] This conclusion is reinforced by the fact that the benefit of water metering is usually linked to the production cost of potable water. And this cost seems to be lower in Montreal than in most other places in Canada (as suggested by figure 4.5 and the numbers produced by the Government of Quebec 2015).

Therefore, although the Quebec Water Strategy reflects a general agreement on the benefit of water metering and the importance of appropriate water prices for industrial, commercial, and institutional use, there is no general agreement about the extension of metering to residential units. Not only is the net benefit of water metering less obvious in the residential sector (Hamel 2012), but some civic groups are also organizing protests against residential metering in Quebec (Eau-Secours, for instance). As Kitchen has mentioned for Ontario (in this volume), many reforms in water management in Ontario were influenced by the tragedy of Walkerton and enforced by the government of Ontario. In Switzerland, federal legislation drives the recourse to water metering and full-cost recovery objectives (see Dafflon in this volume). In Quebec, the government's strategy of 2011 set two main objectives. The first was to lower potable water consumption by 20 per cent in 2016 from its 2001 level. This target was already reached by 2014. The second objective was to reduce pipe leakages or water lost in the network to 20 per cent of treatment plant production volume. This proportion was 26 per cent in 2014 – the objective has not yet been reached, but progress had been made since municipalities are now methodically inspecting their pipes to estimate these losses. Barring some event that would significantly raise the cost of water in the future, it seems plausible that industrial, commercial, and institutional metering will allow Quebec's municipalities to reach their targets. In these circumstances, we don't necessarily expect the government of Quebec to enforce the use of water meters in housing units in the short or medium term.

USER CHARGES IN THE FINANCING OF PUBLIC TRANSIT

Economists distinguish between two types of pure goods: a *private good*, in which consumption by one person takes this good away from other potential consumers (resulting in rivalry for the good and exclusion from the good), and a *public good*, in which use by one person leaves it available for others (street lighting, for example, with no rivalry or exclusion). Transport infrastructure is a semi-public good since it exhibits rivalry in consumption that varies between peak (higher rivalry) and off-peak times (lower rivalry), while exclusion is always feasible using either quantitative rationing (access linked to holding a zone permit or having the proper odd/even plate number) or pricing. As noted by Turgeon and Vaillancourt (2002), roads are also a direct complement to private physical infrastructure. They also need to be physically connected, which is not the case for various types of education or health infrastructure. Roads and vehicles, private or public, are also an input in the production of substitute infrastructure in education and health; roads allow the busing of students to larger, better-equipped schools and the ferrying of sick individuals to larger health centres rather than to basic, less well-equipped health units.

In Canada, in general, there is little federal spending on roads (Turgeon and Vaillancourt 2002; Bojorques, Champagne, and Vaillancourt 2009), although the 2009–2011 infrastructure program saw large but temporary federal transfers to provinces and municipalities for various infrastructure investments including road and public transit. The new 2016 federal infrastructure program (Investing in Canada) also includes investment in public transit as spending to be federally supported.[5]

The Issue of Transit Financing

Figure 4.6 summarizes information at the national level on two types of revenues for bus services in provinces or group of provinces (regions). One finds that subsidies vary in importance by a fair extent across provinces (the most important source of revenue not found in figure 4.6 is for school bus activities). With 30 per cent of revenues for bus services coming from user fees, Quebec stands above the Canadian average, below Ontario, and at a comparable level with British Columbia.

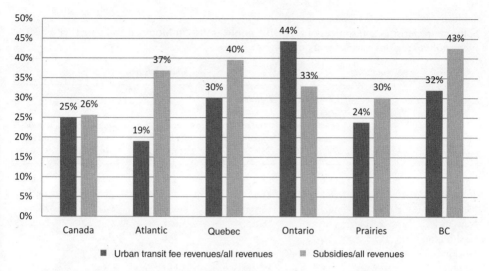

Figure 4.6   Two types of revenues for bus services, Canada and five provinces/regions, 2013

Source: Authors, CANSIM 408-0012, "Canadian Passenger Bus and Urban Transit Industries, Revenue and Expenses, by Selected Provinces and Regions"

Given the higher concentration in Montreal of the urban transit charges collected in Quebec (table 4.4), table 4.5 focuses on a comparison of the financing patterns for public transit in a sample of metropolitan areas. These are not necessarily comparable to Montreal in population size or in the coverage offered by their transit network; they were chosen to reflect a variety of transit financing models. The table presents the financing sources of the major transit authorities in these metropolitan areas. Most of them operate trains, subways, and buses, but not in the same proportion in every metropolitan area. The specific transit authorities are listed in the sources to the table.

Table 4.5 also shows that user financing varies substantially across the ten foreign cases examined. Leaving aside Hong Kong, it varies between 25 and 55 per cent of urban public transit financing. Dedicated taxes play a marginal role in some cases and a major one in others. In the case of New York and Paris, payroll taxes are the main source of funds. Transfers come from both local and regional/central governments. They often target capital expenditures.

The practice of transit charges in Montreal does not seem to diverge from what we observe elsewhere in Canada or around the world. Even

Table 4.5
Some characteristics and sources of financing public transit in Montreal and ten other metropolitan regions, various years, 2009–2012

	Financing			Characteristics		
	Users (%)	Dedicated taxes and other revenues (%)	Transfers by various levels of governments (%)	Annual number of users (000 000)	Single fare $ min./max.	Modal share, public transit %
Montreal	36.0	11.0	54.0	469	3.00	22.0
Toronto	48.3	8.2	43.5	533	3.00	24.0
Vancouver	33.3	38.3	28.5	237	2.75	20.0
New York	40.4	51.6	8.0	2,622	2.50	31.0
Washington	27.7	9.3	62.9	350	1.65/6.20	14.0
Stockholm	40.8	17.8	41.4	739	5.50	30.0
London	35.5	9.6	54.9	3,881	3.50	27.0
Oslo	53.7	12.8	33.4	290	5.25	33.0
Paris	30.8	50.5	18.6	4,132	2.30	34.0
Sydney	24.1	1.3	74.5	513	2.30/3.60	11.0
Hong Kong	100.0	0	–	3,173	0.50/3.50	78.0
Singapore	54.2	9.8	36.0	1,949	0.60/1.70	34.0

Source: Montreal, Agence Métropolitaine de Transport (AMT); Toronto, Toronto Transit Commission (TTC) + Metrolinx; Vancouver: TransLink (SBCTA); NY: Metropolitan Transport Authority (MTA); Washington Metropolitan Area Transit Authority (WMATA or Metro); AB Storstockholms Lokaltrafik (SL); Transport for London (TfL); Oslo, Ruter AS; Paris, Syndicat des transports de l'île de France (STIF); Sydney, Transport for New South Wales (TfNSW); Hong Kong, Mass Transit Railway (MTR); Singapore, Land Transport Authority (LTA). Authors are using an unpublished study collating publicly available information. More than one single fare indicates pricing based on distance, time of use or both.

in France (Paris), where water provision is private and toll roads common, urban transit users benefit from higher subsidies than in Quebec. In this sense, Quebec is not distinct in the way it finances its transit networks.

There are many economic reasons why transit fares should not cover the full cost of transit. Small and Verhoef (2007) note the fact that marginal cost is often lower than the average cost, essentially in off-peak periods. In a world where road pricing is rare, transit ridership also generates external benefits associated with road congestion. It also has environmental benefits by reducing pollution. Finally, since transit is a cheap means of transport it has some redistributive attributes. In a study on major American metropolitan areas, Parry and Small (2009) found empirical support for large fare subsidies. Even starting with fares at 50 per cent of operating costs, they argue that incremental subsidies can result in welfare improvement. A review of the literature in Small and Verhoef (2007) also underlines the difficulties in finding an optimal subsidy or fare contribution for public transit. In this case, by being comparable to what is observed elsewhere in the world, Montreal may display mainstream transit management practices.

The Way Forward: Charging for Roads?

As we have shown in the first section of this chapter, roads are one of the major types of municipal infrastructure in Quebec. By charging fares for public transit or parking, we can argue that some road uses are subject to user charges. But what about charges for the use of roads themselves? Table 4.6 presents examples of road charges for Montreal, . Vancouver, and eight non-Canadian cities. Various instruments are used – from simple one-size-fits-all bridge tolls to sophisticated tolls varying by time of day and vehicle pollution. The technology used to collect tolls consists of either licence plate image capture cameras or transponders. Geolocation technology using cellphone signals is not very common but is likely to be used in the future.

In some cases, the main objective sustaining the implementation of road charges is not financing but demand management. Toll prices in these cases are linked more to congestion than to the cost of road infrastructures. Administrative cost may also be important. In table 4.6, Stockholm, London, Milan, and Singapore use congestion tolls. In San Diego, the toll is only applied on high-occupancy lanes and is also associated with demand management. In Montreal, Vancouver, Oslo, and Sydney tolls are directly associated with road financing. These tolls are usually more cost efficient. Even if data are missing for Montreal, Vancouver, and Sydney, the example of Oslo shows that administrative costs are lower as a percentage of revenues raised than in other toll examples.

Road pricing in the Montreal metropolitan region is not considered a source for financing urban infrastructure. The roads financed are not local but provincial roads (bridges). The tolls are operated by private firms that own transport infrastructure, in this case bridges, in public–private partnership. We have very little information about revenues raised by these private firms. If the tolls generate profit, some of these are shared with the government. Since the government of Quebec has received payments in the first year of operation of the toll on A25, we know that the toll is profitable. Not only does it cover the cost of the

Table 4.6

Examples of road pricing for Montreal and eight other metropolitan areas, 2014

City	Type of road charge	Price	Revenues (one year)	Administrative cost as % of revenues
Montreal	Toll on one access bridge	A25 toll varies by time of day and number of axles: $1.88 off peak and $2.50 per transit per car. Vehicles without transponders pay $5.20 extra for collection costs.	39.1 M$ (2012)	NA
Vancouver	Toll on Port Mann bridge	$3.00 per car and $9.00 for heavy trucks	150 M$ (2014)	NA
San Diego (CA, USA)	Toll for I-15 "HOT Lanes"	$0.55 to $8.80, varying with distance and congestion	1.2 M$ (2007)	67
Stockholm (Sweden)	Access toll on all bridges accessing downtown Stockholm	1.70 $ to 3.40 per trip. Maximum $10.10 per day	125 M$ (2007)	28
London (UK)	Congestion charge to access downtown	$19.20 per day using Congestion Charge Auto Pay (CCAP), 90% reduction for residents	560 M$ (2010)	50
Oslo (Norway)	Numerous tolls country wide: highways, bridges, downtown access	Toll varies between $2.80 to $5.50 depending on entry point for light vehicles; $8.50 to $16.90 for heavy vehicles.	150 M$ (2002)	10
Milan (Italy)	"Area Toll": access toll to downtown with amount linked to pollution by vehicles.	$7.50 per day for non-residents and $3.00 for residents	28 M$ (2012)	36
Sydney (Australia)	Tolls on most bridges and express-ways with some private roads	For some tolls, between $2.50 and $6.00 per transit according to location and in some cases time. In other cases distance tolling from $0.64 to $7.52 per km.	NA	NA
Singapore	Toll to access downtown	Up to $2.60 for motorcycles, $5.20 for light vehicles and taxis, $7.80 for heavy vehicles and minibuses and $10.45 for very heavy trucks and buses.	120 M$ (2009)	18

Sources: Official websites of toll management corporations. TREO (Vancouver), SANDAG (San Diego), Transportstyrelsen (Stockholm), Transport for London, Statens vegvesen et AutoPass (Oslo), Comune di Milano (Milan), ASFINAG (Austria), Sydney Motorways, One Motoring – Land Transport Authority (Singapore), Concession A25 S.E.C. et Nouvelle Autoroute 30, s.e.n.c. Exchange rate of January to June 2014.

infrastructures, it is also a source of revenues for other uses. We estimate revenues from that bridge toll to be $40 million for 2012.

There is a scientific consensus in urban and transport economics about the theoretical benefits of road pricing (Small and Verhoef 2007). Sufficient empirical evidence also exists to support, at least partly, these benefits (de Palma and Lindsey 2011). As Albalate and Bel (2009) state, however, the main obstacles related to road charges are not technical but rather political. Acceptability is the major issue with road charges. As long as road financing is not seen as a political mater and if car drivers continue to underestimate the real cost of congestion, it will take time before transport policies include the objective of road financing and congestion management based on direct user charges.

CONCLUSION

While the definition of municipal infrastructure is imprecise in both Canadian and Quebec statistical sources, we would argue that it should cover both immobile and mobile long-lived assets. A more troubling definitional issue is how charges are defined in Quebec's municipal statistics. This makes it difficult to ascertain the exact role of charges, labelled as such or as taxes on the demand for services and in particular on the demand for water. That said, the use of fees for the financing of public services and in particular for the cost of new infrastructure is not common in Quebec yet similar to practices in the rest of Canada. A greater use of charges in the financing of water provision to industrial, commercial, and institutional properties in Quebec would seem a proper step to take. If some authors have doubt about the efficiency of pricing water for residential use (like Hamel 2012), most agree that the pricing of water for commercial and industrial use should be beneficial.

In the case of public transit, we want to emphasize that there is a key relationship between public transit financing and road financing. Increasing the user-financed share of public transit spending may well decrease its use (Breguet and Vaillancourt 2008) as well as increase the use of private transportation and thus of publicly provided roads. Therefore, fees for roads must be set not only to finance them directly but also to account for private pollution and congestion. Various tools are possible: gasoline taxes that are linked to intensity of road use but do not differentiate by place and time of use; tolls on access points (bridges, expressways, downtown boundaries) that can differentiate by place and time of use; parking fees that can also differentiate by place and time of use; or kilometre charges that, using GPS technology, can be linked to place and time of use. An increase in the price of road usage makes public transit more attractive. It also reduces the need to finance transit with subsidies. Thus road pricing is the key for a better use of charges in the financing of transport infrastructures and services of all modes. Let us hope that these charges will be part of the political agenda in a near future.

NOTES

This chapter was prepared for the October 2016 "Financing Urban Infrastructure: Who Should Pay?" conference of the Institute on Municipal Finance and Governance, University of Toronto. We thank Ben Dachis, our commentator, and participants in the conference as well as Richard Bird and Enid Slack for comments on a first version of the paper.

1   This is the last year for which relevant data were collected by Environment Canada.
2   Some municipalities in the province are not included in Quebec's Water Strategy. For municipalities that are included, 11 per cent of industrial, commercial, and institutional buildings are exempt from metering their water consumption (Government of Quebec 2016, 9).
3   Municipal financial reports, Ministry of Municipal Affairs [Rapports financiers des municipalités, MAMROT]. Analyse des revenus consolidés et non consolidés, S27-1, S27-6, and S27-7, http://www.mamrot.gouv.qc.ca/finances-indicateurs-de-gestion-et-fiscalite/information-financiere/profil-financier-et-autres-publications/rapport-financier-des-organismes-municipaux/exercice-financier-2014/#c628.
4   Net benefit is usually associated with the reduction in water consumption. If the consumption of the unit is already low and the cost of meter installation is fixed, the probability of net benefit is narrow.
5   http://www.infrastructure.gc.ca/plan/about-invest-apropos-eng.html.

5

User Charges for Municipal Infrastructure in Western Canada

LINDSAY M. TEDDS

INTRODUCTION

Municipalities in Canada are grappling with an increasing requirement for infrastructure that is being driven by several factors, including:

- expectations from constituents;
- provincial devolution of responsibility for services;
- provincially and federally imposed service standards;
- population and economic growth that requires new or expansion of existing infrastructure;
- infrastructure that is approaching or has exceeded the end of its lifecycle and is in need of replacement or significant repair;
- climate concerns that put increasing pressure to invest in both mitigative and adaptive infrastructure; and
- changing demographics – including aging population, immigration, and increasing ethnic diversity – that bring unique infrastructure demands.

Municipalities bear the burden of these demands because the majority of infrastructure is now planned, built, and maintained by municipal governments. In fact, since the 1960s the municipal portion of infrastructure has grown 12.5 percentage points, from 30.9 per cent in 1961 to 52.4 per cent in 2002, whereas the federal portion dropped by 16.2 points from 23.0 per cent to 6.8 per cent in the same period (Tindal et al. 2012, 241). This includes such diverse infrastructure as city buildings; convention and sports facilities; police, fire, and ambulance stations and services; libraries; parks; recreations centres; roadways; public transit systems; parking; bridges; sidewalks; streetlights; waterfronts; cemeteries, and sewer, water, storm, and refuse systems. It is important to note that infrastructure is related not just to capital expenditures to create the infrastructure, but also to operating expenditures incurred to operate and maintain the resulting infrastructure.

Municipalities, therefore, face the reality of the complex and joint decision of what infrastructure to build, operate, maintain, and replace and how these decisions should be funded. Municipalities, though, are constitutionally constrained to limited revenue sources. They can finance municipal infrastructure generally through intergovernmental transfers, borrowing, or own-source revenues.[1] Municipal own-source revenues are typically limited to property taxes, user fees, and regulatory charges (including local improvement or development charges).

The funding decision, in essence, boils down to who should bear the burden for the costs. Should it be users (through some form of user charge or special levy), local taxpayers (through property or related taxes), provincial taxpayers (through provincial transfers or revenue sharing), or federal taxpayers (through federal transfers); and, should it be current users or taxpayers (pay-as-you-go) or future taxpayers (repayment of borrowing)? Importantly, the decision of who should pay is not an all-or-nothing decision: funding for any given infrastructure project can be raised through a combination of current/future and local/non-local taxpayers/users.

There has been an increasing reliance on the user-pay model to fund municipal infrastructure in Canada. User fees as a source of own-source municipal revenue have more than tripled since 1965 (Tindal et al. 2012, 262). However, the application of the user-pay model is constrained by two important factors. First, user charges have very specific legal constraints on them that may be at odds with the nature of the specific infrastructure for which funds are being sought. Second, municipal government is known as the "the most varied form of government in Canada" (Treff and Ort 2013, 1:3), which makes it difficult not only to make comparisons of the use of user charges both within and across jurisdictions, but also to make sweeping conclusions about the best way for all municipalities to fund their infrastructure priorities.

These characteristics and constraints mix together to provide a complicated landscape within which municipal infrastructure needs can be and are financed and leads to diverse approaches to financing municipal infrastructure in Canada. In addition, they explain why many municipalities may not adhere to the best practices as outlined in the literature. This chapter examines some of the general considerations regarding the constraints on user charges along with specific contextual environments regarding the municipal user charges in western Canada. The chapter begins by setting out the constraints that user charges must meet regardless of jurisdiction and then considers the specific jurisdictional constraints in two western provinces. The discussion focuses on Alberta and British Columbia, as these two provinces, despite being neighbours, have very different environments within with municipalities operate, leading to different reliance on and uses of user charges. The chapter concludes by discussing some of the comparative complications that arise.

USER CHARGES

The phrase "user charge" generally refers to some form of payment by a user that is directly linked to the use of or rights associated with resources, infrastructure, goods, and services. At the municipal level in Canada, there are, in general, only two types of delegated revenue authorities that meet this general definition of a user charge: user fees and regulatory charges.

As discussed in Athaus, Tedds, and McAvoy (2011), Farish and Tedds (2014), and Alhaus and Tedds (2016), user fees and regulatory charges in Canada have very strict legal limitations on them as revenue tools. These limitations, which will be summarized below, have developed through Canadian case law, which means two important things. First, the limitations apply generally in Canada, to all levels of government in all provinces and territories. Second, similar limitations may not exist in other jurisdictions, like the United States and Switzerland.

User Fees

In Canada, a user fee is a charge for a publicly provided good or service, where the revenues from the fee are solely used to offset the costs of providing the good or service; the size of fee is dictated by the cost of providing the good or service (Althaus and Tedds 2016, 61). These conditions have several implications for the design, implementation, and use of user fees in Canada.

First, the revenues from the fee must be solely used to offset the cost of providing the good or service for which the fee is levied (Athaus, Tedds, and McAvoy 2011, 547; Althaus and Tedds 2016, 54–5). This means that the revenues from user fees cannot be deposited into general revenues to offset general expenditures, but must be earmarked and spent purposefully. There is no requirement for the cost recovery to be complete. Costs may only be partially recovered through the revenues generated from a user fee, but, by extension, that shortfall in revenues cannot be made up from revenues from other user fees.

Does it mean that each and every user fee needs its own account as defined by municipal budgeting and accounting standards? There is no specific requirement in the case law that the revenues from each user fee be physically placed into its own user-fee-specific account (Althaus and Tedds 2016, 55). That said, some judges adhere to the strict interpretation of the requirement to have a specific account (Farish and Tedds 2014, 651). Therefore, the best approach would be to use a specific account. However, when multiple user fees are at play the added costs of having to maintain specific accounts for each and every fee may be prohibitive (though these costs can be factored into the size of the user fee). In this case, a general user fee account may suffice. In this case, there is a need to track the money collected along with how the money is spent.

What costs can be included for recovery by a user fee? Canadian courts have made it clear that governments are limited to the recoupment of actual costs (Althaus and Tedds 2016, 92). This means that a municipality is not at liberty to book any costs it chooses. It must follow accounting rules and procedures and not attempt to mask a surplus through the booking of truly unassociated costs. It also implies that including non-financial costs such as externalities and opportunity costs (costs favoured by economists to be included in any cost assessment) for the purpose of determining costs is likely not acceptable.

Second, there must exist a connection between the cost of the good or service and the fee charged (Althaus and Tedds 2016, 55). The best way to explain this limitation is through example: if the cost of providing the service to each user is a flat amount, the fee cannot vary by user. That is, if the cost of providing the good or service is fixed, then the user fee associated with that good or service itself must also be fixed and not vary by user or units (Farish and Tedds 2014, 643). The takeaway is that there must be a clear rationale for a variable fee, and the clearest rationale would be related to varying costs.

Third, there must exist a reasonable connection between the fee and the good or service for which the fee is being charged (Althaus and Tedds 2016, 56–9). This leads to several limitations on user fees. The most important is that the revenues generated from a user fee cannot exceed the costs of the good or service provided. That is, while both partial and full-cost recovery are permitted, user fees, by law, cannot be used to generate large or ongoing surpluses. The qualifiers on the presence of a surplus are important. Canadian courts acknowledge that costs and consumption can change in ways that cannot be predicted a priori and often adjustments cannot be made in the short term to ensure that surpluses are not generated. This means that small or sporadic surpluses are permissible so long are they are accidental or unintentional. Surpluses that are, instead, an intentional design feature of the user fee regime are not permitted.

Another related limitation is that there must exist a tight link between the activity charged for and the activities funded by the user fee revenues (Farish and Tedds 2014, 661–2). An example is helpful to clarify this limitation (Athaus and Tedds 2016, 155). User fees for residential garbage collection must be used to offset the cost of providing residential garbage collection, including pick-up and disposal costs, operating costs, as well as costs incurred to inform consumers about the service. User fees for residential garbage collection cannot, however, be used to offset costs of other municipally provided services that are unrelated to residential garbage collection, like the provision of recreational services. How tight the link needs to be is not yet settled. Can revenues from residential refuse collection be used to fund broader environmental programs, including leaf collection, compost programs, and refuse collection from other municipal services like transit or recreation? Can revenue from parking fees be used to upgrade streetscapes, including street lights, sidewalks, traffic calming measures, benches, landscaping, and bike racks? The answer to these questions is not perfectly clear, but both of the cases mentioned are questionable in terms of the tightness of the connection between the activity charged for, the costs incurred, and the activity being funded through the user fee revenues.

In summary, user fees are a charge for a publicly provided good or service where, by legal constraints, the revenues from the fee must be used solely to offset the cost of providing the good or service, and the size of the fee is dictated by the cost of providing the good or service. That is, revenues from user fees must be earmarked and spent purposefully, and the size of the fee must be supported by actual costs in-curred. In additional, user fees cannot be used to generate surpluses. Revenues must match costs incurred and must be used solely to offset costs related to the good or service being charged for. The legal con-straints on user fees in Canada make their use to fund capital projects for things like public transit, recreation facilities, water and sewage, and refuse collection potentially problematic, but such fees are ideal to sup-port the operation and maintenance costs of infrastructure. The legal constraints also make user fees use as a general revenue tool or their use to cross-subsidize various publicly provided goods and services very problematic and doing so would not sustain a court challenge.

What would happen if a user fee were found to be non-compliant with these limitations? Althaus and Tedds (2016, 59–61) detail the con-sequences. If a charge were found not to be a user fee, it would likely be found to be a tax, the authority for which was likely not delegated to the municipality by the province. In legal terms, the charge will be found to be ultra vires. The usual remedy to such a decision is either for the court to require the municipality to return the money it collected under the charge or, when doing so would create fiscal chaos, for the court to provide a small window for the municipality to amend its charge to make it valid retroactively, assuming amendments would be possible to make the charge consistent with the limitations of a user fee.

Regulatory Charges

Regulatory charges, also known constitutionally as licence fees, are an alternative way for municipalities to charge users. There is a lot of con-fusion around regulatory charges because: (1) they share similar fea-tures with user fees; and (2) some services can be amenable to both types of charges (e.g., parking, dumping). The features of a regulatory charge are detailed in Farish and Tedds (2016, 653–69) and summa-rized here.

Unlike a user fee, a regulatory charge is not related to the provision of a good or service, but, instead, is related to rights or privileges award-ed or granted by the municipality. Regulatory charges are a broad cat-egory of charges imposed by municipal and other governments and include such charges as development charges, local improvement charges, removal and dumping charges (e.g., sand, gravel, water, landfill, electronics, and beverage containers), fines, inspections, environmen-tal protection, and licences (e.g., liquor and animal).

There are four key components to a regulatory charge: (1) a specific regulatory purpose; (2) a detailed code of regulation; (3) actual costs incurred; and (4) a relationship between the regulation and the person being regulated (Farish and Tedds 2014, 658; Althaus and Tedds 2016, 53). Under a regulatory charge either the revenues are used to recover the costs of the regulatory scheme, in whole or in part, or the size of the charge levied on persons may be set to proscribe, prohibit, or encourage a specific behaviour. If the purpose of the regulatory charge is to change behaviour, then a surplus of revenues may be a permitted outcome.

However, as noted by Farish and Tedds (2014, 667) there are two important limitations to the generation of surplus under a regulatory charge. First, there must still be a reasonable relationship between the charge and the regulation. Second, the presence of a behavioural modification aspect has been found by the courts to mean the regulatory charge meets the criteria of an indirect tax. The authority to charge indirect taxes, however, is not delegated to the provinces and, therefore, cannot be delegated to municipalities. Therefore, a regulatory charge enacted by a municipality must still meet the definition of a direct tax, which, according the courts, means that the objective of behavioural modification as a principal objective of a regulatory charge is not available to Canadian municipalities.

In summary, regulatory charges enacted by municipalities have all of the same limitations imposed on them as user fees, a fact that is clear from examining the last two components of a regulatory charge which are identical to the last two components of a user fee as detailed above. That is, user charges in the form of user fees and regulatory charges require: that the revenues from the fee be used solely to offset the costs of providing the good or service; that the size of the fee be dictated by the cost of providing the good or service; and that the link between the charge and the activities to which the revenues are directed be narrow. This means that for Canadian municipalities, regulatory charges and user fees differ only in purpose. Both are cost-recovery tools: a user fee is a charge for a good or service whereas a regulatory charge is for a right or privilege.

If regulatory charges are a tool to recover costs from a right or privilege, are they relevant to fund infrastructure demands faced by municipalities? In a word, yes. There are a number of applicable uses. First, regulatory charges are suitable when infrastructure demands are driven by development. Municipalities provide the right for developers to develop land for the purposes of residential or commercial development and a detailed regulatory code is required to recover the costs of that right. Development demands expansion of sewer, water, schools, parks, recreation facilities, and roads, among other things, and a regulatory charge ensures that the costs of such expansion are levied on the developers and priced into the development, where the price is ultimately borne by the users of the development through the price of selling or leasing the developed properties. Second, certain behaviours or characteristics incite infrastructure investments. Dogs, for example, need park space in which to run, amenities that support excrement removal, and animal control resources. Municipalities can require dogs to have an annual licence and use the revenues to help pay for these services that are used solely by dog owners. For example, the City of Victoria notes: "Dog licence fees help to offset the costs of operating an animal control and pound service, which shelters, feeds and provides care for lost and injured animals. Dog licence fees also offset the costs of providing dog waste bags in City of Victoria parks" (City of Victoria 2016). Third, removal of resources often means that heavy equipment uses municipal roads, which decreases the road's lifespan. A regulatory charge imposed on the right to remove the resource can help fund the cost of road provision, maintenance, and replacement.

As noted above, there is some complexity in determining what is a service and what is a right or privilege, and these categories can often be interchangeable. For example, a levy imposed on landfill waste could be either a user fee or a regulatory charge. For a user fee, the charge is for the use of the landfill, whereas the regulatory charge is for the right to access the landfill. The same is true for parking, waste, sewer, water, and other related levies. While the lines can be and often are blurred between these two types of user charges, the limitations placed on these charges mean that the blurring may simply pose complexities for comparison purposes. This complexity arises because the levies will be included in different categories and the nature and size of the levy can vary considerably for the same category depending on whether the levy is designed as a regulatory charge or a user fee.

Additional Considerations

The legal limitations on user fees and regulatory charges make them imperfect tools to finance municipal infrastructure. The limitation to cost recovery, where costs are restricted to actual costs incurred, makes it difficult for infrastructure costs to be shared intergenerationally. Instead, user fees and regulatory charges in Canada appear best suited to short-term assets whose benefit accrue to the current tax base within the municipal boundaries. This limitation is also at odds with the nature of municipal infrastructure itself, notably the fact that these projects tend to be big-ticket lumpy expenditures for which it is hard to amortize all the costs or to set the fee or charge to allow the municipality to save for future investments.

A related issue in the use of these revenue tools concerns equity. There are two central principles to keep in mind when considering equity. The first principle is the benefit principle, which can be seen where there is a link between the good or service provided and the benefit the consumer receives. User fees and regulatory charges favour the benefits-received principle as in both cases it is the main beneficiary that pays for the resulting infrastructure. However, if the public places a high value on the provision of the good or service and its broad accessibility, the imposition of a user fee or regulatory charge may not be appropriate unless redistribution can be achieved through such tools as discounts or lump-sum transfers.

The second principle is the ability-to-pay principle. There are two aspects of the ability-to-pay principle: horizontal equity and vertical equity. Horizontal equity is the concept that two individuals who have the same ability to pay should pay the same amount. Vertical equity means that the burden of payment should be higher for those who have a greater ability to pay. When the financial burden of a service falls more heavily on higher-income households, it is referred to as progressive; this is generally the favoured policy direction. When the opposite happens – that is, when the financial burden falls more heavily on lower-income households – the policy is regressive and goes against equity principles. User fees and regulatory charges can often be regressive instruments, because the fee or charge will take up more of the income of a lower-income payer than a high-income payer. Equity may then seem to favour financing through the use of progressive taxes. Of course, regressivity of user fees and regulatory charges can often be offset by careful attention to implementation, including discounts and increased service provision.

What is particularly important to note is that municipalities are provided with very little guidance from provinces with respect to the limitations on user charges. While large municipalities have the ability to rely on sophisticated internal and external advice, the same is not true

Table 5.1
Share of user fees, percentage of own-source revenues, geographic region,
1988–2014

	Western Canada	Ontario	Quebec	Atlantic Canada
1988	28.3	27.3	18.4	20.4
1998	30.5	25.3	19.0	22.9
2008	31.4	27.7	18.7	23.6
2014	30.6	27.5	24.4	26.3

Sources: Data for 1988–2008 calculated from Statistics Canada (1988–2008), *Financial Management System*, catalogue no. 68F0023X, http://www5.statcan.gc.ca/olc-cel/olc.action?objId=68F0023X&objType= 2&lang=en&limit=0. Annual.
Data from 2014 calculated from Statistics Canada (2008–2014), Government Finance Statistics, table 385-0037.

of smaller jurisdictions that lack internal capacity. The lack of guidance is further confounded by the fact that most municipal legislation groups fees and charges, often using the word *fee* and defining it to mean both fees and charges (Farish 2006, 91–2). While academic literature does exist to help guide municipalities, it is scattered across multiple, and often contradictory, sources. Providing clear guidance to municipalities, contextualized to the specific environment they are operating in, is well overdue. Farish and Tedds (2014) provide a detailed discussion regarding the definition of and differentiation between user fees and regulatory charges, and Althaus and Tedds (2016) have included this information in a comprehensive book accompanied by an online interactive guide for practitioners to work through.

USER CHARGES IN WESTERN CANADA

As was mentioned, these general financing tools operate within very specific jurisdictional contexts that result in varying applications of these tools in different regions. This context is dictated by various institutional aspects, many of which are established by the provincial devolution of powers to the municipalities.

One of the challenges in making comparisons on the reliance on user charges across Canadian jurisdictions is a lack of comparable data on the use of user fees and regulatory charges by municipalities across the various provinces. Statistics Canada (1998–2008) used to provide the *Financial Management System*, which provided annual detailed data on local government revenue and expenditures across Canada. This data se-

Table 5.2
Share of user fees, percentage of own-source revenues, western provinces,
1988–2014

	Manitoba	Saskatchewan	Alberta	British Columbia
1988	23.2	23.6	32.0	27.4
1998	27.1	26.4	31.6	31.3
2008	35.4	26.0	29.8	33.5
2014	34.1	34.9	25.7	34.7

Source: Data for 1988–2008 calculated from Statistics Canada (1988–2008), *Financial Management System*, catalogue no. 68F0023X, http://www5.statcan.gc.ca/olc-cel/olc.action?objId=68F0023X&objType= 2&lang=en&limit=0. Annual.
Data from 2014 calculated from Statistics Canada (2008–2014), Government Finance Statistics, table 385-0037.

ries was discontinued in 2008 and replaced with *Government Finance Statistics* (Statistics Canada 2008–2014). The former series was much more detailed on the expenditure side, but is generally comparable across the broad revenue categories report, including user fees (reported as sales of goods and services). However, in both cases the data series do not delineate regulatory charges, which, from the provided descriptions, appear to be included in different categories that include other taxes. As a result, no comparisons can be made regarding the use of regulatory charges.

Table 5.1 shows the share of user fees, as a portion of own-source revenues, by geographic region, for select years over the period 1998–2014. The table shows that municipalities in Ontario have reported a fairly stable reliance on user fees as a portion of their own-source revenue, while the other regions show an increasing portion of user fees forming a share of their own-source revenues. Overall, the western Canadian provinces have relied, and continue to rely, more on user fees as a source of own-source revenues than other regions in Canada. As a result, the western Canadian trend is worthy of greater scrutiny.

Table 5.2 shows how the share of user fees as a share of own-source revenues breaks down across the four western provinces. The table shows several interesting trends. First, Alberta is the only province in western Canada that bucks the trend with its municipalities decreasing their reliance on user fees. Second, municipalities in the provinces of Manitoba, Saskatchewan, and BC report an increasing reliance on user fees and by 2014 appear to have converged to a common share of between 34–5 per cent of own-source revenues. This also makes municipalities in these three provinces the most reliant on user fees by a large amount as compared to all other provinces. Third, it is unclear if the differing reliance on user fees is the result of the devolution of powers or structural differences. Each of the provinces devolves powers to its municipalities in very different ways. In addition, each of these provinces faces different geographic and population pressures. For example, not only do the provinces of Manitoba and Saskatchewan have small populations (between 1.3 and 1.15 million respectively) as compared to Alberta and BC (between 4.25 and 4.75 respectively [Statistics Canada 2016]), but, as reported in Treff and Ort (2011, 1:4–1:14), Manitoba and Saskatchewan have the highest number of municipalities per 100,000 people (16.0 and 80.2 respectively) compared to Alberta and British Columbia (9.4 and 5.0 respectively). If municipalities in Manitoba and Saskatchewan serve a smaller population, then user fees might be higher simply because they are spread across smaller populations.

As a result, it appears to be more appropriate to compare the use of user charges in Alberta and British Columbia. The rest of this paper focuses on these two provinces, which have generally devolved similar revenue authorities to their municipalities, making comparison somewhat simpler. However, while these provinces share some characteristics, they have pursued distinct paths that have led to different approaches to funding municipal infrastructure and the reliance on user charges.

One of the very different paths followed in each of these provinces is that related to intergovernmental grants, which will influence reliance on other revenue tools by municipalities in these provinces. Intergovernmental grants in Alberta account for a much larger share of municipal revenues than in BC. Intergovernmental transfers in Alberta average 22.8 per cent of total municipal revenues over the 2008–14 period (Statistics Canada 2008–2014). These transfers are due in part to the ten-year Municipal Sustainability Initiative that was launched in 2007 which is specifically directed to support local infrastructure projects (Alberta n.d.b). BC stands in sharp contrast as intergovernmental transfers now amount to less than 5 per cent of municipal revenues.

Another difference between provinces pertains to the use of regional districts in BC, which are not used in Alberta. British Columbia is made up of twenty-nine regional districts. As detailed by Smith and Stewart (2009) and British Columbia (2006), each regional district is like a federation in which municipalities within the district are represented on the decision-making regional board. These regional districts provide goods and services that are of a regional nature, including water supply, waste management, recycling, and sewage services, and provide a forum through which regional decisions are made. Regional districts were initially established in an effort to provide a semblance of economies of scale for such infrastructure that is not present in the generally small municipalities that exist outside of Metro Vancouver. Regional districts operate under the user-pay principle and cost recovery and are granted a wide range of cost-recovery tools, including taxes, user fees, and regulatory charges. What is relevant for the data shown above is that for many services, the regional districts charge the municipalities directly for services and then the municipalities then determine how to recoup those charges from the constituents. This means that the regional district can charge its municipalities a user fee for a service (e.g., sewage services, refuse collection), but the municipality is not obligated to pass that charge along to its constituents in the form of a user fee. It could, instead, pass the cost along in the form of higher property taxes. So the reliance on user fees in BC may be more related to the mandate of the regional districts to operate under the user-pay principle rather than the individual municipalities directly charging their constituents user fees.

Both the provinces of Alberta (Alberta 2017) and British Columbia (British Columbia n.d.) release comprehensive annual statistics on revenue and expenditures by local governments within the provinces, including regional districts in BC. This provincially provided data not only matches the data available from Statistics Canada, but also provides greater information about expenditures than provided by the Statistics Canada data presented above.[2]

The data for British Columbia allow for the division of user fees by municipality and regional district. According to the data from 2015 (British Columbia n.d.), user fees account for 52 per cent of own-source revenues for regional districts compared to 34 per cent for municipalities. Combined, user fees represent 37 per cent of own-source revenues for all local governments (municipalities and regional districts) in BC. This confirms the previously mentioned supposition that regional districts, given their mandate, do increase the reliance on user fees in BC, but because regional districts represent a much smaller share of local government revenues, it does not account for the significant difference in reliance between BC and Alberta.

Much like the Statistics Canada data, the provincially provided data do not delineate regulatory charges within its own category. Though

Table 5.3
Share of user fees and developer charges, percentage of own-source revenues, by
province and local government type, 2015

	British Columbia		Alberta	
	User fees	Developer charges	User fees	Developer charges
City	34.2	11.7	29.3	3.0
District	32.9	6.7	9.9	1.3
Town	35.7	3.5	31.8	3.3
Village	39.8	2.1	32.3	0.0
Regional district	52.0	1.1		

Sources: Alberta (2017) and British Columbia (n.d.)

Alberta does provide some ability to examine regulatory charges on
their own, this is not matched by data available from BC. Both, however, detail developer charges in a comparable fashion. Using the data
from 2015 (Alberta 2017; British Columbia n.d.) a similar trend to user
fees is revealed. Developer charges in BC represent a 9 per cent share of
own-source revenues (including both regional districts and municipalities), whereas in Alberta, developer charges amount to only 2.6 per
cent of own-source revenues. This is an interesting finding at a time
when many in BC, including the provincial government, are eyeing local
government developer charges as impeding access to affordable housing. This is because these charges are passed onto buyers in the form of
higher housing prices or renters in the form of higher rents. Yet local
governments must fund significant infrastructure to service new developments, including parks, schools, and sewer and water systems,
through limited revenue tools and a narrow tax base. These competing
interests are difficult to resolve.

The provincially provided data are also delineated by municipality, al-
lowing for comparisons across similar types of municipalities. Table 5.3
shows share of user fees and developer charges by common types of local
government in the provinces for the year 2015. The table shows that the
difference in the reliance on user fees between local governments in Alberta and BC is predominantly driven by lower reliance on user fees by
districts in Alberta. In BC the data also show that villages and regional
districts are much more reliant on user fees than other forms of local
government. The reliance on user fees by regional districts was discussed
above and is likely due to their mandate to favour user-pay models.

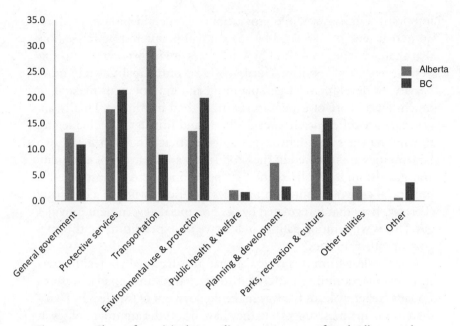

Figure 5.1   Share of municipal expenditures, percentage of total, Alberta and BC, 2015

In terms of developer charges, in BC these are most likely to be used by cities, whereas in Alberta they are most likely to be used by towns, followed closely by cities. BC cities raise nearly 12 per cent of their own-source revenues from developer chargers, compared to 3 per cent by Alberta cities. This difference in the use of developer charges in these two provinces is an area that should be explored in more detail through close examination of authorities, pressures, revenue use, and expenditure pressures, especially in light of the arguments that these charges may be exacerbating housing affordability in BC's major cities.

Finally, the provincially available data also allow a breakdown of expenditures by broadly comparable categories. Figure 5.1 provides this information. Expenditures by municipalities in each of the provinces differ in several notable ways. First, Alberta municipalities spend much more on transportation. This is most likely the result of the responsibility for public transit being devolved to the municipalities in Alberta, whereas public transit is a provincial responsibility in BC. Second, BC spends a higher portion on environmental use and protection. This is despite the fact that Alberta has world-class sewage treatment facilities while many BC municipalities are still dumping primary treated sewage into local waterways. While provincial and federal legislation will require that sewage be treated by 2020, it will be interesting to see how that share changes in BC and how user fees are incorporated into this new provision of services. Third, while BC municipalities rely more heavily on developer charges, planning and development make up a much lower share of expenditures in BC than in Alberta. Finally, another service difference between Alberta and British Columbia relates to who manages and delivers gas and electricity. In Alberta, the two largest cities are involved in the production and delivery of electricity and gas through wholly owned corporations. Across most of BC, a provincial crown corporation provides electricity, whereas a company (FortisBC Inc.) that is regulated by the provincial government provides gas. This is why municipalities in BC have no expenditures in the category of "other utilities."

What is clear from this review is that jurisdictional context matters in terms of examining patterns in user charges in Canada. Western Canada currently leads the way in the deployment of user fees by Canadian municipalities, suggesting they have heard the argument of several economists that the approach to local finance should generally be "whenever possible, charge" (Bird 2010b, 16; Alm 2011, 12–13) so as to ensure the goods and services provided by a municipality are being used by the consumers who value them most and are willing to pay for the use of those goods and services. Comparing two similar provinces, Alberta and BC, however, shows that key differences arise in the use of user charges. Some of these differences are attributable to cost-recovery mandates, municipal size, and differences in the devolution of both revenue tools and service responsibilities. It is, however, difficult to determine what is the most important driver for the reliance on user charges as these differences commingle with numerous context-specific factors unobservable in aggregate data. What is clear is that government expenditure and revenue data for local government available from Statistics Canada are sorely lacking in history and detail to be of any comparative use. Fortunately, the provinces of BC and Alberta have made detailed data available that are very consistent for comparison purposes. Statistics Canada should learn from these provinces and work to provide data that are desperately needed to analyze local government trends such as the reliance on user fees to fund municipal infrastructure.

What has been detailed here is the general use of user charges and the general patterns of expenditures by municipalities in Alberta and BC. A closer look at select cities may yield additional observations. The local

Table 5.4
Share of user fees, percentage of own-source revenues, select local
governments, 2015

	British Columbia		Alberta	
	Vancouver	Metro Vancouver	Calgary	Edmonton
	43.5	83.6	30.3	22.6

Source: Alberta (2017) and British Columbia (n.d.)

governments for Calgary and Edmonton in Alberta and Vancouver and
Metro Vancouver in BC have been selected for the following reasons.
First, two-thirds of Alberta's population (Alberta n.d.a) is now within
the boundaries of either the City of Edmonton or the City of Calgary,
both of which have been experiencing and are expected to continue to
experience substantial population growth. This has put a substantial
pressure on these cities' infrastructure. Unlike in other provinces with
large municipalities servicing a large portion of the population, the
province of Alberta has not established separate legislation for these
municipalities bestowing additional functions or revenue authorities.
However, the provincial government recently commenced consultations on the establishment of charters for these cities, which may de-
volve new revenue tools (Alberta n.d.a). Second, the largest regional
district in BC is Metro Vancouver, which encompases about half the
population of BC and contains twenty-three municipalities. The largest
municipality in this regional district is Vancouver, which is one of the
only municipalities in BC that has its own specific provincial act, called
the Vancouver Charter, which was passed in 1953. Vancouver is struggling with two significant infrastructure requirements: namely affordable housing, due to the significant rise in property values in the last
twenty years, and transit, due to urban sprawl, traffic congestion, and
population growth.

Table 5.4 shows the share of user fees as a share of own-source revenues across the select local governments in the two provinces. The City
of Vancouver and its regional district receive a much larger share of user
fees than the BC average. The City of Vancouver receives 43.5 per cent
of its own-source revenues from user fees and the regional district of
Metro Vancouver receives nearly 84 per cent of its own source revenues
from user fees. Unfortunately, BC Local Government Statistics do not

Table 5.5
Collection and distribution of user fees by function, percentage of user-fee revenues/disbursements, Calgary and Edmonton 2015

Service	Collection		Disbursements	
	Calgary	Edmonton	Calgary	Edmonton
General administration	1.5	1.6	5.6	2.3
Police	1.6	3.3	2.9	2.1
Fire	0.6	0.3	2.2	0.1
Roads, streets, sidewalks, lighting	6.2	3.0	21.5	26.4
Public transit	16.8	18.1	17.0	8.5
Storm sewers and drainage	5.0	7.0	3.9	3.3
Water supply and distribution	24.1	0.0	7.1	0.8
Wastewater treatment and disposal	21.8	16.3	5.1	3.4
Waste management	8.0	24.0	6.4	2.9
Subdivision land and development	9.7	12.1	3.5	0.0
Parks and recreation	4.4	7.2	6.7	5.7
Other	0.3	7.1	18.1	44.5
Total %	100.0	100.0	100.0	100.0
Total $	1,100,837,000	639,976,000	703,806,000	607,740,000

Source: Alberta Municipal Affairs, Municipal Financial and Statistical Data, Schedule E.

break down user fees by function, but, from the expenditure information they provide, it is clear that user fees are much higher for Metro Vancouver. Budget documents for the regional authority show that 80 per cent of its revenues come from water, sewer, and solid waste fees (Metro Vancouver 2017, 8) and it spends 85 per cent of its revenue on these three services as well (9). As mentioned previously, unlike in Alberta, public transit in BC is a provincial responsibility. In Metro Vancouver, transportation is provided by Translink, a statutory authority of the provincial government, so none of the user fees for roads or transit are included in the figures for Metro Vancouver (which spends nothing on these functions) or the City of Vancouver.

The two largest cities in Alberta show very different patterns related to user fees. The City of Calgary's share of own-source revenues from user fees is well above the provincial average, at more than 30 per cent. This is contrasted with the City of Edmonton at below the provincial average, with less than 23 per cent of its share of own-source revenues coming from user fees. Unlike BC, Alberta does provide fairly detailed information about the category of municipal functions raised by user fees and the distribution of these user-fee revenues across municipal functions.

Table 5.5 provides information on the collection and distribution of user fees for Alberta's two largest cities, Edmonton and Calgary, which account for two-thirds of the province's population. For example, provincial data for Calgary show that user fees accounted for 25 per cent of municipal revenues in 2015.[3] Table 5.5 also shows the distribution of user fees by function and indicates the largest proportion of fees are for water and wastewater followed by public transit. The most notable difference between the two cities is that Calgary collects user fees for water supply and distribution whereas Edmonton does not, but this is partially offset by higher fees for waste management in Edmonton. In terms of disbursements (which includes annual and interest expenses), it is interesting to note that total annual disbursements of user fees in Calgary are significantly lower than the total amount collected. In fact, the City of Calgary is reporting a nearly $400 million surplus in user fees. Given the legal constraints on user fees, the City of Calgary would be well advised to carefully review its user-fee policy. The City of Edmonton also reports a surplus, but it totals only $32,236,000, which could be interpreted as a small, sporadic surplus, though also worthy of review. In terms of the category of disbursements, both cities are struggling with ensuring that user-fees revenue is spent on the activities from which it is raised. There appears to be some concerning cross-subsidization of activities that do not appear consistent with the legal constraints. This again points to a need for these municipalities to carefully review the user-fee policies, in terms not only of amounts generated, but also of how those amounts are disbursed.

EMERGING ISSUES IN FINANCING MUNICIPAL INFRASTRUCTURE IN BC AND ALBERTA

There are a number of emerging issues with respect to financing municipal infrastructure that get at the heart of the complexities with financing municipal infrastructure. This section considers two current and intense debates: paying for road infrastructure, and paying for public transit.

Paying for Road Infrastructure

The major cities in the two provinces – namely Metro Vancouver, Calgary, and Edmonton – are burdened with significant traffic congestion due to a mix of geography, urban sprawl, and car culture. There have been calls to implement road tolls or congestion charges (two forms of user charges) in these areas and use the funds to pay for road infrastructure and to fund transit alternatives. While the literature provides a detailed and convincing rationale for road tolls and congestion charges to address these issues, this financing tool has been met with distaste.

In BC, the Community Charter explicitly forbids municipalities from imposing road charges, though the province does collect tolls on two local bridges. Metro Vancouver did consider the idea of a congestion charge to pay for much-needed investments in public transit; however, it preferred a 0.5 per cent add-on to the provincial sales tax. That policy proposal went forward in a referendum and was flatly rejected by voters. After that failed referendum (Johnson and Baluja 2015), the issue of congestion charges has not been refloated as an alternative.

In Alberta, there have recently been some strong messages about the use of toll roads to fund infrastructure. While the former Conservative government was debating the implementation of road tolls in Alberta and a recent report from the C.D. Howe Institute (Dachis 2016) stated that the Canadian provincial governments should be developing and implementing road tolls to help pay for the repairs to current infrastructure and new projects, this approach to raising revenues has been criticized and swept aside by the NDP government. In June 2016, Joe Ceci, the NDP finance minister, stated that although the NDP government was looking for ways to deal with their financial crises, "No to road tolls, unless you know a road that I can make $6.1 billion on" (Wood 2016). The NDP transportation minister Brian Mason further noted: "Our view is that there should not be toll roads in Alberta right now … I think Albertans would not respond well to that" (Wood, 2016).

While the use of a road toll or congestion charge would be an efficient solution to the problem and raise revenues that can and should be reinvested into municipal infrastructure, it is clear that such an alternative revenue tool will not be considered any time soon in either province. This is an interesting dichotomy since user charges are deemed to be appropriate for such municipal services such as utilities and recreation. In this scenario, it appears that "politicians see tolls or other types of road pricing as a political hot potato. They want to be re-elected and instituting a toll or tax is not the most popular thing to do" (Mayer 2011). Moreover, the decision not to support road tolls does not address any social benefit policy considerations in terms of reducing traffic and congestion for either environmental or health reasons.

Public Transit

Many municipalities across Canada have provided the largest share of government funding for the capital costs of expanding and building local transit systems, with British Columbia municipalities being the exception because of the provincial control of the transit system. To pay for the ongoing costs of capital and operating public transit costs, municipalities have adopted user fees (fare box revenue), property taxes, and other sources of funding. Yet many Canadian cities, including those in British Columbia and Alberta, have not been able to keep up with the investment in public transit that is needed to address traffic congestion, long commutes, and air pollution.

With a newly elected Liberal government at the federal level, an NDP government in power for the first time in Alberta, and with a provincial election in British Columbia taking place in May 2017, the time for these three levels of government to make funding commitments to infrastructure has created an opportunity to make a significant dent in the transit infrastructure deficit in both Alberta and British Columbia. As noted earlier, numerous matching grants have been put forward by the federal government, and Alberta and British Columbia have been able to take advantage of such opportunities to invest in much-needed public transit projects across their provinces (see, e.g., Alberta 2016). For example, in a recent announcement made in Alberta about the funds being distributed under the Public Transit Infrastructure Fund, there were "important investments in 46 transit projects across Edmonton to support critical planning for the city's next LRT expansion, as well as buses, LRT cars and significant infrastructure upgrades for the city's existing transit system"(Alberta 2016). Through this specific fund, the federal government states that "funding will be provided to support the rehabilitation of public transit systems; the planning of future system improvements and expansions; enhanced asset management; and system optimization and modernization" (Infrastructure Canada 2016).

Despite the $3.4 billion in public transit funding that was announced
in the spring 2016 budget, there is criticism that this money is not
enough and that it is less than the money promised during the 2015 Liberal election campaign (Lenti 2016). To address the infrastructure deficit,
the Liberals stated they would spend approximately $5 billion in new in-
frastructure spending in 2016 and another $5 billion in the following
year. While there are challenges concerning when municipalities will
start to feel the effects of this investment, Raymond Louie, president of
the Federation of Canadian Municipalities, lauded the government for
providing funding with fewer strings attached and stated: "This is a
tremendous change in policy by the federal government" (Lenti 2016).
The federal funding announcements are still relatively new, and while the
amount of investment in public transit is significant, the provinces and
municipalities will need to work together in the future to determine
what additional funds are needed and what services should be a priority.

CONCLUSION

Municipalities confront complex policy challenges that place a strain
on their fiscal resources, including deteriorating infrastructure and devolution of responsibilities from other levels of government. User fees
may help municipalities generate additional revenue to assist with these
complex policy challenges, either by raising additional revenue, shifting
the funding of a good or service from property taxes to user fees in
order to reallocate those funds, or supporting municipalities to ensure
the best use of municipal resources.

This chapter makes three observations. First, the user charges that are
generally available to municipalities to fund infrastructure, namely user
fees and regulatory charges, are fairly limited, each with its own unique
limitations. Detailing the pros and cons of these tools shows that different tools are suitable for different kinds of projects or problems.

Second, the availabilty and use of the financing tools depend on the
specific environment and jurisdictional reality that the municipality is
operating. Municipalities within and across the provinces are delegated very different responsibilities and revenue tools that either favour
or discourage the use of any given tool, despite its theoretical uses. The
chapter details this by looking at the municipal context in the provinces
of Alberta and BC. These jurisdictions share some similar features, but
also significant differences, and these are important for financing municipal infrastructure in each of these jurisdictions.

Third, there are shared concerns across the jurisdictions that have met with different responses. This demonstrates the importance of flexibility in financing tools. A wide range of financial capacities is available to municipalities in BC and Alberta. This range of financial capacities affects the ability of each municipality to raise the necessary funds within its jurisdiction to deliver the basic bundle of municipal services. Disparities in service delivery abilities may be particularly noticeable when we compare municipalities within a region. BC has attempted to address this through the use of regional districts to fund regional projects. Alberta still relies on individual responsibility, which becomes pertinent for municipalities bordering on large cities. Such municipalities can benefit from the services provided by the large city without needing to raise their own revenue.

Finally, the limitations on user charges make them challenging to apply to cases in which significant up-front investments are needed. User charges come with very specific legal constraints, some of which are at odds with the nature of the infrastructure itself, notably the fact that these projects tend to be big-ticket lumpy expenditures for which it is hard to directly tie the benefits derived from the resulting infrastructure to the source of the financing. In reviewing the data from the cities of Edmonton and Calgary it is apparent that the limitations are not well known and cities need greater guidance in setting user-fee policy. Cities would be well advised to carefully review the guidance provided by Althaus and Tedds (2016).

NOTES

1   PPPs provide another alternative, but these have not yet been used extensively at the municipal level in Canada. The topic of PPPs is covered in chapter 8.
2   The author first obtained the general revenue data for municipalities and regional districts in each province for the year 2014 and was able to obtain nearly identical results, as shown in table 5.2. For Alberta, user fees as a share of own-source revenue was calculated to be 25.9 per cent, compared to 25.7 per cent in table 5.2. For BC, user fees as a share of own-source revenues was calculated to be 35.9 per cent, compared to 34.7 per cent in table 5.2.
3   Source: Alberta Municipal Affairs, Municipal Financial and Statistical Data, Schedule D.

6

The Role of User Charges in Funding the Flow of US Infrastructure Services

ROBERT D. EBEL AND YAMENG WANG

INTRODUCTION

Why This Topic Matters

Twenty years ago, user charges accounted for 18 per cent of US state and local own-source general revenues. That put it well behind the revenue importance of both the sales and gross receipts and property tax categories and on par with the sum of the individual and corporate income tax. Today, charges account for 21 per cent of state/local own-source general revenues – eclipsing the income taxes, nearly on par with the property tax, and closing in on the sales and gross receipts category. There are three reasons why this trend is likely to continue. The first is the "fiscal squeeze," in which the relative revenue productivity of the two large General Revenue categories – the taxes on personal income and property – is being eroded due to a combination of direct discretionary tax-base reductions and changing economic, demographic, and institutional trends that are not being captured in the traditional income and general sales tax bases (Wallace 2015; Fox 2015). Second, in contrast to what is, at least at present, a citizen "anti-tax" mood, state and local policy makers increasingly support local fee and charge activities (Sjoquist and Stoycheva 2012). Third, the technology for employing new charges is improving, particularly in the area of motor vehicle–related activities as revenue collection is facilitated (e.g., smart parking meters that allow governments to accurately monitor and report on the use of public spaces; GPS tracking of vehicle weights and distances driven; highway congestion pricing).

Clearly, for purposes of revenue productivity, user charges and fees matter. In addition, among all the revenue tools available to pay for public services, user charges best fit the benefit principle of public finance that state and local revenue policy should be designed so that the policy outcome is both efficient and equitable.

- Efficiency. Because of their *quid pro quo* character, charges serve as both a rationing mechanism and a long-term public expenditure planning tool. With respect to rationing, there is evidence that greater local reliance on user charges to finance government services leads to a reduction in municipal expenditures – and, in the case of highway use, reduced congestion (Fisher 2016). For similar efficiency reasons, the planner will turn to user charges to ascertain citizen willingness to pay, which, in turn, can guide decisions regarding (1) the type and quantity of public services to promote or cut back; (2) determination of the right price to set for a given service; and (3) a methodology for estimating the economic benefits generated (Gulyani 2005).
- Equity. At the same time, user charges and fees meet the test of fairness that those who benefit from a flow of services are the same person or group of persons who pay the costs of the service (Musgrave 2005).[1]

PURPOSE AND SCOPE

In order to understand and analyze user charges in policy and practice and the role of user charges in funding the flow of current services provided by public infrastructure, one must first have a firm grasp on the nature of the data and how it can be organized intergovernmentally. Accordingly, the purpose of this chapter is to focus on the pattern and performance of user charges as a source for paying for infrastructure services that are delivered to citizens through the highly decentralized US system governance. The associated topics of (1) the capital investment process, (2) the theory of user finance, (3) the price effects of user charging, and (4) the implementation of a user charge policy have been addressed elsewhere.[2]

ORGANIZATION OF THE CHAPTER

This presentation begins by establishing a set of knowledge preconditions that are presented in a logical sequence of four steps that establish the framework for the subsequent discussion of the role of user charges in financing current infrastructure services:

- the need to be explicit as to what one means by the term infrastructure and how it can be empirically defined by an agreed-upon set of types (modes) of infrastructure;
- an awareness that the topic is about paying for a flow of current services rather than adding to the nation's capital stock
- an explanation of why funding in this context is primarily a state and local responsibility; and
- the terms by which one can explicitly define user charges as "current charges" in support of infrastructure.

The chapter then proceeds to work through a set of descriptive and analytical discussions that are accompanied by tables and charts that reveal the highly intergovernmental nature of funding US infrastructure services. The chapter concludes with comments on the short- and medium-term outlook for the use of user charges as part of a strategy for paying for infrastructure services.

TERMINOLOGY, DEFINITIONS, AND DATA

Infrastructure and Its Modes

The first step in setting the context is to recognize that, as Orszag (2008) puts it, infrastructure is notoriously difficult to define. Most often the term applies to some set of general government "hard" physical assets such as roadways, bridges, and sewer pipes (Bird and Slack, this volume; NCPWI 1988; Ulbrich and Maguire 2005). However, other treatments of the topic have included social and even intangible assets (Kim 2016).[3] Moreover, infrastructure that has a "public" nature may be private or public – or some mix of both (Marlow 2012; Siemiatycki, this volume).[4] In addition, one geographical area may be served by a municipal or joint intergovernmental compact, whereas the same services in another area are privately supplied. For example, in the US there is public access to both publicly and privately owned highways, parks and recreation facilities, transit systems, and water and sewer authorities. The same type of infrastructure may show up in the public database ... or not.

For the purposes of this analysis we have followed the US Census Bureau definitions of state and local capital outlay ("infrastructure") and its associated funding streams.[5] There are two important reasons for doing so. First, the Bureau applies a survey-based consistent definition across governments of what constitutes revenues and expenditures even though each type of government – federal, state, and local – may in its own financial documents categorize the stock of capital and flow of user-charges revenues and expenditures differently.[6] This standardization allows one to make consistent statements across all the state/local systems over time for an agreed set – and definition – of modes of infrastructure. According to the standardized Census definitions, there are twelve types of infrastructure: education; hospitals; highways; air transport (airports); parking facilities; sea and inland port facilities; natural resources; parks and recreation; housing and community development; sewerage; solid waste management; and "other" activities not falling in one of the other eleven functional categories (US Census Bureau 2006).[7]

Second, Census standardization further allows one to make statements about the role of user charges in infrastructure financing by type of local government, which, as discussed in this chapter, includes fifty states plus the District of Columbia and the nation's 89,004 local governments (US Census Bureau 2013).[8] These 89,004 local governments are categorized into five types: the first three are general-purpose units and the next two are special-purpose governments: counties (3,031), municipalities (19,522), townships (16,364), special districts (37,203) and independent school districts (12,884).[9]

A Flow, Not a Stock, Concept

A second step in setting the framework is to make explicit that the focus is on paying for the operating of infrastructure services. As used here, the term *funding* is a flow concept, matching the current flow of spending benefits to the users who pay for those benefits.[10] This is distinct from the payments associated with the *financing* of capital stock such as (1) one-time special assessments that come in the form of compulsory contributions collected from property owners who benefit infrastructure improvements that "go beyond' that of routine maintenance (e.g., street paving, sidewalks, sewer lines); (2) developer fees, exactions, and in-kind investments (infrastructure that may be on site such as a sewer hook-up or an off-ramp to a developer's facility or offsite link-

ages such as requiring a developer to build a fire station or school prox-
imate to the development project); (3) spending "linkages" such as requiring a developer to build and transfer to the government or some
non-profit charity organization; and (4) even payments for the right to
name sports stadiums, transit stops, and the use of public utility air
rights (Fisher and Wassmer 2016).

A Topic for State and Local Government Finance

The third step in this sequence is to ask "Which type of government or
governments are functionally responsible for paying for the flow of current infrastructure service?" Here the data show that from both a capital investment and a capital ownership perspective, state and local
governments are the stewards of the vast stock of the public's infrastructure (McNichol 2016). There are three considerations:

Adding to the capital stock. Using a mix of pay-as-you go current revenue, federal grants, and, primarily, long-term debt (Kim 2016), one
finds that the state/local sector accounts for nearly three-quarters (73
per cent) of capital investment spending. Indeed, even in the federal
grant-intensive water and transport sectors, the state and local sector
provides 62 per cent of capital spending and 88 per cent of operation
and maintenance expenditures.[11]

Owning the capital stock. Just looking at the capital investment numbers does not make the case that current funding of infrastructure is a
topic of state and local finance. The more important question that
needs to be addressed is which government sector – federal or state/
local – is the owner of the US stock of public infrastructure?

On this point, the data are clear and convincing that when one examines the state/local vs federal ownership shares of the net stock of
total non-defence public assets in the United States, the provision of infrastructure in the US is primarily a state and local function. Upon examining the data for the net value of structures (one must exclude
equipment), one finds that ownership – and thus the responsibility
for operating and maintaining the nation's capital – is 93 per cent
state/local and 7 per cent federal (figure 6.1). Moreover, this is not a recent development. Throughout its history, the United States has had a
fiscal culture that has assigned state and local government a dominant
role in infrastructure construction and the provision of funds to pay
for its flow of current services (Davis, Hughes, and McDougall 1969;
Walton and Rockoff 2013). A review of the data will reveal that the

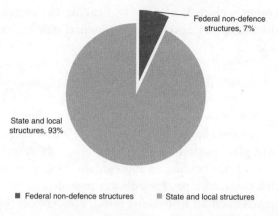

Figure 6.1   Fixed assets owned: federal and state/local governments, 2015

Source: US Bureau of Economic Analysis, author calculations.

percentages shown in figure 6.1 for 2015 have generally held since 1925, when the US Bureau of Economic Analysis (BEA) began tracking fixed assets.

Federal user charges and fees. Although the US federal government has a long list of what it classifies as charges and fees, with some exceptions these charges are not for the purpose of financing the public's stock of physical infrastructure. There are four distinct types of federal charges and fees, including some that the Census categorizes as taxes: (1) *user fees* that fit the conventional textbook definition of a sum of money paid by an individual who voluntarily chooses to access a public service or facility (e.g., national parks, camping grounds, canal tolls) along with payments for insurance premiums and charges for the use of federal land, such as grazing livestock; (2) *regulatory charges* ranging from payments for testing and inspecting equipment and facilities to fees for securing trademark rights, operations of the Federal Communications Commission, food and drug inspection and fees, and charges that derive from the power of the sovereign central state (e.g., passport issuance, patents); (3) *benefit taxes* that mostly relate to transportation (e.g., fuel taxes dedicated to the Highway Trust Fund, a head tax on airport departures and arrivals that is dedicated to the Airport and Airways Trust Fund); and (4) *liability-based taxes* levied for the purpose of abating hazards or compensating injuries (e.g., taxes on mining to fund the Black Lung Disability Trust Fund, a tax on vaccines dedicated to a Vaccine Injury Compensation Fund, and taxes on motor vehicle, aviation, and other fuels dedicated to the Leaking Underground Storage Tank Trust Fund that covers environmental damage clean ups. (Richardson 2005).

User Charges: Define and Measure

So far, so good. Now, how about just going to the textbook definition for a definition of "user charges" and moving on? Well, indeed, the textbook is the right place to start – a charge (and fee – the terms are used together here) is a price paid by an individual or group of people designed to match those who pay for publicly provided goods and services with those who benefit from those goods and services (Bird 1976; Richardson 2005). The principle is similar to a private market transaction *quid pro quo* between the payer for, and the supplier of, a commodity.[12] In the context of this book's question of "who pays?" the task for this chapter is to examine the US practice of spatially matching benefit areas (the flow of infrastructure services to users) with funding areas (the type of government best placed to charge for that flow of services). This is the "matching principle" (Bird 2000).

The detail of the US Census Bureau allows one to make sense of this match. To get started, one needs to be clear on the precise definition of user charges – what Census labels as "Current Charges" – which for purposes of data consistency is adopted in this chapter. Current Charges exclude the following:

- *General taxes*, which are compulsory to government without reference to any specific benefits derived from government expenditures (Bird 1976; Thuronyi 2005).
- *Specific benefit taxes* as compulsory charges levied on a person or group of people assumed to be the principal beneficiaries of certain public services. Examples are motor vehicle licences and motor fuel taxes paid by motorists as a class rather than in direct use of roads and highways, and the excise tax on an airline ticket.
- *Special assessments*, which, as noted above, are compulsory contributions collected from owners of property who benefit from capital improvements to defray the cost of such improvements. These assessments are typically apportioned according to the assumed benefits to the property affected by the improvements and are paid either on a pay-as-you-go basis or through payment of debt service on indebtedness incurred to finance the improvements.

- *Utility revenue.* A fourth Census Bureau exclusion from its definition of infrastructure service Current Charges is revenue from the
  sale of utility commodities and services to the public and to other
  governments. There are four utility sectors: electric power, gas supply, water supply, and mass transit (US Census Bureau 2006).

Unlike the last three exclusions bulleted above, each of which is explicitly linked to the capital construction stage of economic activity and
thus for which there is a reasonably clear "bright line" between a capital and a current charge, the case for separate treatment of utilities is
more blurred since utility operations require users to pay for the current service in the same *quid-pro-quo* relationship that one associates
with a user charge. Thus, there are fare cards at the mass transit system
entry gates (and in some systems also at the exit), and, for water supply,
connection and distribution charges. To make things even a bit more
blurry the Bureau also makes it clear that even though it separates out
utilities from its definition of current charges, what it reports as "utility revenues" are only the user-type fees that are collected from its customers (figure 6.3; US Census Bureau 2006).

It follows that in a strict application of the definition of user charges,
utility revenues would be so classified. However, to include utilities
along with the twelve modes of infrastructure would be misleading.
Utilities (like liquor stores) are operated as enterprises and as such are
accounted for separately in state and local budget accounts – not as part
of general government. Moreover, since most utilities in the US are
investor-owned and investor-operated (thus also not part of general government) and generally self-supporting (through grants from "spon-
soring" general-purpose governments, sale of services, return on own
investments), to treat the sector as general government activity would
distort the infrastructure mode data.

Accordingly, for purposes of assembling intergovernmentally consistent data on how state and local employ user charges for paying for
the flow of publicly provided infrastructure services, "user charges" are
defined and measured by the Census definition of Current Charges
(CC):

Amounts received from the performance benefiting the person
charged, and from sales of commodities and services except liquor
store sales. Includes fees, assessments and other reimbursements for
current services, rents and sales derived from commodities or serv-

ice furnished. Current Charges exclude intergovernmental revenues, interdepartmental charges, license taxes (which relate to
privileges granted by the government) and utility revenues.
(www.census/gov/govs/local/definitions)

Note that this definition encompasses three important features. The
charges are (1) set by state and local governments, (2) part of a cur-
rent/operating budget, and (3) payments for a flow of governmentally
provided infrastructure services. The types (modes) of infrastructure for
which the Census classifies current charges are the twelve identified
above in the discussion relating to the definition of infrastructure and
shown in figure 6.2. Figure 6.3 illustrates the types of charges associated with each of twelve categories. The twelve modes associated with
current charges are the same that Census uses to report capital outlays.

THE NUMBERS

Current Charges are important not only due to their share of state and
local General Revenues Generated (16.5 per cent, table 6.1) but also, as
noted, they can be designed to meet the twin tests of efficiency and equity and efficiency. Moreover, they can be tools for making more effective and transparent public-sector regulatory policy ranging from that
of monitoring "small" local activities such as rip-rapping part of the environmentally protected shoreline to using the state and local-owned
and -managed interstate highway system.[13]
The remainder of this section presents a set of tables and charts
that are as arcane as they are revealing regarding the use and trends
of current infrastructure charges. The purpose is to provide both a
general knowledge base and the intergovernmental story of the role
of infrastructure user charges. To facilitate this, the presentation is
organized on a table-by-table format whereby the information in
each table draws on those previously presented. Thus, the discussion
begins with a presentation of how current charges fit into the total
state and local system of General Revenues and then proceeds to
present current charges by type of infrastructure, the trends over the
past two decades, and the numbers for both the state and local sector, which are then further broken down into state vs local, and then
by type of local government. The empirical work concludes with a
look at the degree to which the state/local use of current charges is
correlated with per capita income and measures of revenue capacity
and revenue effort.

Figure 6.2: Definitions of types (models) of infrastructure

Description	*Definitions*
Education (K–12 as well as post-secondary/higher education)	Schools, colleges, and other educational institutions (e.g., for blind, deaf, and other handicapped individuals), and educational programs for adults, veterans, and other special classes. State institutions of higher education include activities of institutions operated by the state, except that agricultural extension services and experiment stations are classified under Natural Resources. Hospitals serving the public are classified under Hospitals. Revenue and expenditure for dormitories, cafeterias, athletic events, bookstores, and other auxiliary enterprises financed mainly through charges for services are reported on a gross basis.
Hospitals	Financing, construction acquisition, maintenance, or operation of hospital facilities, provision of hospital care, and support of public or private hospitals. Own hospitals are facilities administered directly by the government concerned. Other hospitals refer to support for hospital services in private hospitals or other governments. Nursing homes are included under Public Welfare unless they are directly associated with a government hospital.
Highways	Construction, maintenance, and operation of highways, streets, and related structures, including toll highways, bridges, tunnels, ferries, street lighting, and snow and ice removal. Highway policing and traffic control are classed under Police Protection.
Air transportation (airports)	Construction, maintenance, operation, and support of airport facilities.
Parking facilities	Construction, purchase, maintenance, and operation of public-use parking lots, garages, parking meters, and other distinctive parking facilities on a commercial basis.
Sea and inland port facilities	Canal tolls, rents from leases, concession rents, and other charges for use of commercial or industrial water transport and port terminal facilities and related services. *Excludes* fees and rents related to water facilities provided for recreational purposes, such as marinas, public docks, and toll ferries.

Figure 6.2 (*continued*)

Description	Definitions
Natural resources	Conservation, promotion, and development of natural resources, such as soil, water, forests, minerals, and wildlife. Includes irrigation, drainage, flood control, forestry and fire protection, soil reclamation, soil and water conservation, fish and game programs, agricultural fairs, and agricultural extension services and experiment stations.
Parks and recreation	Provision and support of recreational and cultural scientific facilities and activities including golf courses, play fields, playgrounds, public beaches, swimming pools, tennis courts, parks, auditoriums, stadiums, auto camps, recreation piers, marinas, botanical gardens, galleries, museums, and zoos. Also includes convention centres and exhibition halls.
Housing and community development	Construction and operation of housing and redevelopment projects, and other activities to promote or aid housing and community development.
Sewerage	Provision of sanitary and storm sewers, sewage disposal facilities and services. Sewer services may be provided by a single locality or through intergovernmental coordination. In some parts of the (typically rural) US sewerage is disposed of using private septic tank systems.
Solid waste management	Street cleaning, solid waste collection and disposal, and provision of sanitary landfills.
Other charges	Charges not covered by any of the above categories, such as those derived from court and recording fees, police, fire, correction, defense, public welfare, public nursing homes, public libraries, and health activities. *Excludes* reimbursements and special assessments for capital outlay improvements which benefit specific property owners (e.g., Special Assessments) and sale of used vehicles, surplus equipment, scrap materials that do not relate to any specific function or service.

Sources: US Bureau of the Census Classification Manual (2006) and Census of Government Definitions, www.census.gov.

Figure 6.3: Illustrations of user fees and charges used by state and local governments

Type of public infrastructure services	Description
Education, K–12	School lunch sales, student activity fees, student transportation, sale or rental of books, gymnasium uniforms and equipment use, tuition, sale or rental of text books, revenues from athletic contests. *Excludes* tuition received from other governments.
Higher education	Tuition, general student activity fees, transportation fees, dormitory room and board. Also gross receipts from sales and charges by cafeterias, athletic contests, bookstores, and similarly commercial activities financed wholly or largely through charges.
Highways and roads (includes ferries)	This category includes road, tunnel, and bridge tolls, which may vary (1) for the same facility whether the toll is paid by transponder or at a toll gate, (2) by type of motor vehicle, and (3) according to where on the highway system it is paid (e.g., in the US east coast fourteen states share the same user-transponder, EZ Pass, which is associated with the user's credit card so that each state records each separate use of the transponder, thereby allowing each state to set its own prices; many other states and highway authorities have similar own-systems). This category also includes non-utility governmentally owned and operated subway and bus fare receipts as well as landing and departure fees, congestion levies (e.g., high-occupancy toll lanes that may vary by peak /non-peak times), fees for street cuts and special traffic signs, snow plowing, concession fees to commercial activities (e.g., service stations, restaurants), rights-of-way fees for public utilities, and lease of toll roads (e.g., the Indiana Toll Road, which is concurrent with Interstate 80 and connects Ohio and Illinois). Note: Although US highways are funded in part from the Federal Highway Trust Fund, which is fully tax financed (CBO, 6 May 2014, table 1), there are no federally owned non-defence highways in the US. In 2012 US Highway Trust

Figure 6.3 *(continued)*

Type of public infrastructure services	*Description*
	Fund grants to state plus local governments were $66.8 billion, which was equal to 30.2 per cent of total direct spending for highway finance. For the fifty states and DC, road and crossing tolls accounted for 18.9 per cent of total state highway user fees. The other 82.1 per cent was derived from motor fuel and motor carrier taxes (US Department of Transportation, *Highway Statistics, 2014*). Mass transit systems that are defined as utilities (see text).
Public hospitals	Many states require that public hospitals publish their list of fees. Includes charges and fees from patients, private insurance companies, and public insurance programs (such as Medicare, whereby one is automatically enrolled at age 65 if already receiving Social Security or Railroad Retirement Board benefits), and institutions for the handicapped. Charges include services for special aides, such as a special nursing aide, emergency room fees, operating rooms, and patient rooms that vary by (1) the technical nature of the operating room, or (2) the degree of privacy, whether in a special service such as rehabilitation, intensive care, psychiatric, pulmonary, or recovery for room charges. Other direct charges are assessed for anaesthetics, lab tests, routine medical supplies from bandages to breathing tubes, charges by type of post-operative therapy (e.g., occupational, physical, pulmonary), body scans (e.g., varying by extent, class/level type), and by location on body of heart scan, CT scan, radiology. Hospitals may also pay a Hospital Provider Fee to help finance the state's role in providing Medicaid (a national health insurance fund) and to defray administrative costs of a Department of Health. *Excludes* charges of public university hospitals open to general public, revenues received from other governments for care of patients, medical care provided as part of public welfare programs, fees of state schools for the blind, deaf, or handicapped, and health clinics operating on an outpatient basis only.

Figure 6.3 (*continued*)

Type of public infrastructure services	Description
Air transportation (airports)	Charges include the aircraft landing fees, and take-off/departure fees may depend on type and weight of aircraft. Aircraft charges may also be assessed for de-icing and snow removal. There are also charges for terminal-area air navigation, aircraft parking slots, en-route air navigation, approach and airport control; airport noise (often depends on time of day and/or aircraft noise), passenger service in terminals, baggage and cargo service including special security to monitor the activity; hangar space and ground (ramp and traffic) management. Passengers pay motor-vehicle parking facility charges, and taxi services special airport user access fee. Charges in this category also include airport space-provided concessions (food courts, gift shops, and the like). Note: Other than one regional airport in Missouri (Branson), all major commercial airports in the United States are public and managed by a state local or regional state/local special district authority. There are no federal commercial airports.
Parking facilities	Parking fee/garages (typically peak load pricing) and on-street parking (may also have peak load pricing now that in some urban areas one pays by credit card) loading zone; taxi and commercial ride sharing zones.
Sea and inland port facilities	Canal tolls, rents from leases, concession rents, use of port terminal facilities (wharfage, harbour fees), and cargo facility charges on containers may be based on size (length) or tonnage for bulk of heavy-lift cargo. Cargo charges and fees may vary by distance of cargo shipped and type of cargo (e.g., the Port of Honolulu has different fees for inter-island trans-shipment [at the low end] vs overseas and domestic foreign cargo; plus fees vary by type of cargo [explosives carry a higher fee than dry bulk cargo, animals, and produce]). Inland fees (both state and local) include dockage and mooring fees, and may for some states be

Figure 6.3 (*continued*)

Type of public infrastructure services	Description
	administered in part by a state Department of Natural Resources that are typically fee-for-permit-related (e.g., charges for dredging as well as land infill, mooring/boat lifts, permits for culverts, bulk heading, and piers). The state/local charge policy is coordinated with US Customs. The waterways are jointly administered by the US Army Corps of Engineers and the state and/or local government (or a joint interstate state/local authority) depending on where the waterway is located.
Natural resources	Sale of minerals and other natural products (other than forestry) from public land, laboratory fees (animal testing), permits to remove or add infill to a waterway.
Parks and recreation	Vehicle entrance fees, hiking fees, camping site fees, recreation facility rental fees, greens fees, parking charges, concession rentals, stadium gate tickets, shelter rentals, emergency safety rescue, beach leases, nature tours, access to zoos.
Housing and community development	Gross rentals, tenant charges, and other revenue from operation of public housing, inspection for structural building and renovation/repair, equipment installation charges for access to facilities operated by a state or local government (from zoos to baseball stadiums and convention centres to community centres), and concession fees associated with these facilities. Excludes receipts from the sale of property and payments in lieu of taxes from housing projects operated by other governments, whether independent housing authorities (special districts) or dependent housing agencies of general purpose governments. Further note that the typical "affordable housing" facility is privately owned and operated.
Sewerage	Current fees, such as a flat rates benefits charges and flat or variable usage charges (e.g., in Maryland a Chesapeake Bay restoration fee as part of the quarterly sewer bill).

Figure 6.3 *(continued)*

Type of public infrastructure services	Description
	Some communities also attach to the sewer bill an impervious area charge (e.g., "stormwater fee") based on GPS estimated surfaces such as rooftops, paved driveways, patios, parking lots, and other covered areas (regardless of materials used) that contribute to rainwater runoff entering a sewer system and/or a nearby waterway. Estimated by GPS technology, the fee can be calculated as a statistical median of the amount of impervious area. Because charges are based on square foot area, owners of large office buildings, shopping centres, and parking lots will be charged more than the owners of modest residential buildings (www.dcwater.com).
Solid waste management	Fees and charges for garbage collection and disposal, operation of landfills, selling of recyclable materials, operation of landfills, clean-up of hazardous materials, bulk trash pickup. Excludes fees related to regulation or inspection activities, pay-as-you-use-and-throw bags, bulk trash pickup. One creative way some localities charge for residential solid waste refuse collection is to require that all refuse be deposited in specific bags sold only by the local government. Such bags are usually distinguished by colours and/or insignias (Fisher 2016).
Other charges	Charges not included in the above classifications. Examples include court and recording fees, ambulance services fees, alarm permits, fire response charges, library fees, zoning approval process, loading zone permits, processing service fees for access to various general government services, emergency safety rescue (e.g., boating, hiking). *Excludes* reimbursements and special assessments for capital outlays that benefit specific property owners.

Sources: US Bureau of the Census Classification Manual (2006) and Census of Government Definitions (current), www.census.gov; Fisher (2016); College Board (2016); US Department of Transportation (2014); Sjoquist and Stoycheva (2012), Sjoquist (2015); web search of various state and local government user manuals.

Table 6.1

State and local current charges as share of general revenues, selected years

Type of revenue	2013 $ m	2013 % of general revenue	2002 $ m	2002 % of general revenue	1993 $ m	1993 % of general revenue
General revenue	2,690,427	100.00	1,684,879	100.00	1,041,567	100.00
Intergovernmental from federal	584,652	21.73	360,546	21.40	198,591	19.07
general own-source revenue	2,105,775	78.27	1,324,333	78.60	842,977	80.93
Taxes	1,455,499	54.10	905,101	53.72	594,300	57.06
Property	455,442	16.93	279,191	16.57	189,743	18.22
Sales & gross receipts	496,439	18.45	324,123	19.24	209,649	20.13
General sales	327,066	12.16	222,987	13.23	138,822	13.33
Selective sales	169,373	6.30	101,136	6.00	70,827	6.80
Individual income tax	338,471	12.58	202,832	12.04	123,235	11.83
Corporate income tax	53,039	1.97	28,152	1.67	26,417	2.54
Motor vehicle licence	25,080	0.93	16,935	1.01	12,402	1.19
Other taxes	87,027	3.23	34,087	2.02	32,853	3.15
Charges and miscell. revenue	650,276	24.17	419,232	24.88	248,677	23.88
Current charges	444,153	16.51	253,189	15.03	149,348	14.34
Education	117,647	4.37	72,291	4.29	41,926	4.03
Hospitals	129,820	4.83	65,404	3.88	41,140	3.95
Highways	15,171	0.56	8,196	0.49	4,929	0.47
Air transport (airports)	20,596	0.77	12,331	0.73	6,648	0.64
Parking facilities	2,734	0.10	1,402	0.08	1,002	0.10
Sea & inland port facilities	4,605	0.17	2,685	0.16	1,739	0.17
Natural resources	4,842	0.18	3,001	0.18	2,148	0.21
Parks and recreation	9,916	0.37	7,021	0.42	4,151	0.40
Housing community devl.	6,195	0.23	4,296	0.25	3,354	0.32
Sewerage	50,689	1.88	27,112	1.61	15,998	1.54
Solid waste management	16,843	0.63	11,192	0.66	7,303	0.70
Other charges	65,094	2.42	38,258	2.27	19,008	1.82
Miscellaneous general revenue	206,124	7.66	166,043	9.85	99,329	9.54
Interest earnings	50,837	1.89	67,161	3.99	50,806	4.88
Special assessments	7,154	0.27	4,779	0.28	2,664	0.26
Sale of property	3,685	0.14	2,187	0.13	842	0.08
Other general revenue	144,447	5.37	91,916	5.46	45,017	4.32
Exhibit: utility revenue*	157,747		102,352		61,602	
Exhibit: liquor store revenue*	8,903		5,065		3,641	
Exhibit: insurance trust revenue*	562,791		14,295		163,937	

*The Census data exclude utility, liquor store, and insurance trust from General Revenues. The basis for distinction is not the fund or administrative unit receiving the revenues, but rather the governance of the agency that collects and manages the revenue sources. See text for *(continued)*

Table 6.1   (*continued*)

further discussion of utilities. Seventeen states and jurisdictions have adopted some form of "control" system for the sale of alcoholic beverages. Thirteen jurisdictions (it may be a state or local unit) sell alcoholic beverages at retail either directly or through an agent. These numbers are presented above just to give perspective to the size of these revenues vis-à-vis current charges. Note that the $ amounts of cc far exceed that of utility revenue and special assessments.

Source: US Census Bureau, *Census of Governments: State and Local Government Finances,* selected years, 2016 website, https://www.census.gov/govs/local/.

CURRENT CHARGES IN THE STATE/LOCAL GENERAL REVENUE SYSTEM

To begin laying out the role of current charges in infrastructure finance, table 6.1 provides a two-decade perspective on the quantitative importance of charges relative to total state and local general revenues as well as to the other major revenue categories. The table presents the US$ amounts and the ratio of current charges (cc) to total general revenues by type of general revenue category and for three representative years (1993, 2002, and 2013).[14] To begin, there are some interesting findings:

- For 2002 and 2013 total cc collections are greater than the sum of the collections from individual and corporate net income tax. The data show that total cc exceeded individual plus corporate income taxes for the period 1994 through 1996 and then fell to less than the income tax in 1997–2001. Whereas the growth of total cc has been a consistent feature since 1993, the income tax combination has been volatile. The income tax numbers further attest to the findings elsewhere that as current charges are increasing as a share of own source revenues, the corporate net income tax is disappearing from the state revenue scene: from a high of about 9.5 per cent in 1997 to less than 5.0 per cent in 2016 (Brunori 2012; US Census Bureau 2013).
- Moreover, over the period shown, total current charges not only have been increasing relative to Sales and Gross Receipts (the ratio of cc/Sales and Gross Receipts has increased from 71 per cent in 1993 to nearly 90 per cent in 2013), but also surpassed the yield of the General Sales Tax. As of 2013 total current charge collections are approaching parity with the property tax. So much for the conventional public finance wisdom that the taxes on income, sales

Table 6.2
Broad definition of state and local charges, 2013

Item	$ m	% of total items	% GR	% OSR
Current charges	444,153	85.78	16.51	21.09
Motor fuel taxes	41,401	8.00	1.54	1.97
Motor vehicle licence taxes	25,080	4.84	0.93	1.19
Special assessments	7,154	1.38	0.27	0.34
Total	517,788	100.00	19.25	24.59

Source: US Census Bureau (2016), https://www.census.gov/govs/local/.

and gross receipts, and property make up the "big three" of state and local own-source revenues.

- A large part – but, as will be shown, not all – of the explanation of the growing importance of current charges relative to total General Revenues (from 14.3 per cent in 1993 to 16.5 per cent in 2013) can be attributed to two categories – Education and Hospitals, which taken together have increased from 8.0 per cent of total state/local general revenues in 1993, to 8.2 per cent in 2002, to 9.2 per cent today (2013).

- Before moving on, one last comment is merited, which goes back to the introductory discussion on why, when looking at the user-charge infrastructure topic, settling in on the Census definition of charges works. If one accepts the view that a broad definition of infrastructure user pricing should add in motor fuel taxes and licences along with special assessments, it turns out that even with this broader measure, current charges will still dominate the discussion (table 6.2).

Current Charges Generated
by Type of Infrastructure Service Flows

The next step is to pull the current charges data out of table 6.1 and begin the examination of the charges as a state and local revenue source arrayed by type of infrastructure service. This takes one to table 6.3 and figure 6.4. And again, there are interesting findings. The first, which is also reported (but with a different data context) in table 6.1, is that Education and Hospitals are the major sources of current charge revenues. In 2013 the two categories combine to make up more than half (55.7 per cent) of total collections. The same relative magnitudes are shown

Table 6.3
US state and local current charges by type of infrastructure, 2013

Item	$ thousands	% of total current charges	% of total general revenues	% own-source revenue	% of current expenditure
Total charges	444,152,589	100.00	16.51	21.09	16.83
Education	117,647,102	26.49	4.37	5.59	13.42
Higher education	101,945,211	22.95	3.79	4.84	39.04
All other education	15,701,891	3.54	0.58	0.75	2.55
Hospitals	129,820,391	29.23	4.83	6.16	80.75
Highways	15,171,179	3.42	0.56	0.72	9.56
Air transport (airports)	20,595,949	4.64	0.77	0.98	97.43
Parking facilities	2,733,953	0.62	0.10	0.13	143.61
Sea & inland port facilities	4,604,812	1.04	0.17	0.22	84.64
Natural resources	4,841,537	1.09	0.18	0.23	16.73
Parks and recreation	9,916,241	2.23	0.37	0.47	26.26
Housing & community devl.	6,195,146	1.39	0.23	0.29	12.02
Sewerage	50,689,306	11.41	1.88	2.41	94.44
Solid waste management	16,842,617	3.79	0.63	0.80	68.90
Other charges	65,094,356	14.66	2.42	3.09	5.34

Source: US Census Bureau (2016), https://www.census.gov/govs/local/. Author calculations.

when one calculates the ratios of charges to either General Revenues or General Own-Source Revenue (hereafter referred to as "own-source" revenue, OSR). To get a sense of why this is true, it is helpful to take a glance back at figure 6.3, which illustrates the type of current charges by mode of infrastructure.

But, with table 6.3 and figure 6.4, there are two new results to discuss. First, and still just looking at the revenue dollars and the percentages of total General Revenues (and now the more useful) OSR data, the Education component is seen to be dominated by higher education (take a glance back to figure 6.2 for the definition of scope). The key message that this reveals is that the non-higher education component, which includes elementary schooling (pre-kindergarten through grade 12) along with special programs and training activities, is heavily tax financed (Fisher 2016).

So, education – and, especially, higher education – dominates the discussion; that is, until one goes to the far-right column of the table that shows current charges by mode as a per cent of current expenditures. Now one gets a different picture of the relative importance of current

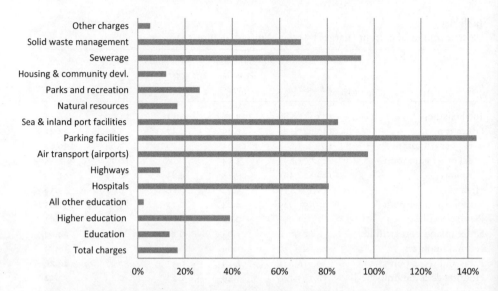

Figure 6.4   US state and local current charges by type of infrastructure as percentage of current expenditure

Source: Table 6.3

charges. Whereas current charges relative to current expenditures are seen to be important relative to total spending on higher education (39 per cent), what shows up is the high importance of current charges to the state and local expenditure components of financing other infrastructure modes – in fact, several of them: hospitals 81 per cent, air transport 97 per cent, sea and inland waterways 85 per cent, sewerage 94 per cent, and solid waste management 69 per cent, and parking facilities, 144 per cent (figure 6.4).

The parking facilities percentage allows a nice transition to two further points that one should keep in mind when looking at the current charges data:

- First, one should not assume that just because a user charge is infrastructure service related (and thus the revenue payer-user matching principle is satisfied) it will therefore follow that the revenues from the charges collected are, in fact, then budgeted to support the services from which the user charge has been derived. Whether or not charges are dedicated to a specific infrastructure mode is a decision made at the discretion of the state legislature, local council, or a legislatively empowered instrumentality (e.g., a special district authority).

- Second, when looking at the CC as a per cent of current expenditure columns, it would be not unreasonable to assume that most, or all, of the CCs for parks and recreation, sewage, and solid waste management are being tagged for the service from which the user charge was derived. But a look at the parking facilities ratio shows that the user charge funds exceed the expenditure made on the activity. In the case of parking, receipts may be directed to special fund support (e.g., in the example of the District of Columbia a fund for making transfers to a tristate mass transit fund) and/or the General Fund (Clark 2016).

Current Charges Trends over Time and by Mode

The next set of data presentations takes a closer look at CC performance by moving on to look at the trends in revenue flows over the past two decades, and, again, selecting the representative years 1993, 2002, 2013. Tables 6.4 and 6.5 look at the changes in revenue collections, by mode, breaking out the numbers to show the nominal change in US$ generated over the time periods 1993–2002 and 2001–13. Among other things, the data show that – not at all unexpectedly – the revenue flows by mode were not static over the time periods examined. Thus, one observes that during the 1993–2002 period, CC from sewerage, hospitals, airports, and highways led the other eight categories.[15] But, for the more recent decade user charges from hospitals, parking, sewage, and highways outpaced the other sectors. Over the entire two-decade period, revenues generated from the activities of solid (and hazardous) waste management, natural resources, and housing and community development increased more slowly that other sectors (table 6.4).

Turning to the trend by mode data when current charges are expressed as a per cent of expenditures (table 6.5), one sees a gets a bit of a different ranking order in terms of which services have generated user charges. Again, recognizing that one cannot assume a 1:1 mapping between user charges generated by mode and expenditures by mode, a comparison of the rankings of where the money may have gone (table 6.5) shows some consistency: hospitals, highways, sewerage, airports, and parking as a likely source of both revenues generated and revenues expended.

What are the policy conclusions and statements that can be derived from these trends? There are a least two. The first is that to fully understand these cross-sector trends requires sector study detail. That said,

Table 6.4
State and local current charges by type of infrastructure as share of total revenues by year, selected years

Item	1993		2002		2013		Exhibit nominal $ change					
	$ m	% of total charges	$ m	% of total charges	$ m	% of total charges	% Increase 1993–2002	Index with TCC set at 100.0	% Increase 2002–2013	Index with TCC set at 100.0	Rank in descending order 2002–1993	Rank in descending order since 2002
Total charges in curr. yr. US$	149,347	100	253,189	100	444,153	100	197	1.00	75	1.00		
Education	41,926	28	72,290	29	117,647	26	181	0.91	63	0.83	Sewage	Hospitals
Hospitals	41,140	28	65,404	26	129,820	29	216	1.09	98	1.31	Hospitals	Parking
Highways	4,929	3	8,196	3	15,171	3	208	1.05	85	1.13	Airports	Sewerage
Air transport (airports)	6,648	4	12,330	5	20,596	5	210	1.06	67	0.89	Highways	Highways
Parking facilities	1,002	1	1,402	1	2,734	1	173	0.88	95	1.26	Education	Seaports
Sea & inland port facilities	1,739	1	2,685	1	4,604	1	165	0.83	71	0.95	Parking	Airports
Natural resources	2,147	1	3,001	1	4,842	1	126	0.64	61	0.81	Seaport	Education
Parks and recreation	4,151	3	7,021	3	9,916	2	139	0.70	41	0.55	Parks and rec.	Nat'l resource
Housing & comm. devl.	3,354	2	4,296	2	6,195	1	85	0.43	44	0.59	Solid waste	Solid waste
Sewerage	15,998	11	27,112	11	50,689	11	217	1.10	87	1.15	Nat'l resource	Housing & CD
Solid waste management	7,303	5	11,192	4	16,843	4	131	0.66	50	0.67	Housing & CD	Parks and rec.
Other charges	19,008	13	38,258	15	65,094	15	242	1.23	70	0.93	****	****

Source: US Census Bureau (2016), https://www.census.gov/govs/local/. Author calculations.

Table 6.5
State and local current charges as percentage of spending by type of infrastructure, selected years

Item	1993		2002		2013		Change		Rank in descending order 2002–1993	Rank in descending order since 2002
	$ m	CC as % of exp.	$ m	CC as % of exp.	$ m	CC as % of exp.	% Increase, 1993–2002	% Increase, 2002–2013		
Total charges in curr. yr. US$	149,347	15	253,189	15	444,153	17	69.53	75.42		
Education	41,926	12	72,290	12	117,647	13	72.42	62.74	Airports	Hospitals
Higher education	34,955	40	61,318	39	101,945	39	75.42	66.26	Education	Parking
All other education	6,971	3	10,972	3	15,702	3	57.39	43.11	Sewerage	Sewerage
Hospitals	41,140	66	65,404	75	129,820	81	58.98	98.49	Parks and rec.	Highways
Highways	4,929	7	8,196	7	15,171	10	66.28	85.10	Highways	Seaports
Air transport (airports)	6,648	72	12,330	76	20,596	97	85.47	67.04	Hospitals	Airports
Parking facilities	1,002	144	1,402	125	2,734	144	39.92	95.01	Seaports	Education
Sea & inland port facilities	1,739	80	2,685	75	4,605	85	54.40	71.51	Solid waste	Nat'l resource
Natural resources	2,147	16	3,001	14	4,842	17	39.78	61.35	Parking	Solid waste
Parks and recreation	4,151	26	7,021	23	9,916	26	69.14	41.23	Nat'l resource	Housing & CD
Housing & comm. devl.	3,354	18	4,296	14	6,195	12	28.09	44.20	Housing & CD	Parks and rec.
Sewerage	15,998	70	27,112	87	50,689	94	69.47	86.96		
Solid waste management	7,303	57	11,192	59	16,843	69	53.25	50.49		
Other charges	19,008	4	38,258	5	65,094	5	18.10	70.14		

Source: US Census Bureau (2016), https://www.census.gov/govs/local/. Author calculations.

Table 6.6
Percentage distribution of current charges by mode and type of government, 2013

Items	State & local	State % of S&L	Local % of S&L
Current charge	100.00	41.30	58.70
Education	100.00	80.03	19.97
Hospitals	100.00	41.01	58.99
Highways	100.00	56.21	43.79
Air transport (airports)	100.00	7.05	92.95
Parking facilities	100.00	0.80	99.20
Sea & inland port facilities	100.00	29.19	70.81
Natural resources	100.00	60.19	39.81
Parks and recreation	100.00	14.01	85.99
Housing & community devl.	100.00	9.73	90.27
Sewerage	100.00	1.23	98.77
Solid waste management	100.00	2.39	97.61
Other charges	100.00	28.82	71.18

Source: US Census Bureau (2016), https://www.census.gov/govs/local/.

there is no apology being made not taking that sector-by-sector study step here; rather, the numbers shown should give sector analysts a start on their work.

Second, the flows reflect both the demand and supply of the infrastructure service category. That revenue flow from hospitals are shown to be increasing over the two decades could reflect several demand variables, perhaps chief among them, the aging of the population (Wallace 2012; Gais, Boyd, and Dadayan 2012; Penner 2012). To identify the supply side variables, experts (e.g., Altman, Kelin, and Krueger 2015; Geddes 2015; McNichol 2016) point to growing deterioration of infrastructure services, which results in increasing costs of operation and maintenance. Other factors – e.g., the increasing use of transponder technology in collecting roadway tolls – may help explain why highways rank at the high end when listing user-charge revenues.

Although the detailed data are not presented here, examination of CC trends in real dollar terms also shows that for all infrastructure modes, CC revenue flows have increased. For the two-decade period 1993–2013, the real revenue flows increased 3.12 per cent above the general rate of price change.[16] The above-average sectors are sewerage, hospitals, and air transport, and highways.

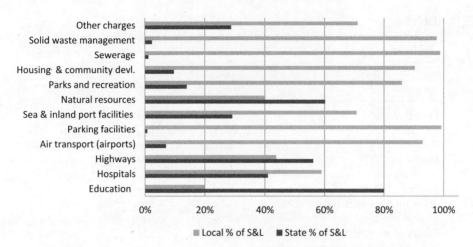

Figure 6.5   Percentage distribution of user charges by mode and type of government, 2013

Source: Table 6.6

Decentralizing the Data: First, State vs Local

The next step in dissecting the nature of CC revenue distribution by mode over the past two decades is to break out the state/local system numbers by State vs Local. The theory of user-charge pricing – that charges have a clear benefits-area character – suggests that by making this state vs local split one should learn a bit more about how the benefit area matching principle is playing out. And, indeed, that the matching principle is the intergovernmental practice is shown not only for the most recent data (2013, table 6.6 and figure 6.5), but also over time, though the detailed data are not included here. The small area services of housing and community development, sewerage, and solid waste management are overwhelmingly local and the services that have a multi-jurisdictional character (natural resources, highways, and the higher education–driven category of educational, natural resources, and highways) are tilted to the state-only column. As for airports, nearly all are local and typically administered as a special district. This pattern of what is shown to be the state/local share in 2013 (table 6.6) is again true when one looks at the same data over the past two decades, although again the detailed data are not presented here.

Table 6.7
Percentage distribution of charges within state and local government
classifications, 2013

Items	State & local % of CC	State % of CC	Local % of CC
Current charge	100.00	100.00	100.00
Education	26.49	51.33	9.01
Hospitals	29.23	29.02	29.37
Highways	3.42	4.65	2.55
Air transport (airports)	4.64	0.79	7.34
Parking facilities	0.62	0.01	1.04
Sea & inland port facilities	1.04	0.73	1.25
Natural resources	1.09	1.59	0.74
Parks and recreation	2.23	0.76	3.27
Housing & community development	1.39	0.33	2.15
Sewerage	11.41	0.34	19.20
Solid waste management	3.79	0.22	6.31
Other charges	14.66	10.23	17.77

Source: US Census Bureau (2016), https://www.census.gov/govs/local/.

A different take on state vs local user charge distribution is presented in table 6.7 and figure 6.6, which look at the distribution of revenue
charges within the state and local sectors. With education (again, higher education dominates) along with hospitals, 80 per cent of state current charge is explained. Hospitals are also important to the local-sector
budgets (30 per cent), but so are sewer charges (19 per cent).

Decentralizing Locally (tables 6.8 and 6.9)

Recognizing the highly decentralized structure of the US federation
works and that the 84,004 local governments in the US account for
nearly 60 per cent of CC collections (table 6.6), a detailed look at the various types of local governments as users of user charges is revealing.

There are two ways to dissect the data. The first is to examine how the
percentage share of total current charges collected are distributed
among the five aggregated types of local governments: counties, municipalities, towns and townships, independent school districts, and
other special districts (table 6.8). The second is to look at each type of
local government and then ask how important current charges are relative to the own-source revenues of that type of government.

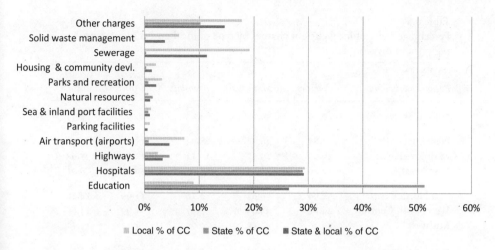

Figure 6.6   Percentage distribution of charges by type of government classification, 2013

Source: Table 6.7

TOTAL CC COLLECTIONS BY TYPE OF LOCAL GOVERNMENT

The data on how the percentage shares of current charges collected break out by region are presented in table 6.8.[17] The four US regions and their divisions are: Northeast (New England and Mid-Atlantic); Midwest (East North Central and West North Central); South (South Atlantic, East South Central, West South Central), and West (Mountain, Pacific). As table 6.8 shows,

- Whereas across the country municipalities are the most intensive users of current charges, there are, of note, variations both regional and, within the regions.
- Counties are the second-largest user/collector with an average collection of 27 per cent, compared to the municipal 40 per cent.
- Though special districts account for the largest number of types of local government, they account for only a fifth of total current charges generated.
- The per cent for school districts (the second lowest of the five types, at 8 per cent) confirms the tax- and grant-financed treatment of elementary education.

Table 6.8

Percentage share of local current charges by type of local government, census region, and division, 2012

Region and division	Counties	Municipal	Townships	Special districts	School districts
United States	26.66	39.90	4.22	20.90	8.33
New England	3.85	46.18	28.94	15.99	5.04
Middle Atlantic	29.06	29.90	10.11	22.99	7.94
Northeast	*12.26*	*40.75*	*22.67*	*18.32*	*6.01*
East North Central	34.99	36.63	2.10	11.99	14.28
West North Central	24.82	43.43	0.07	15.99	15.69
Midwest	*29.06*	*40.59*	*0.92*	*14.32*	*15.10*
South Atlantic	32.00	33.60	0.00	30.89	3.51
East South Central	38.50	30.95	0.00	24.57	5.99
West South Central	28.84	50.20	0.00	11.15	9.81
South	32.78	36.88	0.00	24.76	*5.57*
Mountain	29.12	38.65	0.00	23.94	8.28
Pacific	22.04	48.95	0.00	23.31	5.70
West	26.40	42.61	0.00	23.70	7.29

Note: New England (Connecticut, Maine, Massachusetts, N. Hampshire, Rhode Island, Vermont); Middle Atlantic (New. Jersey, New York, Pennsylvania); East North Central (Indiana, Illinois, Michigan, Ohio, Wisconsin); West North Central (Iowa, Kansas, Minnesota, Missouri, Nebraska, North Dakota; South Dakota); South Atlantic (Delaware, District of Columbia, Florida, Georgia, Maryland, North. Carolina, S. Carolina, Virginia, West. Virginia); East South Central (Alabama, Kentucky, Mississippi, Tennessee); West South Central (Arkansas, Louisiana, Oklahoma, Texas); Mountain (Arizona, Colorado, Idaho, N, Mexico, Montana, Utah Nevada, Wyoming); Pacific (Alaska, California, Hawaii, Oregon, Washington).

Source: US Census Bureau of the Census, State and Local *Government Finance Statistics*, 2016, Author calculations

CURRENT CHARGES EXPRESSED AS A PER CENT OF OSR BY TYPE OF LOCAL GOVERNMENT

There are several further findings one can glean by looking both down and across table 6.9. The top row of table 6.9 shows the percentage of total own-source revenue that each separate type of local government generates from current charges. To get a sense of how things work by type of local government and by regions and regional division, go down the rows.[18]

- Across the country, current charges generate close to the same proportion of total own-source revenues for counties (31 per cent) and municipalities (28 per cent).

Table 6.9
Current charges as percentage of general revenue from own sources by region
and regional division, 2012

Region and division	Counties	Municipal	Townships	Special districts	School districts
United States	30.88	27.56	12.53	63.12	8.98
New England	22.45	23.07	10.44	64.50	30.60
Middle Atlantic	28.79	17.52	17.67	70.46	3.90
Northeast	24.56	21.22	12.85	66.49	21.70
East North Central	39.26	32.82	12.18	44.41	10.92
West North Central	30.56	34.01	2.90	59.90	14.07
Midwest	34.19	33.52	6.77	53.45	12.76
South Atlantic	23.37	29.69	0.00	74.27	10.47
East South Central	40.07	36.73	0.00	74.12	16.41
West South Central	30.38	35.32	0.00	52.68	11.98
South	28.95	32.67	0.00	69.15	12.23
Mountain	28.46	39.35	0.00	55.06	10.82
Pacific	26.08	32.54	0.00	48.79	7.47
West	27.54	36.73	0.00	52.65	9.53

Source: US Census Bureau (2016), https://www.census.gov/govs/local/. Author calculations.

- Townships, which are characteristic of the "old" regions of the country (as one goes west, states do not have township government), rely on current charge revenues in the Northeastern and Midwestern states.
- Special Districts, as intended when established by a General Purpose government or governments, are heavily reliant on user funding. These numbers further support the case that the matching principle is at work.[19]
- School Districts, which are largely local property tax plus state grant financed, are classified as either *dependent* or *independent*. Dependent school systems are part of county, municipal, township, or state government and are not counted as school district governments for Census purposes. Of the 14,178 school systems in the US (2012), 12,880 (91 per cent of the total) are independent and are thus included in the school district data of current charges. Charter schools, which are publicly funded independent schools under terms of a charter with the establishing

state/local government authority (thus a government entity) are included in the school district data (US Census Bureau 2014).

Although state-by-state details are not included here, for those interested in this sort of fiscal decentralization data, it is both a very rich and hard-to-interpret data set. To illustrate:

- Effective 1 October 1960, Connecticut county government was abolished and county functions were transferred to the state government. The only thing that remains of Connecticut county governments is that boundaries have been retained for election of county sheriffs and for judicial purposes. Towns in Connecticut provide the services that are associated with counties and municipalities in most states.
- Connecticut, Massachusetts, and Virginia show high school district reliance on current charges. But, here special caution is advised in interpretation because of data anomalies that arise because (1) education agencies collect data at different levels of detail and (2) a state's mix of dependent vs independent school systems will influence ratios of CC/School District own-source general revenues. For example, in Connecticut the entire area of the state is encompassed by town areas, which are counted as towns except for areas in which the town is consolidated with a city or borough government. Under this arrangement 87 per cent of schools are dependent on general-purpose governments; the other 13 per cent are independent regional schools organized by a joint action of two or more towns after a referendum. Census designates these regional schools as independent.
- Massachusetts has 327 public school systems, but only 84 – which include some regional and independent vocational-technical schools – are counted as separate governments. Virginia has 136 public school district governments, only one of which is independent.[20] Hawaii and Alaska schools are fully state funded.

One must thus be careful in interpreting the data especially when making interjurisdictional comparisons of user charges. When observing an out-of-line school district number, for example, it is a good idea to delve into the detail of the intergovernmental organization of the state before drawing any policy conclusions.

Table 6.10
Rank correlation results

	# of states	Rank correlation*	t	Significant level %
All states	51	−0.5943	−5.1727	99
All states other than non-income tax states	43	−0.6226	−5.0947	99
All states other than non-sales tax states	46	−0.5631	−4.5201	99
All states, education & hospitals excluded	51	−0.1757	−3.6129	not significant
All states other than non-income tax and non-sales tax States	40	−0.6311	−5.0159	99
All states CC as % of direct current spending	51	−0.4586	−3.6129	99
Revenue capacity, CC as % of own-source revenue	51	−0.6248	−5.6015	99
Revenue effort, CC as % of own-source revenue	51	−0.0711	−0.4992	not significant

Source: Author calculations.

Correlation Coefficients

Having dissected the CC numbers by type, trend, mode, and for different forms of government, one must ask: do current charges for infrastructure finance vary significantly when one looks at the broader aggregates of state income, revenue capacity and revenue effort? In order to get some answers, eight rank-order correlations were run. A first set examined the relationship between state and local current charges as a percentage of own-source revenue, direct current expenditure, and state per capital income. The second set of two rank-order correlations were calculated to learn if there is a systematic relationship between states' use of current charges for infrastructure and recently released estimates by the Tax Policy Center (Gordon, Auxier, and Iselin 2016) of measures of state-by-state revenue capacity and revenue effort. The results are provided in table 6.10.

Spearman's rank-order test, which givesus a correlation coefficient in the range of values −1 to +1, was applied. A negative (positive) sign indicates an inverse (direct) relationship between the data sets being tested. For our purposes here, it was necessary to initially develop three sets of state-by-state rankings. The first set ranks the dependent variable for all fifty states and DC for their use of current charges as a per cent of own-source revenue, and the next two independent variables, first by (1) an economic measure (per capita income) and then (2) fiscal measures of revenue capacity and effort.[21]

Table 6.11

Percentage of current charges relative to own-source revenue, per capita income, revenue capacity, and revenue effort ranks, all states, 2012

State	CC as % of own-source revenue		Revenue capacity		Per capita income		Revenue effort	
	%	Rank	$	Rank	$	Rank	%	Rank
Alabama	34.52	2	5,229	49	36,176	45	98.05	27
Alaska	11.87	49	9,567	4	51,259	9	200.62	1
Arizona	21.61	26	5,344	46	36,723	42	92.07	40
Arkansas	21.04	29	5,259	48	36,529	44	97.10	28
California	21.91	24	7,007	18	48,125	12	100.91	18
Colorado	25.30	12	6,930	21	46,746	15	92.46	38
Connecticut	9.54	50	8,694	5	62,112	2	96.33	31
Delaware	20.82	31	7,731	8	44,819	21	101.11	16
District of Columbia	8.24	51	11,404	1	68,606	1	107.79	8
Florida	26.85	9	5,854	34	41,309	29	95.73	33
Georgia	23.88	18	5,437	44	37,596	41	90.90	42
Hawaii	20.33	33	7,427	14	44,314	23	99.42	24
Idaho	24.45	14	5,287	47	35,641	47	89.30	44
Illinois	14.13	46	6,685	24	46,477	16	101.01	17
Indiana	24.68	13	5,624	38	38,291	39	100.47	20
Iowa	28.71	4	6,990	20	43,735	26	99.87	21
Kansas	26.03	10	6,332	27	44,311	24	105.95	11
Kentucky	22.12	22	5,353	45	35,967	46	96.31	32
Louisiana	24.42	15	5,922	32	40,819	30	99.67	22
Maine	15.59	42	6,366	26	39,562	33	97.06	30
Maryland	15.69	41	7,625	10	52,545	7	92.09	39
Massachusetts	15.18	43	8,472	6	56,549	3	90.27	43
Michigan	25.70	11	5,527	41	39,197	37	104.00	13
Minnesota	17.69	38	7,038	16	47,410	14	102.71	14
Mississippi	31.62	3	4,776	51	33,629	51	111.15	5
Missouri	22.74	21	5,916	33	40,297	32	87.43	46
Montana	20.31	34	6,780	23	38,884	38	79.90	49
Nebraska	22.04	23	7,078	15	46,254	17	90.94	41
Nevada	21.51	27	5,767	36	39,223	36	93.53	35
New Hampshire	17.21	39	7,575	11	50,535	10	76.82	50
New Jersey	14.69	45	7,950	7	55,194	4	100.59	19
New Mexico	18.22	37	5,599	39	35,254	49	107.58	9
New York	13.68	48	7,659	9	53,606	6	134.87	2
North Carolina	28.49	5	5,938	31	37,774	40	94.25	34
North Dakota	14.09	47	10,229	2	54,373	5	97.06	29
Ohio	21.47	28	5,751	37	40,749	31	105.54	12
Oklahoma	23.10	20	5,847	35	41,962	28	93.43	37
Oregon	27.17	7	6,131	29	39,426	34	102.06	15
Pennsylvania	20.87	30	6,442	25	46,028	19	98.64	26

Table 6.11   (*continued*)

State	CC as % of own-source revenue		Revenue capacity		Per capita income		Revenue effort	
	%	Rank	$	Rank	$	Rank	%	Rank
Rhode Island	15.12	44	6,866	22	46,145	18	107.80	7
South Carolina	35.11	1	5,218	50	35,472	48	108.98	6
South Dakota	18.36	36	7,495	12	44,772	22	70.48	51
Tennessee	24.12	17	5,571	40	39,312	35	85.06	47
Texas	20.55	32	6,213	28	43,807	25	89.08	45
Utah	28.20	6	5,506	42	36,542	43	99.15	25
Vermont	16.33	40	7,008	17	44,839	20	99.46	23
Virginia	24.22	16	7,467	13	48,956	11	83.55	48
Washington	26.98	8	6,994	19	47,468	13	93.53	36
West Virginia	21.81	25	5,461	43	35,163	50	118.17	3
Wisconsin	19.79	35	6,121	30	42,737	27	106.63	10
Wyoming	23.74	19	9,628	3	51,791	8	112.41	4

Source: US Bureau of the Census, https://www.census.gov/govs/local/; US Bureau of Economic Analysis, https://www.bea.gov/; Gordon et.al. (2016). Author calculations.

ALL STATES AND ALL CURRENT CHARGES

In the first case – testing the relationship rank-correlation of the use of CC and per capita state income for all fifty states and the DC, the rank correlation coefficient comes in at –0.5943 with a confidence level of 99 per cent.[22] This allows one to assert that a negative relationship exists between the two variables – that is, the higher (lower) a state ranks in per capita income, the lower (higher) such state ranks in current charges as a percentage of own-source revenue.

The same negative and significant relationship exists for Current Charges as a per cent of direct current spending relative to state per capita income. While this appears to "fit" with the All States revenue and per capita relationship, one must be careful not to make a 1:1 match with the CC revenue finding to spending. As noted above whether or not user charges to pay for infrastructure services are, in fact, allocated to an infrastructure mode is a political decision that will be influenced by the availability of alternative financing options.

STATES WITHOUT A BROAD-BASED INCOME OR SALES TAX

With these results the question then arises as to whether one might find the same or a different result for three fiscally interesting sub-groupings of states; that is, what would be the rank correlation if one omitted from the list of states (1) the seven that do not levy a broad-based personal income tax (Alabama, Florida, Nevada, South Dakota, Texas, Washington, and Wyoming); (2) the five non-sales-tax states of Alaska, Delaware, Montana, New Hampshire, and Oregon; and then (3) a combination of these two sets. The findings for all three cases were essentially the same as for "All States" – the use of current charges is inversely related to per capita income and significantly so. Among these four cases, the strongest correlation (–0.6311) was found using the sample of all states excluding both non-income-tax and non-sales-tax states.

ALL STATES AND EXCLUDING HOSPITALS AND EDUCATION

Recognizing that in the CC data not only do Education and Hospitals taken together dominate the CC data, but also that the Education data are largely explained by higher education (85 per cent), rank correlations were run excluding these two general sectors from the charges data (from both the Current Charges numerator and Own-Source Revenue denominator). The finding is that although there is still a negative relationship between reliance on user charges and state per capita income, the relationship fails the test of significance. That is, when one considers only the "physical infrastructure" one cannot make a robust statement that there is higher reliance on user charges in low-per-capita-income states.

Why this is the case is beyond the scope of this chapter. However, one can hypothesize for future work that what one is observing may reflect a public choice decision: when policy makers turn to user charges as a source of financing, they are relatively more reluctant to turn to user charges on activities for which there is seen to be a significant element of general benefits to their public than to charges on those who presumably are able to shift the cost of the charge to others. This focus seems to be particularly true for hospital services, the initial payment for which can be offset by those who have access to private or public insurance.

A similar way of thinking may be at play for higher education if the policy maker views users of higher education as relatively high-permanent-income persons who can turn to debt finance (student loans) and thus defer the user-charge payment requirement until they have a higher expected income in their post–higher education days.[23] Three other factors may come into play in explaining the trend to the increase in tuition for higher education. The first is that the US has a long-standing policy – introduced in the late eighteenth and early nineteenth centuries – of charging tuition and fees (room, board, books, clothing) as part of a system of private and publicly subsidized colleges and universities. The second is that today's tuition-levying policy makers are acting on incomplete information by failing to recognize that there are externalities (e.g., research) in higher education (Fisher 2016). The third factor is that unlike most of the other modes for which current charges are made, higher education is more voluntary in character – unlike, for example, elementary education, which is mandatory.

REVENUE CAPACITY AND REVENUE EFFORT

Once one has the results for per capita income, the next step is to rank-order the fifty-one states (including DC) in terms of (1) current charges as percentage of own-source general revenue and of (2) state revenue *capacity* by using the standardized Representative Revenue System (RRS). Here the analysis reveals a negative and significant rank correlation coefficient: –0.6248. However, when a rank correlation between use of current charges and revenue *effort* (actual revenues collected/revenue capacity) is calculated, the rank-order correlation is not robust.

So, what can conclude from all this? At least two things. First, one can say with confidence that the reliance on the use of current charges in support of the financing of infrastructure flows is a policy that is significantly associated with states that have lower per capita income and, as one might expect from the per capita income data, a lower capacity (the standardized RRS) to generate total revenues. Moreover, an examination of the state-by-state data (which are not presented here) suggests some supporting statements regarding user charge policy on a state-by-state basis. The anecdotal evidence is there: Mississippi ranks 51st in per capita income and 3rd in use of current charges. Ohio is ranked 31st in per capital income and 28th in use of user charges. And New York in 6th in per capita income and 48th in use of charges.

Second, as Fisher (2016) warns, one should not be too quick to make a state-by-state comparison regarding the use of current charges, or, at least, to be very careful when doing so. As discussed above, education and hospitals dominate the data that show the relative importance of current revenues to a common denominator such as general revenues from own sources. In 2013, these two categories accounted for 55.7 per cent of current charges (table 6.3). Thus, whether or not a state has large public hospital and/or public education facilities (and in the case of education, a small or large system of higher education) will affect the state cc rankings. So, whereas the rank correlation findings presented here are of merit – and they do allow one to make a general statement regarding income and revenue capacity as has been done – just be careful when leaping into a state-by-state discussion.

The finding that there is no significant rank correlation between the use of user charges and the total revenue effort also implies that one cannot conclude that because a set of states may not use one or both of the broad-based state taxes (income and sales), these states will turn in a significant way to the use of current charges. Just as it was noted above, that caution is advised due to the fact that states have different mixes of user-charge-related infrastructure services (Alabama is not Alaska; South Dakota is not South Carolina). States also have different ways of substituting other tax sources for those broadly levied on sales and income. Thus, Washington State does not have an individual income tax and New Hampshire eschews the general sales and user tax, but both have a much broader business entity tax (Washington's tax on gross receipts; New Hampshire's on value added) than do the other states.

Nonetheless, as a group, the states with higher per capita incomes and higher revenue capacity rely less intensively on current charges in financing infrastructure services.

CONCLUDING COMMENT

As the data have shown, the US use of user charges in support of local funding has risen in real terms over the years examined (1993–2013). Moreover, this growth and pattern of financing the flow of infrastructure services is a state and local story.

Whether this historical practice will continue or whether there will be some dramatic changes over the next years is difficult to pin down. It is reasonable to expect that the relative federal (largely grant-making) and state/local (generating current charges) roles will not change – the federalism, history, and institutions are well established and working. If there is any significant uncertainty it has to do with whether the federal sector will continue to be a partner in infrastructure policy or become more and more of what one observer has noted is an army (defence spending) with an insurance company (Zakaria 2011). Of particular concern is the long-term outlook that increasing federal entitlement spending will crowd out federal infrastructure spending (Penner 2012; Ebel, Petersen, and Vu 2013).

Some developments, however, are occurring and indeed arriving at such a quick pace that even if the federal/state and local balance does not change, the sources and uses of state and local infrastructure user charges may see some important changes. To note:

- Education. Systems of higher education, which, as demonstrated, account for most of the current charges in the education sector, are under growing political scrutiny, especially when it comes to the matter of tuition levels at both four- and two-year institutions. This may be changing, at least for two-year community colleges. As of 2016 Oregon and Tennessee have newly instituted programs for "last dollar" free community college education, with state governments providing additional funding for needy students when federal grants do not suffice to cover the gap between financial capacity and costs.
- Hospitals. If one is looking for a representative literature on US public policy, just turn to the topic of growing US health care system costs – costs that are often paid for by user charges (paid both directly by the individual user and her or his insurance plan). If these costs cannot be controlled – the next few years will be telling – hospital user fees may increase exorbitantly. Whether new health care technologies will reduce costs, and thus the user-fee cost-recovery revenues, is not known. Suffice it to say, expect little slowing of hospital user charges in the US in the near future.
- Highways. It may be that the bad news regarding the stresses inherent in US highway user tax funding may lead to an increase in user charges. Despite a combination of more efficient motor vehicles and, for now, low oil prices, motor fuel taxes appear to be in an inexorable real-dollar downward trend; new highway transponder technologies appear to have great promise to generate increases in current/user charge revenues. Other important developments are the expanded use of vehicle charging for highway as well as local road access (electronic toll collection), congestion charges (high-occupancy toll lanes), and a more aggressive use of fees based on vehicle miles travelled and road usage weight-distance charges.
- Parking facilities. Again, new technology has its promises. With new software, some cities can monitor the demand for parking on a real-time basis such that when the parking spaces begin to fill up (congestion begins), software-linked electronic monitors can

automatically trigger a higher peak-load price on a city block-by-block basis.

• As for the other types of infrastructure listed in figure 6.2, it's hard to say. For perverse reasons sewer charges for operations and maintenance can be expected to rise in the absence of new capital (largely debt-financed) outlays. Otherwise, one should look to a more creative and intensive use of types of charges and fees as described in figure 6.3, which may contribute to an increase in charges.

As a final comment, the US can expect to see continued real increases in current charges combined with a combination of some dramatic, charge-enhancing activities along with existing practices.

NOTES

The authors wish to acknowledge the advice and comments of David Allen Clark, Catherine Collins, George Guess, Bartley Hildreth, Ronald Fisher, Joseph Pennachetti, Jim Regimbal, David Sjoquist, James Spaulding, Leslie A. Steen, Selbe Tibeu, and Robert Zuraski. Special acknowledgments are also due to Elliott Dubin, who reviewed drafts of this chapter, and to the expert practitioners in the Governments Division of the US Census Bureau. The views expressed in this paper are solely those of the authors.

1 Note that application of the benefit principle does not necessarily require full-cost recovery or the restriction of levying the tax or fee on only residents of the taxing jurisdiction since the beneficiaries of the net fiscal benefits of a flow of subnational public services may or may not reside in the tax- or fee-levying jurisdiction. Further, as Musgrave (2005) discusses, the claim of fairness for a revenue system (including taxes) as a whole requires the further premise that the distribution of income, out of which purchases of services are made, must be just.

2 For example: Munnell and Cook (1991); Gramlich (1994); Fisher and Wassmer (2015); Dannin and Cokorins (2012); Gifford (2012); Marlow (2012); Kim (2016); Siemiatycki (this volume); Lindahl (1958); Mushkin and Bird (1972); Downing (1999); Bailey, Falconer, and McChlery (1993); Sjoquist and Stoycheva (2012); Fisher (2016); Bird (1976, and this volume); Lindsay (2006); Slack and Tassonyi (this volume).

3 In the *Handbook on Urban Infrastructure Finance*, Kim (2016) identifies a list of economic sectors that "generally include" transportation, water and wastewater, education and health care, plus the power and energy, telecommunications, petroleum and mining, chemical, petrochemical, pulp and paper, metal processing, and cement sectors.

4 One estimate is that the public/private split in the US is 57 per cent public and 43 per cent private (Orszag 2008).

5 US Bureau of the Census (2016), www.census.gov/gov/local/ definitions/html.

6 Unlike all state and most local governments, the US federal government does not have a capital budget.

7 For discussion and application with respect to state local fiscal comparisons, see Bourdeaux and de Zeeuw (2015). For financing public capital, see Dannin and Cokorins (2012); Fisher and Wassmer (2015); and Kim (2016).

8 The data cited as of 2012. The sixteen US territories, each with its own governing structure, are not included in this discussion. https://www .census.gov/history/www/programs/geography/island_areas.html.

9 In aggregating, the Census will assign joint activities (e.g., city-county hospitals) to one or more of the co-operating jurisdictions following a set of standardized rules whereby Census considers factors such as the magnitude of financial (e.g., "substantial authority") or employment activity by co-operating jurisdiction (US Census Bureau 2006, sec 3.14 and 114). A state-by-state description is published at five-year intervals (US Census Bureau 2012). Tribal governments are recognized as sovereign nations under the auspices of the federal government and therefore do not meet the definition of a state or local government.

10 Some experts refer to "funding" as the extent to which the flow is financed by charges vs taxes infrastructure as distinct from the "financing" of replacing and extending the capital stock, including earmarking to pay for current expenditures for administration, debt servicing, and repair. Others refer to "funding" as specific to the capital construction process. Still others use the two terms interchangeably. In most cases, user charges may contribute to both. What is important in this matter is to carefully make clear how the terms are being used. See Bird and Slack chapter in this volume.

11 The 73 per cent/27 per cent split is for 2004 data provided in Congressional Budget Office (CBO) director Peter Orszag's testimony before the Committee on Finance, United States Senate, 10 July 2008 (Orszag 2008).

In his testimony, Orszag also breaks down, by category, the public (57.3 per cent) vs private (42.7 per cent) split on capital spending on infrastructure. The bulk of private capital investment (78.4 per cent) is for energy and telecommunications systems. Schools account for an added 13.5 per cent of infrastructure spending.

12 Note that the question of whether the payment is compulsory or voluntary is not relevant here. For discussion see both Bird (1976) and Henchman (2013).

13 The 46,876-mile interstate highway system, the financing of which has been a federal–state matching share of 90–10, is owned by the states and for some segments by local authorities. The states establish operating rules and requirements (e.g., speed limits) and are responsible for toll collection and enforcement. Federal law still prohibits states from establishing tolls, but waivers are allowed for highway sections the state initially owned, or when a state expands the system and/or makes other improvements such as the introduction of high-occupancy toll lanes (HOT lanes). The tolls collected are designated to retire bonds and pay for bond debt service and other operating and maintenance costs. www.fhwa.dot/interstate.

14 General Revenues include all revenue except liquor stores, insurance trust, and utility revenue. The basis for distinction is not the fund or administrative unit receiving particular amounts, but the nature of the revenue sources concerned. www.census.gov/govs/local/definitions.html.

15 The "Other Charges" category, though shown in the tables, is omitted from this ranking discussion.

16 For this purpose, the CPI-U index is used. However, in carrying out sector studies of capital investment, one can draw on sector-specific price indexes provided by the US Department of Commerce. https://www.census.gov/econ/construction.

17 See www.census.gov.

18 The US Census Bureau (2016) provides state-by-state details of all forms of state and local governments.

19 Special Districts are independent, special-purpose units that exist as separate entities with substantial administrative and fiscal independence. In most cases (90 per cent of the total) these are single-purpose entities that provide education (e.g., libraries); social services (e.g., hospitals, public welfare, health services); transportation (e.g., highways, airports, parking facilities, water transport and terminals); public safety (e.g., fire protection); sewerage and solid-waste management; public water supply; sewer-

age and sanitation services; and natural resource services ranging from ir-
rigation and drainage to flood control and soil conservation. Multiple-
function districts typically have some degree of water supply function.
US Census Bureau (2002, 2012).

20 The one school that is treated as a school district is the Eastern Virginia
Medical College (US Census Bureau 2012), which leads the US Census
Bureau (2013) to show a cross-subsidy of current charges from the classi-
fication of higher education to school districts.

21 2012 data from US Bureau of Economic Analysis (BEA) and Gordon, Auxier, and Iselin (2016), respectively.

22 Netzer (1992) and Fisher and Wassmer (2015) reach a similar conclusion.

23 Fisher (2016) recognizes this increasing trend for a share of higher education to be covered by tuition (user charges), but argues that the decision
to turn to tuition is based on incomplete information.

7

Financing Environmental Infrastructures through Tariffs:
The Polluter/User-Pays Principle, Swiss Way

BERNARD DAFFLON

This paper questions how environmental infrastructures can be – and in the Swiss case are – financed through tariffs based on the benefit principle: beneficiaries should pay for the services they obtain. It is based on the expertise that local governments have developed during the last three decades, forced to find innovative practical solutions in order to assume local environmental responsibilities with limited taxation power and under hard budget constraints. The argument is developed in four sections. The first section looks at the importance and financing of investments at the cantonal and local levels. It evidences which functions can possibly be financed through tariffs instead of taxes. It also shows how much investments are loan financed and how user charges and fees have a significant place in local public finances. The second section deals with the institutional economy of user charges. Services financed through user charges must at the same time display both "public–private" characteristics of joint production. Thus financing services (and the related investments) through the user-pays principle needs a clear and indisputable legal framework and a precise accounting system so that joint production can be identified and their costs correctly traced. The third section is about implementation: we consider the tariff design for water resources, wastewater, and solid wastes in the Swiss case. What are the legal and financial requirements and how are these requirements vertically coordinated for coherence, efficiency, and equity? Though the chapter refers to the Swiss situation, the intended message is not parochial: economists need to pay attention to the institutional, political, and technical context if they wish the user-pays principle to be successfully implemented. The fourth section analyzes the performance of the polluter-/user-pays principle in the Swiss communes for the period 1996–2014. It estimates the costs-coverage ratio for (1) the production and distribution of drinking water, (2) sewage and wastewater treatment, and (3) solid waste collection, sorting, and disposal, inclusive of operating and investment costs. The last section outlines our conclusions.

PUBLIC INVESTMENT EXPENDITURES AT THE CANTONAL AND LOCAL LEVELS

In this section, we analyze successively the importance of public investments at the cantonal and local levels and the functional categories of investments. This double approach permits focusing on those particular investments in social services and public utilities for which pricing and user charges are a common source of financing. We also explain the importance of the "golden" rule of balancing the budget/accounts and limiting debt in the Swiss cantons, which influences the position of taxes and tariffs in the global public finance of local government.

Importance of Public Investments in Total Public Expenditures

Whereas cantonal public investments used to correspond to 11 per cent of the cantons' total public expenditures (TPE) around 2000, they decreased continuously to 7.5 per cent in 2014 (figure 7.1). This fall has two origins: first, a drop in investment expenditures in nominal value from 6,529 millions CHF in 2000 to 6,217 millions CHF in 2014 and, second, a 40 per cent increase in current cantonal public expenditures[1] over the same period from 59,338 millions CHF in 2000 to 82,989 millions CHF in 2014. In the period 1995 to 2005, cantonal public investments corresponded to 1.5 per cent of GDP; since 2006 it has continuously decreased to around 1 per cent in 2014.

At the local level, the time path of public investments consists of two periods. Between 2000 and 2007, communal investments amounted to 5,341 millions CHF on annual average; that is 12 per cent of TPE. In the period 2008–2013, it increased to 6,551 millions CHF in annual average. This last amount corresponds to 16 per cent of the communes' TPE and 1.2 per cent of GDP.

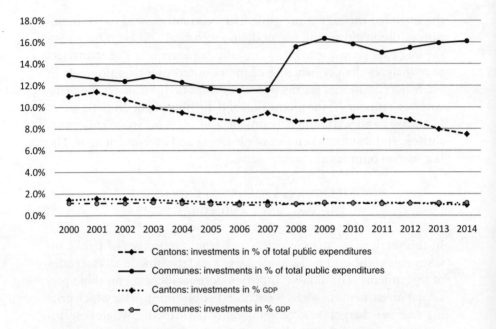

Figure 7.1   Cantonal and communal investments as percentage of TPE and GDP

Source: Author, from http://www.bfs.admin.ch/thèmes/18 Finances publiques/Rapports/tous les fichiers. Also see Annex for details on selected years.

Functional Investments

The allocation of investment resources within the various decentralized responsibilities is crucial for the focus of this chapter. Table 7.1 identifies the functions where public pricing and user charges are possible: hospital, home for elderly people (HEP), and urban public transportation in the cantons; children care, kindergarten, out-of-school facilities, and environmental policy at the local level. In the distribution of functional investments, communes have dominant positions in [3] culture, leisure, and sports (for this function, the communal expenditure share is 87.6 per cent of the added cantonal and local expenditures in line), [5] social aid (72.6 per cent), [7] environmental policy (85.8 per cent), and [8] the exploitation of natural resources (91.1 per cent).

In sub-functions, investment expenditures are important in [21] compulsory education (88.1 per cent), mainly school buildings, and in [54] kindergarten and out-of-school facilities (82.1 per cent). The com-

Table 7.1
Functional investments, average, 2010–2014

HPAS	Function	Cantons average 5 years	Communes average 5 years	in % (horizontal) total	subtotal
0	Administration	458,039	539,146	54.1	
1	Security, justice	346,945	178,331	33.9	
2	Education	1,007,803	1,223,248	54.8	
21	*Compulsory education*	*162,568*	*1,202,870*		*88.1*
22	*Special schools*	*7,283*	*2,016*		*21.7*
23	*Professional schools*	*173,239*	*18,362*		*9.6*
3	Culture, leisure, sports	87,668	621,667	87.6	
4	Health	221,537	11,447	4.9	
41	*Hospital, HEP*	*205,122*	*4,512*		*2.2*
5	Social aid	39,178	103,560	72.6	
54	*Child care, pre-school facilities*	*10,620*	*48,699*		*82.1*
6	Roads, transports, communication	2,218,475	1,340,830	37.7	
62	*Public transportation*	*156,255*	*35,693*		*18.6*
7	Environmental policy	192,210	1,159,230	85.8	
71	*Water delivery*	*30*	*314,102*		*100.0*
72	*Wastewater management*	*22,339*	*529,087*		*95.9*
73	*Refuse/garbage collection and treatment*	*3,400*	*62,749*		*94.9*
74	*Land zoning*	*103,275*	*150,576*		*59.3*
79	*Regional/local territorial planing*	*3,268*	*50,339*		*93.9*
8	Economy (agriculture, forestry, fishing, tourism)	19,935	204,079	91.1	
	total	4,591,789	5,381,538		

Source: Author, from http://www.bfs.admin.ch/thèmes/18 Finances publiques/Rapports/tous les fichiers. Italic lines evidence some sub-functions of a given main function. Functions are numbered according to the Swiss Harmonized Public Accounting System HPAS, called MCH1 for "Modèle comptable harmonisé pour les collectivités publiques," 1st ed.

munes, alone or organized in specific service precincts, are responsible for all investments related to the protection of the environment [71, 72, 73, 79]. Land zoning [74] is the exception since it has to be vertically coordinated and harmonized at the cantonal level in order to gain in

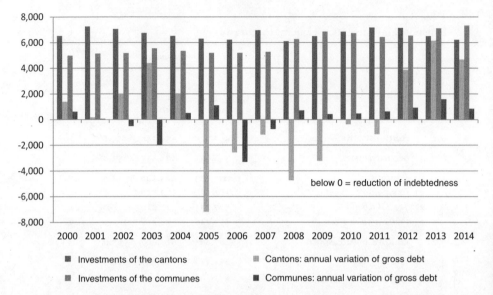

Figure 7.2   Financing public investment, 2000–2014, in millions CHF, 2000–2014

Note: The annual variation of the gross debt in 2005 in the cantons, and in 2006 in the communes (negative part of Diagram 3) mirrors an exceptional one-shot situation. In 2005, the Swiss National Bank sold on the market 1,300 tons of gold that was no longer necessary for its monetary policy. This yield was distributed one-third to the federal government and two-thirds to the cantons. The large majority of the cantons used this resource to reduce their debt; some transferred part of the yield to the communes (in 2006) under the condition that it should also serve for reducing their debt.

Source: Author, from http://www.bfs.admin.ch/thèmes/18 Finances publiques/Rapports/tous les fichiers.

coherence and efficiency. The cantonal shares are dominant in [23] professional schools (and also in high schools and university – not specified under [2] in table 7.1), in [4] health and hospital, and in [6] roads and transportation.

Financing Investments

During the last decade, the general public finance situation at the cantonal and local levels was healthy in comparison to other European states. Investments were often financed through capitalization of the surpluses in the current annual accounts. Figure 7.2 illustrates this for the period 2000–2014 by comparing the total annual investments of

Table 7.2
Sources of public revenues, average, 2010–2014 (%)

	Confederation	Canton	Communes
Income and wealth taxes	15.4	37.9	46.3
Corporate taxes	13.5	8.8	9.1
Other direct taxes	8.4	3.8	2.6
Immovable property taxes		0.4	1.7
A. Total direct taxation	37.3	50.9	59.7
VAT, consumption	55.2	2.8	0.2
B. Total indirect / consumption taxes	55.2	2.8	0.2
Patents and concessions	1.3	2.4	0.8
User charges and fees	2.7	8.7	19.1
Financial yields of assets	3.2	4.3	7.6
C. User-pays/benefit principle	7.2	15.4	27.5
Revenue sharing	0.0	5.9	1.6
Functional payments	0.0	5.4	1.7
Equalization	0.0	4.6	3.5
Grants-in-aid	0.3	15.0	5.8
D. Transfer payments	0.3	30.9	12.6
Total	100.0	100.0	100.0
Own resources A+B+C	97.7	69.1	87.4
(A+B+C) in % GDP	10	8.6	6

Source: Author, updated 9 September 2016 from http://www.bfs.admin.ch/thèmes/18 Finances publiques/Rapports/tous les fichiers.

the cantons or the communes (column left) and the annual variation of gross debt (column right); the difference between the left and right columns indicates the proportion of investments that were financed through budget surpluses.

At the cantonal level, investments were partly financed through loans from 2000 to 2004 and in the last three years (2012 to 2014). In the period 2005–2011, current surpluses were sufficient to finance investments and, in addition, reduce indebtedness (columns are negative). The cantonal situation deteriorated considerably in the last three years. In 2014, for example, cantonal public investments amounted to 6,217 millions CHF; the cantonal debt increased by 4,676 millions CHF. The difference, 1,541 millions CHF, was financed through budget surpluses. At the local level, surpluses in the current budgets pay for more than three-quarters of annual investments. In 2002, 2003, 2006, and

2007 budget surpluses were sufficient to finance investments and reduce the debt.

In the context of quasi-permanent healthy budgets/accounts, the large variety of cantonal and communal public finance resources plays a fundamental role. Relying on many sources gives local government the capacity to diversify its financial resources and distribute the burden of its expenditure needs to respond to local conditions. Table 7.2 summarizes this issue on the basis of the last five years.

Particular features include the following:

1 The power for direct taxation is shared among the three levels of government without constitutional or legal provision. Sharing direct tax power is the result of a long history, starting in the early twentieth century, and of political bargaining between the Confederation and the canton. For the years 2010–14, the proportions of direct tax yield were 26 per cent for the Confederation, 45 per cent for the cantons, and 29 per cent for the communes.[2]

2 Another remarkable feature in international comparison (OECD 2015, tables 77 to 88) is the very low revenue from the property tax: less than half a per cent for the cantons, and below 2 per cent at the local level.

3 Consumption taxes are almost exclusively federal (94 per cent) and minor in the cantons and communes (mainly vehicle and boat registration).

4 Transfer payments, distributed in four categories, are relatively important for the cantons (30.9 per cent), less so for local governments (12.6 per cent).

5 Own resources (total A+B+C in table 7.2) represent 24.6 per cent GDP.

6 User-pays and the benefit principle play a prominent role in financing specific services, including operating costs and investments. At the local level, user charges and fees amount to one-fifth of total public finances, and, more important in comparative terms, to one-third of direct taxation. Financial yields also correspond to market pricing (interest from movable properties, rental values of patrimonial properties of cantons or communes).

Balancing the Budget/Account

In the last two decades, funding services through user charges have increasingly alleviated the burden of direct taxation. Two motivations can be given. One is allocative and productive efficiency: charging for public services introduces a link between payers and beneficiaries. It increases consumers' responsibility and reduces free-rider behaviours. In Olson's (1965) terms, it matches the political accountability of deciders vis-à-vis the residents, who are at the same time beneficiaries and payers. The second reason is that cantonal and local budgets must be balanced under hard budget constraints, as explained next.

The requirement of a balanced budget and borrowing limits in local public finance is not new. But the detailed set of rules applied in most cantons, for themselves and the communes, deserves some attention (Novaresi 2001; Yerly 2013). At the federal and cantonal levels (for the cantons and the communes), the constitutions or the financial laws, sometimes both, require balancing the budget/account and limiting indebtedness in order to guarantee sustainable public finance in the long term. The usual ("golden") rule contains the obligation of balancing the current budget (and account) and limits loans to investment financing. It contains strict rules for amortization and debt reimbursement.

Amortization is founded on the expected investment's time horizon, taking into consideration the risk of obsolescence. In most cases, the technical rates of amortization are written in the law. Rates of amortization correspond to the physical depreciation of assets and usually follow professional prescriptions (see note 7 for a practical example). Debt reimbursement must follow: the banks or lending institutions have to contractually respect the technical amortization rates written in the law and cannot adapt the duration of annual repayments to the availability of funds on the capital market. Amortization, debt service, and the recurrent costs resulting from a new investment (maintenance costs and the cost of the additional services that the investment allows) have to be included in the current budget, which must be presented in balance.

The complication is that there are two levels of implementation: one for the global current budget/account and the other for each of the specific services whose provision is financed through user fees and charges. For those investments subject to the "benefit principle" and financed through user fees, the above rule applies individually for each service provided by the public sector and "sold" to those who receive them; as we shall detail later, compensation between those services is not permitted. The accounting system must separate each function and balance each account. All entries in the balance sheet must be sufficiently detailed to establish a relation between specific infrastructure facilities, financial costs, and the revenues yielded by such sales. Investments subject to pricing and user charges are capitalized in the balance sheet and thereafter annually amortized according to the usual economic rules. In addition to the running costs, debt service and amortization are included in the user charge tariffs in order to obtain full-cost coverage of the services (Dafflon 1998). The cost coverage ratio (CCR), discussed later in this chapter, measures the connection between spending and revenues.

THE INSTITUTIONAL ECONOMY OF USER CHARGES[3]

Services financed through user charges and fees must at the same time display both "public–private" characteristics of joint production. Each service must present one part that is collective with non-rival, non-excludable characteristics and another "marketable" part that is rival and excludable so that beneficiaries can be identified and the service can be individually billed. One immediately sees the difficulties (Kitchen and Slack 2016, 3–5). How much of a "collective" service is also marketable – or the inverse? Who determines where the line is drawn between the collective and the marketable part of the service? How is that line estimated for particular services? If it was only marketable, there would be no reason for the public sector to deliver the service. If it was only collective, it could not be charged. If both characteristics apply, once the collective part has been recognized and evaluated, then the remaining part of the cost must be paid through user charges. Yet, as described below, the evaluation of the collective portion is far from easy since economic theory is controversial about its designation and its measurement.

Three categories of public services have both collective and marketable characteristics: (1) public utilities traditionally belong to the historical category, and were later followed by (2) social and (3) health services. Figure 7.3 summarizes the three categories and outlines the collective and marketable parts of each service. In the rest of the paper, we consider financing current and capital environmental expenditures (table 7.1 function [7]; table 7.6, block 1) through user charges. Pricing child care and nursery, kindergarten, and out-of-school services is discussed in Dafflon (2009); hospital and HEP financing in Dafflon and Vaillancourt (2017).

How are the collective and the marketable proportions of a joint "public–private" service evaluated since it follows that their pricing will be different: the general budget (taxes) for the collective part; tariffs

		Collective	Marketable
1/	**Public utilities***		
	Drinkable water	general municipal development, avoid health problems due to bad water	private household or industrial consumption
	Sewage and waste water treatment	protection of the eco-system and natural resources	treatment of household and industrial wastewater
	Solid waste collection and disposal	recycling, protection of the eco-system, clean air and landscape	sorting reusable items, collection of individual household garbage
	Urban transport	less air pollution and less city traffic jam due to the use of private cars	individual public transportation from one place to another
2/	**Social services***		
	Nursery	enlarge the female labour market	time for individual professional work,
	Kindergarten	female labour market, socialization of children	social inclusion of one's child
	Out-of-school services	school meals, homework surveillance, prevention of social disturbance	individual service benefit
	Medical aid at home	insurance value against risk and temporary difficulties, avoid cost in homes for the elderly	individual service benefit
3/	**Health care***		
	Hospital care	insurance value against risk and	individual service benefit
	Home for elderly people (HEP)	uncertainty, network ready to accept emerging individual situations without announcement or pre-selection	individual service benefit

Figure 7.3   Domains of possible application of the benefit principle

Sources: *Dafflon (2013, 2015); **Dafflon (2009); ***Dafflon and Vaillancourt (2017).

and charges for the marketable part? In the case of Switzerland, the answers for each specific function where the "benefit principle" could apply can be grouped in two categories. For social services and health care (figure 7.3, 2/ and 3/), the line between "collective" and "marketable" results from collective bargaining between the concerned parties and is finally legitimated through parliamentary decisions and written in the law. The "collective" part, measured in proportion of the total costs or through a monetary amount, is financed through taxation or third parties' contributions. The "marketable" part of the service – that is, total costs minus the collective part – must be financed by the yield of the charges so as to guarantee full-cost coverage. The following practical example, in figure 7.4 and the next paragraph, for nurseries and kindergarten, gives a flavour of the "collective" political evaluation.

The average cost (AC) includes salaries and contributions to social security, insurances, operating costs, including normal equipment and facilities, and the rental value of the premises. The residual average cost or RAC equals AC minus the contributions of the canton and employers.

Cantonal reference	"Collective"			"Marketable"
	Canton	Communes	Employers	Parents
	Socialization	Redistributive policy	Labour market	Service delivered
Fribourg [law 2011]	10% of accepted average cost AC [9]	difference RAC – parental payment [11]	0.04% total wages [10]	Residual AC = RAC or less according to financial capacity [8]
Vaud [law 2006]	annual budget [45] 24 million CHF in 2014	5 CHF per habitant [46] = 3.72 million CHF in 2014	0.08% total wages [47] 21,6 million CHF 2014 0.12% 2017, 2018	RAC or less according to financial capacity [29]
Ticino [law 2008]	40% of accepted AC [14] 23.7 million CHF in 2014	◄ 1/3 of the cantonal contribution [30] 7.9 million CHF in 2014	Not mentioned	RAC or less according to financial capacity

Figure 7.4   "Collective" and "marketable" in practice: nursery and kindergarten

Source: Dafflon (2009, 190); for 2014 figures: author, on the basis of the cantonal legislations. In the cells, [number] indicates the article of the law.

The price paid by parents varies with regard to their financial capacity but cannot be higher than the RAC. No cross-subsidization between users is permitted; that is, the price billed to one particular user cannot exceed the RAC in order to obtain a surplus that would serve for reducing the price for users with low financial capacity. Redistribution must be financed through the general budget of the commune. In the three cantons, communes contribute for the difference between the RAC and what the user pays according to his or her financial capacity.

For *public utilities* (figure 7.3, 1/), the investment costs are shared between the "collective" and the "marketable" parts following the nature of the joint products in the production function. This is will be explained in more detail in the third part of this chapter. Of course, if the investment function permits a joint production (for example, drinkable water and fire defence), the investment costs are first distributed between the functions on the basis of the costs of the specific technical equipment and the engineers' calculation. Then, based on the benefit principle, the current and capital costs of the "marketable" part of the public service must be apportioned between economic agents according to the benefit each of them receives from the potential or actual consumption of the service. Thus the more user charges finance specific public services, the less such services absorb ordinary tax resources. There is nothing new under the sun: Bird (1976) and Buchanan (1968) were forerunners in advocating that "current and capital costs of a public service are [should be] apportioned among economic agents according to the exact benefit each of them derives from the consumption of the service" (OECD, 1998, 9). Dafflon (1998, 111ss) followed, but the user-pays principle still remains to be politically accepted and technically implemented in many countries.

The benefit principle comprises five rules in order to mirror the true "price" of the service and achieve allocative efficiency (Dafflon and Daguet 2012, 78).

Equivalence: the charges must be proportional to the benefits received by the user.

Equal treatment of equal: user charges are related to the services provided and cannot be apportioned following other not-related criteria.

No profit: on a medium time horizon, total charges cannot excess total costs. User charges cannot be disguised taxes; any annual excess of revenue must be duly reserved for the same function and appears explicitly in the balance sheet. One important point is that the "no profit" rule is truly financial. If the investment is paid through borrowing, the interest of the loan is considered. If the government uses savings, the lost interest is taken into consideration. No allowance is made in the project analysis or at any other point for a "normal" (social) rate of return.

No cross-financing: there can be no compensation between the functions. Excess of revenue in water distribution, for example, cannot be used to soften user charges in wastewater treatment. Financial reserves, if any (see the previous rule), can be used for levelling out possible imbalance through time. The reason is that cross-subsidies give a wrong price signal with negative consequences for efficiency. Also within-function cross-subsidization is not possible: between users, see the example given above for figure 7.4 for nursery and kindergarten. Between sub-functions, if any (for example, within water supply – Dafflon 2013, 13), the true investment and operational costs of each sub-function must be calculated and billed consequently.

Time causality defines the moment when the obligation to pay arises in relation to potential benefit or effective use of the service.

Apart from these requirements, the Federal High Court issued case laws adding criteria to be respected in implementing the polluter-/user-

pays principle.[4] The reason is that despite the fact that the communes
have the competence of deciding user-charge tariffs in a formal legislative act, debtors can challenge local tariffs at the administrative court
of their canton, then at the Federal Court, on the basis of the bill later
received from the commune. The federal High Court's jurisprudence is
interesting in that it coincides exactly with the economic approach of
the benefit principle. Tariffs decided by the local legislative (people's
assembly or local parliament) must explicitly state four points:

1 the definition of who are the beneficiaries of the service subject to
   the charges; if the tariff contains several distinct charges and fees,
   this regulation counts for each of them;
2 the precise designation of the services which are submitted to the
   user-charge tariff (investment, running costs, lump services);
3 the criteria for the calculation of the individual charges in the tariff;
4 the maximum amount of the user charges.

The consequence of the rules and requirements set out above is that
the implementation of the polluter/user-pays principle requires robust
legal frameworks and transparent accounting.

IMPLEMENTATION

In this third section we consider the tariff design for water resources,
wastewater, and solid wastes and the related policies. In Switzerland,
environmental policies are shared responsibilities among the three lay-
ers of government. In conformity with articles 73 to 76 of the federal
Constitution of 1999, objectives, implementation, and financing have
been assigned "top-down." The federal legislation sets out the objectives and service standards: for example, quality requirement for
bottled and tap water, the maximum residual pollution admitted for
wastewater, the qualitative and quantitative targets for the removal, recycling, and disposal of solid wastes. The cantons coordinate the implementation and the territorial mapping of the services. They also
issue the production regulations, control, and sanctions. The local level
(individual communes or communes associated in service precincts) is
responsible for investments, the production of the services, service delivery, the issuance of the user-charge tariffs, and the financial management. This organization corresponds to a double-agency model,
between the Confederation (first principal) and the cantons (agents)

and, for each canton, from the canton (second principal) to the communes (agent), in which the local governmental layer has almost no room of manoeuvre and is assigned executive powers in managing and financing the three services.

For financing investment and operating costs in drinking water, sewage and wastewater treatment, solid waste collection and treatment, local governments apply three environmental user-pays or polluter-pays tariffs. In addition to the case law issued by the Federal Court, the federal and cantonal legislations contain legal rules that restrain local choices in the design of tariffs.

Federal Rules

For the production and distribution of bottled or tap drinking water, the federal government has issued quality requirements, based on its health policy, but no rules for tariffs. This is left to the cantons. Thus, potentially twenty-six systems are possible. In fact, the cantons' room of manoeuvre for this function is largely constrained by the Federal High Court case law and the federal rules applicable for wastewater sewage and treatment since the production functions are similar.[5] Also, due to the complexities of these legal requirements and the compliance with local/regional/cantonal development plans,[6] local solutions are also self-restricted in mimicking "best practices."

From 1997 onwards, the federal rules for financing (1) solid waste collection, sorting, and disposal, and (2) sewage and wastewater treatment, are the same. It is worth underlining that the federal legislation requires the implementation of the polluter/user-pays principle and lists the production costs that must be included in the calculation of the tariffs. But it leaves open the questions of how the charges must be apportioned and whether the tariff should offer a charge break for possible sub-services.

User charge tariffs must be designed in order to cover:

1 full costs of infrastructure investment and maintenance;
2 amortization in order to maintain the capital value of the assets (capitalization of the amortization or debt instalment according to the initial source of financing the investment);
3 debt service (interest);
4 capitalization of future investments necessary to compensate for obsolescence and for new quality standards;

5 user charges that also mirror the type and quantity of solid waste (volume, weight) or wastewater (meter).

The particularity of this list, and a novelty in the 1997 law, is item (4). Local tariffs should include a "charge for the future" that is not related to the service delivered but to future investments. One can understand that the depreciation of productive capital and, to a certain degree, the probability of obsolescence are taken into account in the amortization rate of the investment.[7] But it was more difficult to anticipate what would be "new quality standards" and why the future costs of these standards – often using rule-of-thumb evaluation – should be paid in advance through capitalization rather than through amortization once they have been implemented. Resistance to introducing this part of the tariff has been rather strong in legislative local assemblies and parliaments since its "value for money" is not clear. It also means that the present generation of users is paying twice for the investments, past and future.

These difficulties have been perceived at the federal level. From 2016 onwards (time limit is year 2040), the federal government perceives a fee to a maximum of 9 CHF per habitant from "the owners of wastewater treatment plants" (in fact the communes that belong to the service precinct) that have not yet invested in treating micro-organic residuals. The yield of the fees finances grants-in-aid in order to accelerate the implementation of the related technology. Communes are exempted from the fee once the investment is realized.[8]

Cantonal Legal Rules for Tariffs

Owing to the federal legislation and the Federal Court case law, the cantons' legal rules for tariffs for drinking waters, wastewater, and solid waste are very similar. Without going in too many details, the main legal features of the legislation in the Canton Fribourg, summarized in figure 7.5, correspond to the general trend in the other twenty-five cantons. Based on the cantonal legislation, each communal tariff contains four categories of charges described below.

CONNECTION CHARGES

Connection charges are "one-off" charges for connecting public and private properties to the water supply and the sewage system. Its purpose is the full coverage of total costs resulting from the investments (infrastructure and technical equipment) of the first generation. Since the public investments must include not only built zones but also the reserve of land for future housing and activity zones, individual charges are calculated on the construction potential of individual plots of land and not on their effective use. The construction potential corresponds to the maximum building capacity of a given surface in the local development plan.[9] There are two methods of payment. In a majority of communes, the connection charge is a unique charge to be paid at the time of connection of the plot of land to the network; it means that the billed charge is de facto privatized in the owner's mortgage loan. Otherwise, connection charges are distributed in annual instalments, including annual interest for the open debt.

Connected public properties, school buildings, cultural and sport centres, public administrative buildings, and the like, held by all levels of government, must also be accounted for in the base for the calculation of the charges. The concerned institutions receive a bill for each property, based on the same regulations and tariffs as private owners. The government pays the bill through its budget.

Note that with sufficient pressure, the water distribution network can also be used for fire defence – which has the collective characteristics of no-rivalry and no-exclusion within the service precinct. Thus, that part of the investment costs must be assigned to this function and not paid through the water tariff (also the example given for figure 7.6).

ACCESS CHARGES

When a plot of land situated within the perimeter of the water distribution or wastewater networks can be connected but is not because it is not yet built, potential beneficiaries (owners of the land in the zone reserved for development) must pay up to 70 per cent of their share of the investment costs. The remaining 30 per cent portion will be paid later by the owners when the building is realized and connected. In the meantime the commune has to support the interest of the remaining 30 per cent. The maximum ratio 70/30 per cent was pulled from the Federal Court case law.

Two arguments can be used to justify that access charges, considered as prepayment of the connection charges, must be paid though at a lower percentage. First, potential beneficiaries have to pay the access charge as a sort of insurance premium in exchange for the guarantee to get connected and to benefit from the service when needed. But the amount of the access charge must be lower since the benefit of the service is potential and not fully exploited. Second, since the decision to build cannot be forced on private owners, it would be unfair for the commune to support their total share of investment, whereas their plots benefit from a value added due to public infrastructure in development zones. In the meantime the commune supports the interest payment for the difference since the "not yet built plots of land" are part of the "village or urban development," which is considered a collective good.

There are no connection or access charges for solid waste collection, sorting, and disposal because there is no fixed network for this service and, in consequence, no possibility to identify potential beneficiaries.

BASIC ANNUAL CHARGES

At the origin, the basic annual charges (BAC) took into account the fixed operating costs, whereas the annual consumption charges (ACC) (next) would account for the variable operating costs. The BAC was based on the potential use of the service, whereas the ACC was calculated on the effective use or consumption of the service (volume or weight for solid waste, cubic metre for water and wastewater). This has changed with recent legislation that introduced new references for investment costs: (1) the replacement value (at current price) of existing investment and (2) the "costs" of future investments in response to the federal law foreseeing "new qualitative requirements."

The present-day tendency is therefore to abandon the distinction between fixed and variables operating cost distributed in the basic and operational charges to reserve the basic annual charge for capitalizing both (1) the difference between the historical and the current replacement value of the existing investment and (2) "future" investments for improving the quality of services.

But, in the case of the canton Fribourg, it is interesting to observe that in the 2009 law on water only 60 per cent of the estimated future investments could be taken into consideration. Two years later, in the 2011 law on drinking water, this proportion was set at 50 per cent. These two different minimal thresholds and the 10 per cent difference received no explanation from the government and in the parliamentary debates. But a reasonable explanation is that the canton anticipated the difficulty for the communes to obtain from local assemblies or parliaments a positive vote for taking into account the "evaluated future costs" of not yet clearly designed investments.

ANNUAL OPERATING CHARGE

As a result of the modification in the previously described charge, the annual operating charge includes fixed and variable operating costs, including maintenance. And in all three functions, it is proportional to the individual use of the services. The only practical question is how to measure or quantify the service benefits. It is self-evident for tap water and wastewater where cubic metres exist, but more difficult for solid waste (volume, bags, weight have each pros and cons – not to be discussed here).

For solid waste, the law does not make an explicit distinction between annual basic or operating charges. The legal requirement that the yield of the charge based on volume or weight must correspond to at least 50 per cent of the total user charges and cover at least 70 per cent of total cost (art. 23 of the law) has been interpreted so that the other 50 per cent can take the form of an annual basic charge in order to cover fixed costs. Costs of communal waste reception centre treating waste according to category ("déchetterie") are fixed for a large part; thus, these costs plus financial costs if any (interest and amortization) are tariffed in the basic annual charges. Solid waste incineration plants are legally organized in separate corporate entities because they produce energy and district heating services that are commercial. Thus the net costs of the sub-function "solid waste incineration" are apportioned between the communes proportionally to the volume/weight of household solid wastes. The communes include this payment in the annual operating costs. Disposal and incineration of commercial and industrial solid waste are paid directly by the private customer; the financial system does not transit through the communes. ·

PERFORMANCE

Before analyzing the performance of the polluter/user-pays principle, this section develops a few considerations about the accounting rules necessary for its implementation. Accounting principles have to be clear so as to guarantee a quid-pro-quo correspondence between expenditures and charges. Second, the cost-coverage ratio must be explicated.

Accounting

Transparent accounting information is a key component of environmental management issues, more so in the Swiss case for at least four reasons:

	Drinking water	Sewage and wastewater treatment	Solid waste
Federal law	No rules on tariffs	Federal law of 24 January 1991 on the protection of waters (RS 814.20, art. 60a); article 60a was added to the federal law on 20 June 1997 and enforced on 1 November 1997. 9 CHF per habitant, law of 21 March 2014, enforced from 1 January 2016	Federal law of 7 October 1983 on the protection of the environment (RS CH 814.01, art. 32a); article 32a was added to the federal law on 20 June 1997 and enforced on 1 November 1997.
		(a) full costs, (b) amortization, (c) debt service (interest); (d) capitalization of future investments necessary to compensate for obsolescence and for new quality standards; (e) user charges (volume, weight)	
Federal court case law		*The jurisprudence is the same for the three services*	
Cantonal law RS FR	Law of 6 October 2011 on drinking water (replaces the 1979 law) RS FR 821.32.1 art. 27-33	Law of 18 December 2009 on water (replaces the 1974 law) RS 812.1 art. 40 - 43	Law of 13 November 1996 on solid waste management (replaces the reference articles in the 1974 cantonal implementation law of the 1971 federal law on the protection of waters against pollution) RS FR 810.2 art. 42, 43
Connection charge	art. 28-29 potential building capacity	art. 41 potential building capacity	none
Access charge	art. 31 70% of the connection charge	art. 41 70% of the connection charge	none
Annual basic charge	art. 32 *for the realized equipment:* fix costs (amortization and interest) capitalization of the current replacement value (50%) *for future equipment:* cost estimation according to the local development plan (minimum threshold 50% of the "estimated" future costs)	art. 42 *for the realized equipment:* fix costs (amortization and interest) capitalization of the current replacement value (60%) *for future equipment:* cost estimation according to the local development plan (minimum threshold 60% of the "estimated" future costs)	art.23 based on volume or weight. The yield of the tax must correspond at least to 50% of the total user charges and cover at least 70% of total cost art. 24 For some categories of solid waste sorted out in communal waste reception center treating waste according to category (e.g., used oil, batteries, metal etc), local government can levy a specific charge. The law does not distinguish annual basic or operating charge.
Annual operating charge	art. 33 maintenance and operating costs must be apportioned on the basis of consumption (cubic meter)	art. 43 maintenance and operating costs	

Figure 7-5   Legal base for user charges in environmental services

Source: Author, Recueil Systématique du droit fribourgeois, RS FR, www.fr.ch/Etat et droit/legislation/BDLF/8 Environnement (reference number)

1 There cannot be one single general "environmental function": the law does not permit financial compensation between one service and the other. This is the "no cross-subsidy" rule.
2 The local assemblies or parliaments must be given the possibility to verify in the successive annual budgets/accounts and in the balance sheet the correct implementation of the federal and cantonal legislations and the respect of the rules issued from the Federal High Court case law.
3 The various costs of each environmental function must be visible because they are distributed in different charges in the tariffs (see figure 7.6). Individual payers can contest the bill if the categories of charges are not respected.
4 Local assemblies and individual beneficiaries must be given the opportunity to verify the cost-coverage ratio (CCR).

The accounting system provides two classifications, functional and economic nature, that correspond to the needed information. In the Swiss Harmonized Public Accounting System (HPAS) (CCMF, 2007, 271–2), the chapter 7 heading is "protection of environment and land planning" and comprises the following major heads: 71 water distribution, 72 wastewater management, 73 solid waste management, 74 protection against natural disasters, 75 fauna, flora, and landscape protection, 76 protection against air and noise pollution, 77 cemeteries. Also, if the production function contains sub-products or services, it could be further divided into minor heads: thus for 72 wastewater management, the HPAS gives 720 sewage (communal) and 721 wastewater treatment (most often, special service precincts with several communes within the same watershed). The second classification in HPAS gives the economic nature of expenditures and revenues (line-item in the budget and account such as: personal, insurance, vehicle maintenance, administrative material, energy, etc.).

Connection and access charges are accounted for in the investment section of the budget/account for the respective functions. Then the corresponding values are reported in the closing balance sheet in deduction of the historical values of investment. The closing balance sheet thus indicates the residual value of the investments at the end of each year. All other accounting operations are included in the annual current budgets and accounts.

These points of analysis are not simply purely technical assemblage of words and numbers. It is absolutely necessary to establish the true costs of the production functions, possibly with a distinction between

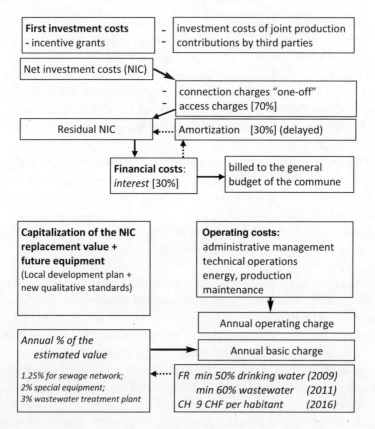

Figure 7.6   Relations between costs and charges

functional major and minor heads. With this information, it is possible to calculate the true activity-based costs, the average and marginal costs, and to distinguish between financial, fixed and variable operating costs. The organization of the tariffs depends from these calculations.[10] Figure 7.6 offers a simplified illustration of the relations between costs and charges.

Cost-Coverage Ratio

In common definition, the coverage ratio (CR) is a measure of a company's ability to meet its financial obligations. In broad terms, the higher the coverage ratio, the better the ability of the enterprise to fulfill its obligations to its lenders. The trend of coverage ratios over time is also studied to ascertain the change in a company's financial position. Here, we use a derivative of CR applied to local government and, in specific terms, to environmental policies. What we want to analyze is how much expenditures for each specific environmental function in the current budget is covered through user charges or other third parties' earmarked contributions, within the rules fixed by law and jurisprudence.

If correctly applied, the cost-coverage ratio [CCR] equals 1 for each of the three functions. The CCR corresponds to the ratio

$$\frac{\text{tariff yields (+ possible third parties' earmarked contributions)}}{\text{current expenditures}}$$

without accounting for double entries. The requirement of full-cost coverage corresponds to the logic of the benefit principle in political economy and to the polluter-/user-pays legal requirements. With CCR=1 or 100 per cent, the revenues from the tariffs and contributions exactly cover expenditures: the function is self-financed via the corresponding user charges. Three points must be cleared.

First, if the production function allows for joint products – drinking water and fire defence, for example – then the joint product must be excluded from the cost basis. If in figure 7.6, the main calculation concerns the supply of drinking water in the top-left box, the investment costs of the joint product in the top-right box – fire defence – must be deducted from the calculation. If the joint product is also "marketable," a separate calculation is run for this joint product.

Second, pursuing the previous example, let us admit that one-fifth of the total area in the local living and activity zones of the commune contains not-yet-built plots of land. At the time of zoning, owners of the unbuilt plots paid access charges corresponding to 70 per cent of the connection charges. Thus the value of 30 per cent of one-fifth of the investment costs remained unpaid. The equivalent amount is written in the balance sheet of the commune until payment at the moment of building. Amortization will be paid gradually with the effective occupation of land. In the meantime, reserves of land are considered "collective" goods since the future development of the commune is of general concern. For this reason, the equivalent interest is billed to the general budget of the commune.

Third, the CCR is not conceptual. It is calculated in the account book. This also explains the importance of a precise technical description of the production function in order to isolate joint products and of the accounting system, which has to trace exactly the origin and importance of costs attributed to each item within a function (Dafflon 2013).

Global Performance: All Communes in All Cantons

Table 7.3 presents the average results for years 2008 to 2013 for all communes in the twenty-six cantons. What we observe are relatively significant differences from one canton to the other. For drinkable water and wastewater, the communes in four cantons present a CCR below 70 per cent, which is the lowest limit admitted by the Federal High Court in case law.[11] Of course the difference has to be paid through the ordinary resources in the current budgets, that is, through taxation. For solid waste, the communes in ten cantons present scores below the 70 per cent threshold. Geneva is a particular case: the communes have externalized the production and distribution of drinking water, the treatment of wastewater and solid waste to the "Services industriels de Genève";[12] the information about the CCRs is not accessible.

In the time series, the CCR in the two bottom lines of table 7.3 are progressing, though slowly, from 2008 to 2013: 4 percentage points for drinkable and wastewater, 5 percentage points for solid waste.

While these results are comparable – the computation method is the same for all cantons – the analysis suffers from important statistical drawbacks for three main reasons (AFF, 2012). First, the statistical data are aggregated for drinkable water and wastewater despite the fact that the legal regulations on user charges are federal for wastewater and left to the cantons for drinkable water. And this aggregation is contrary to the High Court case law which forbids cross-financing between the two functions. Second, financial costs (amortization and debt interest) are often accounted in chapter 9 of the account (HPAS) concerning the general finance of the communes, without being internally imputed to the correct functional chapters [71 drinking water], [72 wastewater], and [73 solid waste]. In the communes where the imputation is not applied, the CCR percentage is overestimated. Third, in several cantons, some environmental sub-services are not included in the data because of their particular legal status (for example, when the service is externalized to a public law autonomous institution or a "private" corporate entity – though entirely in public hands). There is no CCR indication for these "privatized" services.

At this stage, an obvious question is: who enforces the rules? Again the Swiss way of doing things is parochial: the answer is "persuasion"

Table 7.3
Cost-coverage ratios in the cantons, average, 2008–2013

Communes in the canton of:	Drinkable water, wastewater (%)	Solid waste (%)
Basel-Town	135.8	89.3
Neuchâtel	98.4	67.7
Solothurn	97.1	88.2
Obwalden	96.1	89.8
Luzern	95.8	81.7
Fribourg	93.4	81.1
Bern	91.6	84.3
Vaud	87.2	39.8
Jura	86.2	74.4
Basel-Land	84.6	80.0
Nidwalden	84.2	93.9
Aargau	83.0	68.1
Zug	81.0	47.0
Schaffhausen	79.2	80.6
Appenzell Rh.Ext.	79.2	56.9
Glarus	76.9	114.7
Schwyz	76.8	80.4
Grisons	78.6	111.8
Valais	75.8	75.7
Thurgau	72.8	50.8
St Gallen	71.2	66.6
Zurich	70.3	74.2
Ticino	55.4	43.9
Appenzell Rh. Int.	28.5	81.4
Uri	28.4	3.7
Geneva	9.4	5.5
AVERAGE	79.6	63.3

	2008	2009	2010	2011	2012	2013
Drinkable water, wastewater	77	77	79	81	82	81
Solid waste	63	62	63	64	61	68

Source: Author; www.efv.admin.ch/Thèmes/Statistique financière/Indicateurs/Financement par les émoluments.

not "legal force," but in practice, the cantonal monitoring authorities (ministry of health for water, ministry of environment for wastewater and solid waste) are busy with the technical implementation of the laws, insisting that investments and equipment be realized within the time limits and maintenance flows. They also care for the quality of water (fixed in the federal legislation), either at the tap, for wastewater entering the sewage system,[13] or for water returning from the treatment plant to the river. Financial control, notably the respect of the CCR, through the cantonal authorities, is absent. For example, the overall result for communes in the canton of Fribourg (next) are well known from the "Service des Communes," but this supervisory agency has authority to control the communes' bylaws and regulations, but no power in obliging them, for example, to reach a CCR = 1. Yet individual taxpayers have this power if they complain to the administrative tribunal (first cantonal, then federal) about the non-respect of the rules. There are two possible ways they can do this: to complain that the communal by-law is not respected or that direct taxes are higher than necessary because charges in one of the three environmental domains do not cover the costs. In several cases, the Federal Court compelled the commune to correct the situation within a period of time (three to five years in general).

Overall Results for the Communes in Canton Fribourg

The performance analysis for all communes in the canton Fribourg is illustrated in figure 7.7 for the period 1996–2014. The results are slightly different and better than the corresponding line in table 7.3, and also more robust due to the technical controls in the annual accounts of the communes. First, separate statistical data, commune by commune, are accessible for each function so that the three CCRs can be measured. Second, communal accounts are detailed [function and accounting classification by nature of revenues and expenditures], which is important to verify whether all current and capital expenditures are correctly accounted for and entered in the respective functions or sub-functions. Third, the annual results can be lined in time series since the accounting system based on HPAS was introduced in 1981 and has not been subject to major changes during the nineteen years of the referred period.

The performance analysis consists of two measures: accuracy in accounting costs and revenues in the right functions and sub-functions, then estimation of the CCR. The analysis was conducted for all the communes in the canton, and also for communes distributed in seven groups corresponding to the seven administrative districts – in order to see if the results differ in urban, suburban, or rural areas.[14]

The overall results approximate the objective set by law. In the first measure about accounting accuracy, more than 85 per cent of the communes adequately recorded the environmental costs covered by user charges. There is no behavioural strategy of underpricing – for example,

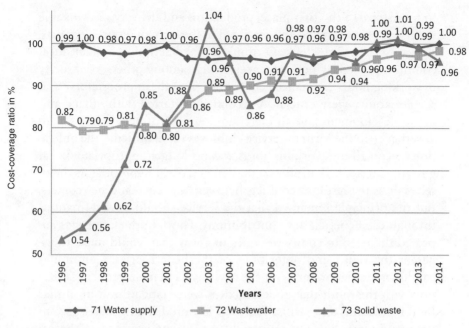

Figure 7.7   CCR for functions [71][72][73], 1996–2014, canton Fribourg, all communes

Source: Author, www.fr.ch/Etat et droit/communes/Service des communes/Statistiques/Finances communales.

in accounting for amortization and interest of debt in chapter [9 Finance] and omitting the internal computation under the right function [71, 72, or 73]. Errors are residual and mainly due to misunderstandings of the accounting system. The most common error is that when the annual basic charges are capitalized, the total amount is correctly identified in the balance sheet, but the interests of the capital remain as general revenue in chapter [9 finance] and are not always imputed under the referred environmental function. These errors have been corrected for the analysis. The CCR test, over the period 1996–2014, shows a clear trend towards full-cost coverage.

Drinking Water

Figure 7.7 confirms that water supply has traditionally been totally financed by user charges. As in many cantons, local tariffs for drinking water in the canton of Fribourg are the result of a historical evolution in four steps. In the first place, production and delivery of drinkable water were appropriated and managed in the form of service precincts, the "consortages," much like Ostrom's (1990) description of stable local common pool, in which trust, reciprocity (among others, reciprocity in working hours or financial contributions of the appropriators), and accountability were crucial. A second step started with village and urban development and an increasing number of beneficiaries. Self-governance in the form of service clubs was more difficult; the obligation to contribute working hours was no longer appropriate. Local government stepped in, often at the demand of the appropriators themselves or as the result of conflicts between "ancients" and newcomers. But the principle remained that the service should be self-financed through the beneficiaries' contributions. Third, in the late 1970s appeared the need to codify the rules in a way that would make transparent the rights and obligations of the beneficiaries. Communes would serve as laboratories for the new legal and managerial organization with the result that good practices were standardized in similar local regulations and tariffs. The 1979 law on drinking water gave to the communes the right to introduce a unique connection charge: water delivery could be "charged." These legal prescriptions were insufficient in the eyes of the Federal Court, so in 1981 the cantonal law on the communes reconsidered the issue and determined that the requirement of the Federal Court should be detailed in the local implementation decree. Fourth, in 2011, the canton of Fribourg issued a law that fixes in detail the rules of financing the production and distribution of drinkable water (see figure 7.5). It could not be privatized, and for this public service CCR should equal 1.

Wastewater and Solid Waste

As can be seen in figure 7.7, the CCRS in 1996, the starting point of time for this analysis, were at 54 per cent for solid waste collection and treatment, and 82 per cent for sewage and wastewater – compared to 99 per cent for the production and distribution of drinking water. Over the period 1996–2008, important efforts were accomplished in order to improve the financial performance. In 2009, the CCRS were at 94 per cent for wastewater, 97 per cent for solid waste. The situation has remained sustainable for the following five years 2010–2014. However, for wastewater, a closer sampling of local accounts and the corresponding local regulations shows that in a large number of communes, the annual basic charge (figure 7.5) takes into account the capitalization of the current replacement value, but not future qualitative investments. Thus, the CCR is performant in the comparison between the user-charge revenues and the "costs/expenditures" they finance, but is less so with regard to the rules set by law.

Three arguments, namely environmental awareness, equity, and tax competition, are usually proposed for explaining the trend approximating CCR = 1. The first reason would be a better awareness of environmental issues: the message is that care for the environment starts at the doorstep. Saving water and recycling solid wastes are easy daily behaviours which also have efficiency effects: consuming less and sorting solid wastes for recycling result in lower user charges. The second argument is the concept of equity embedded in the benefit principle: you pay for the service from which you benefit. Put the other way round: why should one pay through taxes the individual services that others obtain? This thinking is self-evident for public utilities.[15]

The third argument is the pressure of tax competition, which obliges communes to maintain or even lower their tax coefficient on individual income taxation and corporate profit taxation, and partly compensate the loss of revenue with higher earmarked user charges (Dafflon 2014). This substitution is the result of a combination between vertical tax externalities and the constitutional or legal obligation to balance the budget and limit indebtedness. The design of direct taxation belongs to the federal layer for the definition of taxable income or profit and the list of possible tax deductions. The cantons decide the ceiling for each deduction, the tax rate schedule, and the threshold for the taxable income or profit. The communes have no room for manoeuvre in this design. They apply a piggyback taxation in deciding only the tax coefficient as a percentage of the cantonal tax. When the cantons engage in tax competition, the communes have to support the vertical tax externality, which means a loss in tax revenues. Local competition, though limited, makes it difficult to increase the tax coefficient for compensating the loss of revenue in order to respect the legal requirement of balancing the current budget/account. User charges offer a possible substitute. This was clearly the case in the period 2000–2008, but this becomes difficult when the CCRs approximate 1 in the three environmental functions and is impossible with CCR = 1.

CONCLUDING REMARKS

The Swiss way of financing environmental policies through the polluter-/user-pays principle suggests four concluding remarks. First, it has been and still is a long process: at the federal level, thirty-three years between the first and last law on the protection of water (1983, 1991, 1996 and 2016); fourteen for solid waste (1983, 1997); and thirty-two years at the cantonal level for drinking water. Most legal changes were taken at the federal level. But rules cannot simply be imposed from the top down: the political and participatory decision process makes it impossible without the voters' consent and a majority of cantons. The system as it exists today has been created gradually over three or four decades, but was also founded initially on a non-governmental solution for the production and distribution of water.

The second conclusion emphasizes the need for (1) a clear legal framework, with a strong vertical coordination that draws a clear line in the sharing and distribution of responsibility; (2) a precise accounting system in which the traceability of the benefit principle is guaranteed between functions and within function for joint product and sub-product; (3) a judicial system that, in one way or another, permits users, beneficiaries, and payers to make their point in case the principle is violated.

The third remark concerns the absolute necessity for economists implementing the benefit principle to collaborate closely with environmental and network engineers and professionals in land zoning and development planning. Without transversal professional co-operation, economists are simply not in a position to make any proposal or formulate any recommendation in pricing environmental services.

Finally, performance in the implementation of the polluter-/user-pays principle is not possible without the people's consent. With a few exceptions (Geneva, for example) or with reluctance (Vaud for solid waste), voters have accepted these instrumentalities in order to determine and implement a well-thought-out charging policy in several public services; to achieve better efficiency (no waste: you pay for what you use; you use what you pay for) and equity ("Why should I pay through taxes for others?"); and to alleviate the budget constraint for other not-pricing policies.

Table 7.4
Cantonal public-sector expenditures, selected years, 2000–2014

HPAS	Economic classification	2000	2005	2010	2011	2012	2013	2014
30	personal	21,633	25,968	24,641	25,339	26,302	26,740	27,103
31	goods and services	7,374	9,234	8,409	8,433	8,599	8,998	9,219
34	finance, interest	2,341	1,796	1,191	1,133	1,076	1,052	982
36	grants-in-aid	21,461	26,817	34,034	35,728	37,646	38,431	39,467
3	current expenditures	52,809	63,815	68,274	70,632	73,623	75,221	76,772
50	cantons: own direct investment	4,814	4,842	4,721	4,891	4,794	4,393	4,158
51,52,55	external investments			111	185	548	270	264
57	investment grants	1,715	1,456	2,009	2,091	1,799	1,843	1,795
5	cantons: investment expenditures	6,529	6,297	6,841	7,166	7,142	6,505	6,217
3+5	Total Public Expenditures (TPE)	59,338	70,112	75,115	77,799	80,765	81,726	82,989
	Cantons: gross debt	63,141	64,558	52,460	51,310	55,166	61,311	65,987
	GDP	458,779	507,463	606,146	618,325	623,611	634,776	643,784
5/(3+5)	Total investments in % of TPE	11.0	9.0	9.1	9.2	8.8	8.0	7.5
50/(3+5)	Own direct investments in % TPE	8.1	6.9	6.3	6.3	5.9	5.4	5.0
	difference [51,52,55,57]	2.9	2.1	2.8	2.9	2.9	2.6	2.5
5/GDP	cantons: investments in % GDP	1.4	1.2	1.1	1.2	1.1	1.0	1.0

Table 7.5
Communal public-sector expenditures, selected years, 2000–2014

HPAS	Economic classification	2000	2005	2010	2011	2012	2013	2014
30	personal	15,480	18,192	13,512	13,858	13,827	14,024	14,279
31	goods and services	8,530	9,831	9,189	9,367	9,623	9,682	9,561
34	finance, interest	2,093	1,501	1,409	1,354	1,261	1,165	1,122
36	grants-in-aid	9,256	10,276	12,229	12,735	13,098	13,596	13,876
3	current expenditures	35,359	39,800	36,339	37,314	37,808	38,468	38,838
50	own direct investment	4,621	4,845	5,370	5,088	5,159	5,503	5,747
51,52,55	external investments	0	0	69	141	235	293	313
57	investment grants	360	341	1,291	1,206	1,146	1,310	1,268
5	investment expenditures	4,981	5,187	6,729	6,436	6,540	7,105	7,329
3+5	Total Public Expenditures (TPE)	40,340	44,987	43,068	43,750	44,349	45,573	46,168
	Cantons: gross debt	49,054	48,237	45,784	46,420	47,345	48,935	49,788
	GDP	458,779	507,463	606,146	618,325	623,611	634,776	643,784
5/(3+5)	total investments in % of TPE	12.3	11.5	15.6	14.7	14.7	15.6	15.9
50/(3+5)	own direct investment in % TPE	11.5	10.8	12.5	11.6	11.6	12.1	12.4
	difference [51, 52, 55, 57]	0.9	0.8	3.2	3.1	3.1	3.5	3.4
5/GDP	cantons: investments in % GDP	1.1	1.0	1.1	1.0	1.0	1.1	1.1

Source: Author, from http://www.bfs.admin.ch/themes/18 Finances publiques/Rapports/tous les fichiers; updated 1 September 2016.

NOTES

The author wishes to thank Enid Slack, Richard Bird, Harry Kitchen, and the participants at the conference for their comments and suggestions.

1 This corresponds to an average expenditure increase of 2.86 per cent annually, whereas during the same period, the nominal annual GDP growth was 2.47 per cent. Detailed data are given in tables 7.4 and 7.5 for selected years.

2 For direct taxation, there is no rule of power sharing between the three levels of government except that the maximum tax rates for federal income and business taxes are written in the federal Constitution (art. 128 Cst: 11.5 per cent for income taxation and 8.5 per cent for business profit taxation) for a limited period of time (actually end of 2020: Cst 196/13 – but always prolonged since 1934, usually for a period of fifteen to twenty years, submitted to popular vote with the double majority of the cantons and the voters). The cantons received 40 per cent of the federal direct tax yield from 1934 to 1940, 35 per cent in 1941, and 30 per cent from 1941 to 2007 (17 per cent on the basis of origin and 13 per cent earmarked for revenue equalization). Since 2008, the cantons receive 17 per cent on the basis of origin; the federal contribution to revenue equalization is financed through the annual budget without earmarking (table 7.2, line "revenue sharing"). All the cantons restrict the communal power to tax through limits in the piggyback tax supplement (or coefficient). For example, in the canton of Fribourg, the ceiling is fixed at 125 per cent of the cantonal direct tax.

3 Adapted from Dafflon and Daguet (2012) and Dafflon (2015).

4 On this, for example the decision of the Swiss Federal Supreme Court, 7 July 2003; reference in BGE 129 I 290 "considérant" 3.2; more recently the decision of 4 July 2011, reference ATF 2C_740/2009.

5 Drinking water requires a production infrastructure and a distribution network; wastewater requires a sewage network and a wastewater treatment plant. See Dafflon (2013).

6 As is the case for most environmental policies, local development plans are largely constrained by the cantons' law on planning, which considerably limit the communes' room for manoeuvre in defining activity zones (industry, small and medium enterprises, commercial zones), residential areas, mixed activity-residential areas. In turn, the cantons have to respect the rules of the federal law, in particular the obligation to preserve agriculture land and natural sites ("strict separation of building from non-building

portions of territory") introduced in the law following the federal vote of 15 June 2012 and enforced on 1 May 2014 (Federal law of 22 June 1979 on land zoning and planning, as on 1 January 2016, RS CH 700). www.admin.ch/droit federal/recueil systématique/droit interne/700 LAT.

7 The amortization rate corresponds to the allocation of the costs of assets to the periods in which the assets are used (20 years = 5 per cent for linear amortization). The amortization is based on the historical value, which is the amount of expenditure at the time the asset was realized. Depreciation takes into consideration the replacement value at current prices of the assets for the same quality and quantity of service. Obsolescence considers that a new technology for producing the same service will occur before the normal time horizon of the asset use (twenty years in the example). Before 1997, there was no dilemma: the historical value was the reference for amortization. After 1997, the obligation to pre-finance future investments due to new technologies (for example, the actual requirement to introduce techniques capable of removing organic and chemical micro-pollutants) is fiercely debated in local assemblies and is not yet implemented in a majority of communes. Keep in mind that tariffs have to be voted at the local level and that voters are payers and have already paid the existing investments. Thus they believe they are being "taxed" a second time. The equity argument is "Why should we pay in advance and why not the future beneficiaries through connection charges or amortization, as was the rule for us for the investments' first generation?" As one can appreciate, the answer "because this is the requirement of the federal law" does not satisfy the equity argument.

8 This legal change has been introduced by the law of 21 March 2014, enforced from 1 January 2016 (Official Register of Federal Laws RO 2014, 3327).

9 Gross Index of Land Use, that is $\text{GILU} = \dfrac{\Sigma \text{ built surfaces}}{\text{surface of the plot of land}}$.

For example, 1,000 m² of land with a building rate $\text{GILU} = 0.65$ permit a construction with a total built surface of 650 m² (floor surfaces and basement). If the building effectively uses only 400 m², then the calculation is based on 650 m² and not 400 m².

10 Detailed information on user charges tariffs can be found in Dafflon and Daguet (2012) and Dafflon (1998, chapter 4; 2013).

11 In a 2011 decision (ATF 2C_740/2009), the Federal High Court admitted that a maximum 30 per cent of the solid waste total costs be financed through the general budget of the commune – that is, through taxation. The argument is that public administration, schools, all communal

buildings, leisure parks, street dustbins, etc. also produce solid wastes that have to be treated in the normal process. It corresponds to a "collective" production of solid waste, thus paid by the general budget. Within the 30 per cent limit, the budget contribution most often results from a "rule-of-thumb" evaluation; a number of communes prefer administratively charging their own services as ordinary users. The same argument has been extended to drinking water and wastewater in communal public buildings and facilities.

12 The SIGs are organized in the form of a public-law autonomous institution. Its capital belongs 55 per cent to the canton, 30 per cent to Geneva City, and 15 per cent to the other forty-four communes.

13 The sewage system must separate rain and stormwater (including water from the roofs or from open-air and surfaced places) from wastewater. The quality benchmark for wastewater is the normal use of a household (household equivalent = 1). Dirtier wastewater from commercial and industrial activities receives a higher coefficient in terms of household equivalent – that is, [produced cubic meter × coefficient]; pretreatment may be required. The norms are fixed at the federal level.

Rainwater of streets and open public places enters separate storm sewers going directly to the river. Owners of properties (public or private) must first solve the evacuation of "rain" water from the premises. If this is not possible, the rainwater can enter the public storm sewers. In this case, they have to contribute to financing the public storm sewers. This is obtained through an increase of the surface of the plot of land (s). The increasing coefficients are $s \times 1.3$ for open-air surfaced places, $s \times 1.6$ for roof surfaces and $s \times 1.2$ for drainage. Increasing the surface normally increases the connection charge and the basic annual charge.

14 Accuracy in accounting and also cross-verification per district are not detailed in this paper; only global results are given. For the technical details of the accuracy test, see Dafflon and Daguet (2012, 83–5).

15 In more recent times, the benefit principle has been tentatively extended to social services such as kindergarten, pre-school, and out-of-school facilities. Once the externalities of the services have been evaluated and paid from the general budget, the remaining costs must be financed through tariffs. Beneficiaries pay for the service; those with low financial capacity receive targeted individualized financial aid (Dafflon 2009). The same applies for medical and hospital care (Dafflon and Vaillancourt 2017).

8

The Role of User Fees in Urban Transportation Public–Private Partnerships: Canada in a Global Perspective

MATTI SIEMIATYCKI

INTRODUCTION

In the face of tight public budgets and diminishing tax revenues, governments around the world are increasingly looking to the application of direct user fees as a way to fund the construction and operations of major urban transportation infrastructure. When it comes to public–private partnerships (PPPs), however, the charging of user fees may serve a wider range of public interest functions than simply raising money to pay for infrastructure. Depending on the way that user fees are charged and the revenues allocated between the partners in the PPP, they are intended to solidify risk transfer arrangements, encourage innovation and life-cycle asset management, and even provide a screen against politically motivated but wasteful government investment decisions. Nevertheless, the application of user fees has been a contentious topic in general, and particularly so when they are integrated into public–private partnerships to fund the construction and operations of infrastructure. The application of user fees in transportation infrastructure PPPs has sometimes resulted in unintended consequences that diminish the public benefits derived from large urban infrastructure projects and create political risks.

The purpose of this chapter is to examine the role of user fees in PPP arrangements to deliver large urban transportation infrastructure, and situate the Canadian experience within a global perspective. The next section defines PPPs, provides an overview of the wide range of models that have been applied worldwide, and explains the various ways that user fees can be applied. The third section examines the varied rationales for integrating user fees into urban transportation PPP arrangements, while the fourth section identifies the potential drawbacks. The fifth section documents the practice of applying user fees in Canadian urban transportation PPPs and highlights evolutions in the models that have been followed. Finally, the paper concludes by discussing the lessons learned from the Canadian experience with user fee–based PPPs and reflects on the optimal role of integrating user fees into urban transportation PPPs.

DEFINING PPPs

In the broadest terms, public–private partnerships are guided by a belief that government and firms working collaboratively together will deliver better infrastructure project outcomes than any one party could realize on its own. In practice, PPPs in the infrastructure sector are more akin to a form of long-term contracting arrangement whereby a private-sector partner provides a range of project delivery services as well as some capital investment in the project (Tiesman and Klijn 2002).

In the classic free-standing PPP, the government bundles the design, build, financing, operations, and maintenance of an asset into a single contract with a private-sector concessionaire. In North America this is commonly referred to as a DBFOM-style partnership, while in the UK it is known as the private finance initiative. In an infrastructure PPP, the private concessionaire is typically a consortium of firms that form a new special-purpose vehicle (SPV) company to undertake the project. The formation of an SPV limits financial liability in the project for the parent companies (Boardman, Siemiatycki, and Vining 2016).

In exchange for making an upfront investment in the design and construction of the project and financing its operations and maintenance, the private-sector partner is repaid its initial investment over the life of a long-term operating and maintenance concession period that typically lasts from twenty to thirty-five years. This concession period is selected because it is long enough for the private investors to earn a sufficient return on their initial investment and matches the major life-cycle maintenance requirements of large infrastructure projects. The private-sector partner is remunerated in one of three ways: by collecting user-fee revenues that are charged on the facility; through payments

Table 8.1
PPP payment mechanisms

	Real user fees	Shadow tolls	Availability payments
Are user fees charged on facility?	Yes	No	Yes/No
Payment model description	The concessionaire recovers all of its financial investment in the infrastructure project through user-fee revenues generated on the facility.	The private-sector partner is paid more by the authority depending on the number of users on the facility. Shadow tolls are typically applied on projects where the government authority wishes to transfer demand risk to the private-sector partner but no interest in applying real user fees, either for political or socio-economic reasons.	Government authority pays a fixed amount to the concessionaire provided that the facility is operational and available to users. Availability payments can be mixed with real tolls/user fees such as toll roads in Ireland or transit lines in Canada. In this case the authority receives the user-fee revenue generated on the facility and pays a pre-set amount to the concessionaire. Or availability payments can be applied on facilities where user fees are not collected. In such projects the authority makes payments to the concessionaire from other revenue sources.
Risks transferred to concessionaire	Construction, availability, demand	Construction, availability, demand	Construction, availability

from the government that vary depending on facility usage levels, which are called shadow tolls; or through preset availability payments made by the government at regular intervals, provided that service standards are met (Siemiatycki and Friedman 2012; World Bank 2016) (see table 8.1).

A key benefit to government of the bundled DBFOM-style partnership is that it provides a mechanism to potentially transfer significant project risks to the private-sector partner. This includes the construction risk of cost overruns and delays; the availability risk that once operational the infrastructure does not function as expected and is out of service; and the demand risk that traffic or ridership volumes on the facility will not meet forecasted levels, resulting in lower than expected revenues from user fees. At the end of the concession period control of the facility is transferred back to government, which can then either contract out the service on an ongoing basis or provide it in house with public employees (Siemiatycki and Friedman 2016). Due to the high cost of structuring, executing, and privately financing PPP arrangements, they typically are used only for the largest infrastructure projects with capital costs of at least $50 million.[1]

Beyond the classic DBFOM-style PPP, there are many different partnership models that are used, which range on a spectrum from greater public to greater private responsibility (table 8.2). Each of these models can be applied with or without user fees. One common variation of the classic DBFOM-style PPP that involves a significant level of private-sector responsibility is the design-build-finance-maintain (DBFM) approach. In this model there is a long-term concession for facility maintenance bundled into the PPP concession, but the public sector retains control over providing the public service. In the transportation sector this model is most commonly used for urban rail transit projects such as the new Eglinton Crosstown line in Toronto, where the private-sector partner maintains the physical buildings and system components while government employees operate the trains and stations. Another PPP model that is applied to monetize the value of existing transportation infrastructure funded through user-fee revenue is the long-term lease of brownfield facilities. In this model, the operation and maintenance of an existing transportation infrastructure facility such as the Highway 407 toll road in Greater Toronto or the Chicago municipal parking meters is leased to a private-sector partner for a period lasting from fifty to ninety-nine years in exchange for an up-front payment to government.

At the other end of the PPP spectrum where the public sector maintains greater responsibility is the design-build-finance (DBF) model. The DBF-style PPP is being used to procure the Evergreen rapid transit line in Metro Vancouver, the VIVA rapid bus expansion in York Region north of Toronto, and the Lachine Train Maintenance Centre in Montreal. In this model the private-sector partner is repaid its full capital investment towards the design and construction of the project shortly following substantial completion of the build period. The facility is then operated and maintained by public-sector employees or contracted out separately. The DBF model would not strictly be considered a PPP based on common international working definitions that require both private-sector risk capital and a long-term concession period (see Garvin and Bosso 2008). However, many Canadian government agencies that deliver PPPs such as Infrastructure Ontario and Partnerships BC consider DBF partnerships part of their suite of alternative procurement options.

Importantly, PPPs are distinguished from private infrastructure and outright asset sales in that service quality and standards, user-fee rates, dispute-resolution protocols, and the relationship between the public- and private-sector partners are established by a concession agreement that is signed at the outset of the project. Conversely, when transportation infrastructure is entirely private, be it a private shipping company such as the Canadian National or Canadian Pacific freight railways or the Ambassador Bridge at the Canada–US border, the asset is owned and operated in perpetuity by private-sector investors. In such cases the state has input into the operations of the asset only as a regulator or possibly as a minority shareholder, while the private owner controls operational and pricing decisions within the limits of the legal and regulatory requirements.

PPPs are also distinguished from the traditional model of public-sector procurement for large megaprojects. Traditional procurement in North America, known as the design-bid-build approach, is highly disaggregated and involves the government contracting each element of facility design, construction, and operations and maintenance separately while financing the project through government borrowing. In Canada, recent traditionally procured transportation megaprojects include the Toronto-York Spadina subway extension, the Laval Metro extension in Montreal, and the southwest section of the Anthony Henday Drive ring road in Edmonton. Design-bid-build projects have upfront costs that Blanc-Brude and his colleagues (2009) estimate are 24 per cent lower than delivering a similar project through a bundled PPP; however, in traditional procurement the public-sector client bears considerably greater risk that often offset any initial cost savings.

As a final point, it is critical to recognize that user fees may or may not be applied to infrastructure projects delivered through any type of procurement model. As illustrated in table 8.2, in Canada there are examples of traditional procurement, DBF, DBFM, DBFOM, and privately provided transportation services that do charge direct user fees and others that do not.

Table 8.2
Transportation infrastructure procurement models

	Greater public-sector responsibility			Greater private-sector responsibility		
	Traditional procurement	DBF	DBFM	DBFOM		Long-term asset lease/private infrastructure
Transport infrastructure with user fees	• Laval Metro Extension, Montreal • Sheppard Subway Extension, Toronto	• VIVA Rapid Transit Extension, York Region • Evergreen LRT, Metro Vancouver • Union-Pearson Express, Toronto	• Eglinton Crosstown LRT, Toronto • Ottawa Confederation Line LRT, Ottawa	• Billy Bishop Airport Pedestrian Tunnel, Toronto • Canada Line LRT, Vancouver • A25 and A30 Highways, Montreal		• CP Rail • CN Rail • Highway 407, Greater Toronto • NAV Canada Air Traffic Control Service
Transport infrastructure without user fees	• Anthony Henday Drive Southwest, Edmonton	• Lachine Train Maintenance Centre AMT, Montreal	• GO Transit East Rail Maintenance Facility, Toronto • Herb Grey Parkway, Ontario	• Anthony Henday Drive, NE, NW, Edmonton • Northeast Stoney Trail, Calgary		• School bus services

THE DRIVERS AND RATIONALES FOR USER FEES IN PPPs

Within a historical and international context, PPPs that include user fees are nothing new. For centuries private-sector firms have been financing and providing public infrastructure. This includes turnpike arrangements with private companies that date back over 150 years in North America and Europe, and twentieth-century toll road concessions that were common in European countries such as France and Spain. However, the current incarnation of PPPs began in earnest in Britain in the early 1990s and took hold globally through the 2000s. To date there have been upwards of 1,110 transportation PPPs worldwide worth more than $650 billion. Canada is considered one of the most active markets for PPPs globally. To date more than fifty-five major Canadian transportation infrastructure projects have been delivered through PPPs, or are currently in various stages of project delivery. And Canada is internationally recognized as a sophisticated PPP market, with extensive government institutions, legal frameworks, and firms to support the delivery of PPPs (see Siemiatycki 2015).

The rationales for delivering large public-works projects through PPPs have varied by jurisdiction and evolved over time (Pollock, Shaoul, and Vickers 2002; Leiringer 2006). As Hodge and Greve (2010) explain, PPPs are applied as both a legitimate project delivery method aimed at realizing value-for-money benefits and as a governance tool that produces significant political benefits to the political parties in power. Against this backdrop, the section below provides a range of economic and political explanations made globally for why governments may proceed with PPPs that include user fees.

Additionality of Funds for Critical Infrastructure

The most common rationale for PPPs with user fees is that they provide governments with a self-financing mechanism to provide public infrastructure while freeing up public resources for other uses. Such a motivation for using PPPs was especially strong in the early 1990s and into the 2000s but has remained a driving force motivating the use of PPPs through to the present. Traditional taxes that have been used to fund transportation infrastructure in a diverse range of countries such as the United States and Nigeria – especially gas tax revenues – are in decline and collecting less revenue than in the past (Raimi, Fadipe, and Shokunbi 2015). And in many jurisdictions raising general taxes is political anathema for governments and widely opposed by voters. The result is an acute funding crunch for transportation infrastructure at a time when urban populations are rapidly growing and current public infrastructure is aging and in need of urgent rehabilitation.

PPPs that include user fees provide a resolution for governments to this perfect storm that is placing increased pressure on the budgetary position of contemporary urban transportation infrastructure. When user fees are included in a free-standing classic PPP, the private-sector partner finances the up-front facility design and capital costs of building the infrastructure without the need for major public investment or a government guarantee. The initial private capital investment in the project as well as the annual operating and maintenance costs and a profit are recouped through user-fee revenues. In such arrangements, the asset is privately *financed* and *funded*. The private investment is additional to *existing public money* dedicated to infrastructure, though the infrastructure is by no means "free" to society; the cost has been shifted from general taxpayers or all payers of gas taxes to facility users.

In PPPs with user fees the government can thus delegate the financing and provision of much-needed public infrastructure to the private sector, where there is a vast pool of investors seeking stable, long-term returns from a viable user-fee revenue stream without having to tie up tax dollars that can be invested in other worthwhile ventures (Regan, Smith, and Love 2010). This makes free-standing PPPs politically attractive (Boardman and Vining 2012). Spain, Australia, Ireland, France, Mexico, and Chile are among the leading countries where free-standing PPPs with tolls have been used to fund urban transportation infrastructure and add to government financial capacity to deliver projects. International agencies such as the World Bank, United Nations, and OECD have also identified private investment through user fee–based PPPs as a way to expedite the delivery of much-needed infrastructure in developing countries (Siemiatycki 2011).

Of course, governments can also charge user fees in the form of road tolls or transit fares on urban transportation projects that are financed with public borrowing that is typically at a lower cost than private borrowing and generate public profits that can be used to cross-subsidize other state investments. Indeed, there are many publicly owned and operated toll roads globally. In the United States, in particular, public financing is given an additional advantage by the availability of tax-exempt municipal bonds, which create a significant financial spread between the cost of public- and private-sector infrastructure borrowing and make the privately financed alternative less favourable. Never-theless, the free-standing PPP model supported by private finance and user fees is politically attractive for cash-strapped governments and politicians promoting austerity budgets that at the same time want to continue invest in high-quality infrastructure.

Off-Balance-Sheet Accounting

In many countries, another key financial and political rationale for in-tegrating user fees into free-standing PPPs is that the full capital cost of the infrastructure project does not necessarily appear on the public bal-ance sheet. According to the European statistical agency Eurostat, PPPs qualify for off-balance-sheet accounting if the risks and rewards of the project reside primarily with the non-governmental partner (European PPP Expertise Centre 2010). In this context, if private investors finance the full capital cost and assume the risk of project construction, and the upfront capital investment is repaid in full by user-fee revenues without a government guarantee, then off-balance-sheet accounting is permissible.

Off-balance-sheet accounting strategies are politically attractive be-cause they enable heavily indebted governments to approve popular public infrastructure while presenting improved current budgetary po-sitions and sidestepping internal or externally imposed debt limits (Brown et al. 2009). The European Union, in particular, has imposed strict criteria through the Maastricht Treaty on permissible levels of na-tional government debt among EU member countries. Faced with structural pressures to limit public debt, achieving off-balance-sheet ac-counting has historically been a key driver of toll road PPPs in Euro-pean countries such as the UK, Spain, Portugal, and Greece.

Risk Transfer

Proponents argue that a key benefit of PPPs is the potential to transfer project risks to the party that is best able to manage them, at the low-est cost. The classic free-standing PPP arrangement where the private-sector concessionaire recoups its initial investment in the project through user-fee revenues provides a strong mechanism for the con-cessionaire to manage construction, availability, and demand risks that are transferred to them through the contract. The concessionaire is highly incentivized to manage construction risk and avoid cost over-runs and schedule delays because its revenue source from user fees does not begin until the project is open and tolls or fare revenues are generated. When project construction is delayed, the bank or bond lenders who provide the majority of capital to fund the project construction are not repaid on time and interest and late repayment penalties escalate on the concessionaire. The threat of these costly penalties creates an incentive for the concessionaire to assign the necessary resources and complete the job quickly (Grimsey and Lewis 2004).

Managing availability and revenue risk is also strongly incentivized in a free-standing PPP with user fees, because any event that either takes the facility entirely out of service or lowers the utility of the service to users will diminish demand and user-fee revenues for the concessionaire. As such during the procurement phase of free-standing PPPs, the bidders are incentivized to carefully scrutinize the initial demand forecasts to ensure that projected facility usage and revenues are realistic. They are also motivated to design the facility to maximize availability over the entire life cycle of the asset. Once operational, the concessionaire is motivated to take measures, such as investing appropriately in facility maintenance and developing systems to quickly respond to unexpected disruptions that take the facility out of service, so that revenue-generating operations can be restarted (Engel, Fischer, and Galetovic 2011). The PPP agreement then ring-fences user-fee revenues for facility operations and maintenance, which is important in a context where infrastructure maintenance budgets are especially vulnerable to government cutbacks.

To be sure, governments have designed pay-for-performance–type mechanisms to transfer construction, availability, and revenue risk to the private sector in shadow-toll and availability-payment–based PPP arrangements that do not include user fee revenues. This includes: holding back payments to the contractor for construction expenses until substantial completion has been reached, annual availability payments during facility operations tied to performance, and shadow-toll–type systems where the size of the government payments to the concessionaire are based on actual traffic volumes on the non-tolled facility. However the user fee–supported free-standing PPP is the simplest way of transferring construction, availability, and revenue risk to the private sector because it is most significantly driven by market mechanisms that do not require government interventions to be enforced.

Life-Cycle Asset Management and Innovation

In free-standing PPPs where the private-sector partner recoups its initial investment through user-fee revenues, the bidders are incentivized to design the facility to maximize the attractiveness to users to increase revenue levels, make it buildable as quickly as possible to expedite the start of revenue collection, and emphasize durability to ensure long-term asset availability (Roumboutsos and Saussier 2014). Moreover, PPPs are intended to encourage a life-cycle asset management approach, where sufficient investment in facility maintenance and rehabilitation is made by long-term private facility operators in order to ensure that the infrastructure is consistently available and attractive to users. This contrasts with a common critique of traditionally delivered infrastructure where politicians may underinvest in infrastructure operations and maintenance because it is not highly visible to voters.

The incentives within PPPs that encourage a whole-of-life perspective to infrastructure have tended to spur innovations that have primarily focused on construction means and methods and material selection decisions that optimize the balance between durability and cost, and make the facility quicker to build. PPPs have also been used in some cases to incorporate novel automated toll-collection technologies into major highway projects, as was the case with Highway 407 in Greater Toronto, which was the first entirely automated open-access toll road in the world, and the PPP to operationalize the London congestion charging toll system. At the same time, and perhaps paradoxically, the incentives built into the free-standing PPP also encourage a level of risk aversion among private-sector bidders, because the concessionaire does not want to propose the inclusion of novel technologies, architectural features, or construction methods that may not function as expected and thus create risk or lost revenues. Thus PPPs have tended to encourage the realization of evolutionary rather than revolutionary innovations in facility design and the provision of infrastructure (Yuan and Zhang 2016). Indeed, the more revolutionary policy and technological innovations in the urban transportation sector, such as the research and development of autonomous vehicles, the rise of ride-sharing services, and the application of big data and the internet of things have been undertaken separately from classic infrastructure PPPs.

A Screen against Politically Motivated Projects

Free-standing PPPs funded by user-fee revenues empower private-sector investors as a screen against wasteful, politically motivated projects that do not serve sufficient demand or generate enough revenue to warrant the investment. As Flyvbjerg, Bruzelius, and Rothengatter (2003) argue, a key accountability mechanism in project selection is created when the decision to proceed with a project is made contingent upon the willingness of a private-sector investor to participate in the project as a commercial concession, where their capital investment is only repaid through user-fee revenues. In such cases, the investors have a strong incentive to cut through the optimism biases and political rhetoric that result in suboptimal projects being selected for development, and instead realistically assess the merits of the project based on sufficient usage and profitability.

Maximizing Revenues from Toll Projects

PPPs can be attractive to governments if they make it politically feasible to set user-fee rates on privately operated facilities that are higher than those likely to be charged if the government provided the facility directly. In free-standing PPPs and long-term-asset leases the government can delegate the responsibility for setting user-fee rates to the private-sector partner, or lock in predetermined rates through a contractual agreement with the concessionaire. The imposition of user charges on urban transportation infrastructure and the setting of fee rates pose a significant political risk to government. Users of transportation infrastructure do not like paying tolls, fees, or high transit fares. There is often significant public backlash when the rates on roads or public transit are raised, even when the money is allocated to fund the construction, operations, and maintenance of the asset. Higher user fees on transportation infrastructure also serve to manage facility demand; on road projects this provides societal benefits in terms of lower levels of congestion and reductions in polluting emissions. In this context, the added distance from the ratepayers that PPPs provide can insulate governments from the politically unpopular decisions to include user fees on a facility, or charge market or true cost-recovery rates for the provision of infrastructure services (Boardman, Siemiatycki, and Vining 2016).

DRAWBACKS OF USER FEES IN PPPs

Despite the proposed advantages, the inclusion of user fees in PPP arrangements also pose some distinctive challenges to the effective provision of transportation infrastructure. These challenges are identified below.

Supporting Auto Dependence

PPPs in the transportation sector have not been widely used to invest in sustainable mass transportation such as subways, light rail, commuter rail, and rapid bus systems that provide low-energy intensity and low-polluting urban mobility. Rather, transportation PPPs have been primarily used to build infrastructure projects that support auto dependence in cities. Between 1984 and 2009, 70 per cent of all urban surface transportation PPPs built worldwide were roads, highways, and tunnels, while only 30 per cent were transit projects that provide transportation alternatives to the car (Siemiatycki 2011). A key reason for this unequal pattern is that toll roads can often recover their entire cost through user-fee revenues, making them politically attractive since infrastructure can be provided without requiring the allocation of government funding. Conversely while transit projects provide broad economic and social benefits, they typically require public subsidy and are thus not as attractive in a political context where cash-strapped governments are looking to PPPs with user fees to augment scarce public funds for infrastructure.

Uneven Infrastructure Development

Within cities, Graham and Marvin (2001) argue that privatized infrastructure and PPPs with user fees contribute to a splintering pattern of urbanism. Investors favour premium networks such as airport rail connections, express commuter rail lines, or high-occupancy toll lanes. These premium networks where high user fees can be charged are often in the wealthiest parts of the city or target high-income users. However, by unbundling such profitable assets from the wider transportation network and placing them under private control, governments lose a profitable source of revenue that has historically been used to cross-subsidize unprofitable infrastructure assets such as off-peak transit service. While often unprofitable, off-peak transit service in many cities provides the primary transportation mode for low-income and female transit users and a critical vehicle for social inclusion (Garret and Taylor 1999). Overall, the prioritization of user fee–based PPPs can contribute to an unequal and sometimes suboptimal pattern of infrastructure investment, where careful coordination and service planning are not carried out.

Reduced Equity and Societal Benefits

The charging of user fees on urban transportation infrastructure through PPPs can exacerbate social-equity issues that are ever present when applying user-pay models to infrastructure. The application of user fees on transportation infrastructure, whether levied by government or the private sector in PPPs, creates an unequal burden on users with low incomes and may price some users off of the facility. In PPP arrangements where the private-sector concessionaire controls the toll or fare rate, they are likely to be set at a high price to maximize up-front concession payments to government and corporate profits, rather than broader social goals such as maximum levels of ridership on a transit system. And in PPPs with fixed-toll escalation agreements built into the concession, these may prescribe increases that are above what current or future governments would deem politically acceptable. A further challenge is that PPPs which are designed to maximize user fee revenues from the asset are less likely to provide concessionary rates to low-income users, youth, or seniors, which may cut into profits. They also may eschew environmentally preferable but revenue-cutting programs like providing free travel on a tolled motorway for high-occupancy or zero-emission vehicles. Finally, when user-fee profits are captured by the private-sector partner rather than government in a PPP arrangement, they reduce the amount of money that government has to cross-subsidize other socially valuable but unprofitable infrastructure (Siemiatycki 2010).

Loss of Policy Flexibility

Long-term PPP concessions that can last up to thirty-five years inherently limit the flexibility of future governments to make changes to the infrastructure service that is being provided by a private-sector partner. This creates a form of policy lock-in for future governments. It can be costly for the government partner in a PPP to subsequently reopen the contract to alter any of the prescribed aspects of the service provision agreement, regardless of the merits of the policy rationale. In a long-term free-standing PPP, governments pay a significant premium to the private-sector partner to alter facility service levels, adapt the facility structure, or revise maintenance requirements in the face of changing circumstances. The negotiations of such contract revisions take place in the absence of any competitive pressures from other bidders and are prone to overpayments by government (Guasch 2004).

Free-standing PPP concessions where the private-sector partner bears all revenue risk and recoups their entire investment in the asset through user-fee revenues without a government guarantee are especially restrictive on future government policy. In such PPPs, the setting of rates is either transferred to the private-sector partner or carefully prescribed in the concession contract, which can become a political risk for current or future governments as public sentiment about the toll rates change. In the case of the Manchester Metro PPP, for example, public opposition to a concessionaire-initiated fare increase led the public authority to cancel the PPP concession prematurely (Siemiatycki and Friedman 2012).

PPP highway concessionaires assuming revenue risk have also often required governments to sign non-competition agreements that restrict the public authority from building new infrastructure within the same travel corridor that would reduce traffic volumes on the PPP. In southern California, for instance, the state transportation authority bought out the PPP concessionaire that built and operated express toll lanes in the median of SR91 in order to override a non-competition agreement and expand the highway's general-purpose traffic lanes. In Sydney, Australia, contractual terms restricted the local government from reversing local road closures that motorists complained were funnelling them into the tolled Cross City Tunnel PPP (Siemiatycki 2010). And in PPPs to operate city parking meters, like in the city of Chicago where the contractor is paid from parking fees, the concession agreement restricts the local government from removing or altering the availability of on-street parking spots, as this would lower the contractor's revenues. While the restrictions imposed on governments through PPPs are logical from a business profitability perspective, they challenge the capacity of future governments to make plans that serve the public interest.

Innovation for Whom?

While PPPs have been shown to spur private sector–initiated innovations, the benefits of innovation realized through PPPs do not accrue equally to all stakeholders (Leiringer 2006). The types of innovations that tend to be encouraged by PPPs are those that lower construction and operating costs, and reduce construction and availability risks borne by the private-sector concessionaire. At the same time, innovations catalyzed through the PPP can create adverse impacts on a wide range of stakeholders. Construction means-and-methods innovations that lower cost may in some instances be more disruptive on the surrounding community, as was the case with open trench tunnelling method used to build the Canada Line rapid transit project in Vancouver. And in a drive to save building costs, some transit PPPs have reduced the quality of facility integration into the wider transportation network by not constructing convenient connections between transit lines or with adjacent buildings. Another trade-off in PPPs has been architectural and design innovation. The architecture and design of transportation facilities delivered through PPPs has tended to be average though not necessarily exceptional, as concessionaires aim to meet the minimum design standard accepted by the public authority and win the concession on price. Worldwide, very few infrastructure projects delivered through PPPs have won major architectural or design awards. This is significant in a context where the iconic design of public transit systems and bridges can become imbued with important symbolic meanings and key features of city branding exercises (Siemiatycki 2006).

Risk and Contract Renegotiations

Despite the risk transfer protocols that are prescribed in PPP concession agreements, PPP contracts globally in the transportation sector have been unstable and faced frequent contract renegotiations. Guasch (2004) finds that in Latin America, 57 per cent of all transport concessions are renegotiated. The majority of these concession renegotiations are initiated by the private sector and result in improvements to the contract terms in favour of the operator, adverse impacts on users, and reduced efficiency of the concession for government. In European PPPs, frequent contract renegotiations that are initiated by and benefit the private-sector concessionaire have been observed as well (Cruz and Marques 2013).

Free-standing PPP concessions that include user fees paid to the concessionaire and transfer revenue risk to the private sector are especially prone to contract difficulties and renegotiations. In such PPP arrangements, although the private-sector partner has assumed revenue risk, it controls few of the policy levers that impact on transportation system demand such as land use policy, transportation network integration, and regional economic growth. In the face of traffic volumes and revenues falling short of projections, PPP concessions have been renegotiated to provide public subsidy to the concessionaire, raise toll rates, or extend the concession period to provide the operator with a longer revenue-generating period. In other cases such as the Croydon Tramlink or State Route 91 Express Lane projects, a public authority has stepped in to buy out troubled PPP concessions at considerable cost (Siemiatycki 2010).

Is Government Risk Holder of Last Resort?

Beyond contract renegotiations, in PPPs there is always a risk that the private-sector concessionaire or one of the firms in the consortium could go bankrupt. Some level of private-sector bankruptcy is socially desirable as a marker that the private-sector partner is sufficiently assuming risk in PPP arrangements. However, a general critique of PPPs is that they are prone to bankruptcies because they are highly leveraged financial transactions, where in practice the primary private-sector concessionaire has relatively little of its own equity capital invested in the project.[2] The risk of bankruptcy is especially acute in projects where the private-sector concessionaire assumes revenue risk on PPPs with user fees, as forecasting long-term demand is unpredictable and largely beyond the control of the concessionaire to manage (Shaoul, Stafford, and Stapleton 2006).

Over the years, there have been a number of high-profile PPP bankruptcies, including the Las Vegas Monorail, the Kuala Lumpur light rail system, State Highway 130 in Texas, and the South Bay Expressway in San Diego. When a PPP bankruptcy does occur, a key question is whether there is a completely private-sector solution to resolve the matter, as has been the case with the Cross City Tunnel in Sydney, Australia. Or is the government ultimately the residual risk holder and compelled to bail out the project, either by retendering the concession, taking over the operations of the concession in house, or decommissioning the project? In the case of a spate of bankruptcies on PPP toll roads in the Madrid area in 2012, the Spanish government was compelled to purchase or bail out the PPP concessionaires, at significant cost to government.

High Private-Sector Profit Margins

While PPPs are always at some risk of bankruptcy, successful projects can generate high profit margins for the private-sector partner and its investors. Studies of PPP projects around the world have documented excessively high returns for investors above the weighted average cost of capital, as well as the practice of governments commonly underpricing the value of public assets in long-term lease arrangements (Vecchi, Hellowell, and Gatti 2013; Ashton, Doussard, and Weber 2012; Loxley 2012). PPPs with user fees, where the private-sector partner assumes revenue risk, can generate particularly large profit margins. A significant factor influencing the level of profitability on a PPP is the competitiveness of the bidding process and the degree of risk assumed by the private-sector partner. As PPP models become more complicated and include user fees and revenue risk for the private sector, the number of bidders tends to diminish and the rates of return increase (Soliño and Vassallo 2009). Importantly, public reports of high profits on PPPs not only are a financial matter but have also created political risk for the concession. User groups have mobilized to oppose high toll rates and pressured public authorities to reopen concession agreements to drop or eliminate user fees on the facility.

PPPs WITH USER FEES: THE CANADIAN EXPERIENCE

This section examines the ways in which PPPs with user fees have been applied in the Canadian urban transportation sector, and compares them with the international experiences described above. The data on Canadian transportation PPPs reported below are compiled from the PPP Project Database maintained by the Canadian Council for Public–Private Partnerships. In Canada, there have been shifting philosophies about which risks government transfers to the private sector and how tolls are applied to fund infrastructure PPPs. This reflects an ongoing evolution in the rationales for using PPPs in the country over the past quarter-century.

First Generation of PPPs

The Canadian experience with transportation PPPs can be effectively divided into two generations of projects. The first generation of surface transportation PPPs in Canada took place in the 1990s and early 2000s, involving eight projects. This includes such high-profile projects as the tolled Confederation Bridge connecting Prince Edward Island and New Brunswick, the Highway 104 toll motorway through the Wentworth Valley of Nova Scotia, a highway connecting Fredericton and Moncton in New Brunswick, and the express tolled Highway 407 north of Toronto. PPPs planned during this period sought to transfer as much responsibility for project delivery and risk as possible to the private-sector concessionaire. Each PPP was a variation on the free-standing DBFOM model, ensuring a high level of private-sector responsibility within the PPP.

During this period, PPPs were widely seen as a strategy for cash-strapped governments to deliver high-quality infrastructure without taking on additional public debt. There was also a prevailing view that PPPs could leverage the ingenuity and expertise of the private sector to deliver innovative infrastructure solutions while reducing the required involvement of government. Governments thus sought to fund, not merely finance, infrastructure through PPPs, and user fees were a common feature of PPP-delivered infrastructure. In the case of the Confederation Bridge, the PPP deal was specifically structured to achieve off-balance-sheet accounting treatment for the federal government. And PPP models were designed to transfer construction, availability, and demand and revenue risk to the private-sector partner (Siemiatycki 2015).

Overall, the experiences of these first-generation transportation PPP projects highlight the limitations of PPPs. These early Canadian transportation PPPs faced scholarly, user, political, and media criticism about poor transparency and accountability, high private financing costs, and loss of public control over crucial infrastructure assets. First-generation transportation PPPs were also especially vulnerable to political risk related to the application and setting of tolls on privately operated highways, in a country where motorways typically do not include user fees. In New Brunswick, for instance, the CBC News (McHardie 2011) reports that the initial proposal to include tolls on the Fredericton-Moncton Highway and community opposition to privatization "ignited one of the bumpiest political debates in the last two decades." This ultimately resulted in a subsequent government removing the tolls from the project and replacing them with government availability payments to the private contractor, a move that has exacerbated high debt levels in the province. And in Ontario, there has been long-standing public outcry about the high toll rates, aggressive toll collection strategies, and profitability of the private operator of Highway 407, leading to unsuccessful efforts by the provincial government to reopen the tolling agreement. In sum, from this first generation of projects, free-standing PPPs funded by user-fee revenues became widely identified as an unpopular form of privatization that put private benefit ahead of the public interest.

Second Generation of PPPs

The experience with the first generation of PPPs in Canada has been central in shaping the design of the second wave of projects. Between 2004 and 2016, thirty-seven urban surface transportation PPPs have been built or are currently in various stages of procurement. The rationales put forward by Canadian PPP proponents have evolved such that PPPs are not being widely applied as a strategy to infuse additional money into infrastructure projects through user fees or move investments off of the public balance sheet. Rather, second-generation PPPs in Canada are conceptualized as a "modern" procurement method designed to encourage the realization of value for money through innovation, life-cycle asset management, and the allocation of risks to the party best able to manage them (Cory 2016). At the same time, promoters of PPPs have recognized the political risk of conflating PPPs and asset privatization, alongside the loss of public control over user-fee rate setting and long-term policy flexibility. The impact of this shifting perspective on Canadian PPPs has resulted in a number of key trends.

First, Canadian PPPs are not generally being used to build exclusive premium infrastructure services initiated by private investors and funded through high user fees that spur splintering patterns of urbanism, as has been experienced internationally. Rather Canadian governments have maintained a strong level of control over infrastructure network planning and project selection decisions. PPPs are being applied as a model to procure government priority projects that are integrated into the overall transportation network and designed for general public usage.[3]

Second, in the urban highway and bridge sector, where user fees have been widely applied internationally and have the capacity to cover the full cost of building and operating the infrastructure, only six of twenty-three second-generation urban transportation PPPs include road tolls. This means that Canadian PPPs are playing a limited role in raising additional money to fund public infrastructure. The decision to eschew charging tolls on most of the second-generation urban road PPPs has been a policy and political choice on the part of the commissioning government.

- In Alberta and Saskatchewan, where one-third of the new urban road or bridge PPPs are located, provincial governments with large budget surpluses from natural resource extraction when the projects were commissioned had no fiscal need or political interest in charging road tolls. With resource revenues in decline, governments in these provinces continue to oppose road charges, arguing that they are highly unpopular (Wood 2016).
- In British Columbia, the provincial government sought to manage the political opposition to road tolling by instituting a policy that tolls could be applied only on new or significantly upgraded roads where a free alternative route was available (BC Ministry of Transportation 2003). As a result only one of four urban road or bridge PPPs in the province includes tolls.[4] However, in Metro Vancouver, this strategy has been criticized for creating regional inequality whereby motorists in one part of the city with new bridges are required to pay tolls while others in areas with existing bridges do not (CBC 2015).
- At the federal level, in 2015 the incoming Liberals reversed a decision by their predecessors and removed tolls from the planned Champlain Bridge in Greater Montreal. While popular with motorists in the region, this policy shift has required a renegotiation of the PPP contract with the concessionaire and the addition of new public funding for the project. This decision has led residents in PEI to question the equity of the federal government continuing to levy tolls on the Confederation Bridge.

As can be seen, second-generation PPPs are not immune to political pressure on the inclusion of user fees or the rates charged.

Third, even when tolls are included on recent Canadian highway or bridge PPPs, the demand and revenue risk is retained predominantly by the public authority. None of the second generation PPPs are fully freestanding concessions where the private partner recoups its entire capital investment through user fees on the facility and bears all of the revenue risk. Rather, the private concessionaire typically operates the toll collection system and remits the toll revenues to the public authority. The public authority then pays the concessionaire a fee that combines a construction fee, plus a fixed annual availability payment to cover operating and maintenance costs of the facility. In some cases such as the Autoroute 25 and Autoroute 30 projects in Montreal, a portion of the concessionaires repayment is a fee that varies based on facility revenues (World Bank 2016). Retaining ownership and demand risk in Canadian highway PPPs has been a political strategy to overcome public opposition to privatization and loss of public control over user-fee rate setting. As the premier of Ontario explained when announcing a new PPP project to extend the controversial Highway 407 toll highway: "The people of Ontario will own this highway ... We'll be setting the service standards, and the people of Ontario will benefit from the tolls" (O'Toole 2012). At the same time, the allocation of risk on Canadian PPPs has also been driven by the private sector. Increasingly, greenfield PPPs that transfer revenue risk to the private sector are not bankable with investors due to the recent international wave of toll road bankruptcies and a growing recognition that the private-sector partner does not control the policy levers necessary to manage demand risk.

Fourth, PPPs are being used to deliver far more public transit projects than during the first generation of PPPs. Since 2004, fourteen public transit PPPs have been built or are in procurement, comprising nearly 40 per cent of the total portfolio of urban surface transportation PPPs delivered during this period in Canada. This includes nine rapid transit mega-projects, and five large transit maintenance facilities. The rise of transit PPPs in Canada has been made possible by an increase in public spending on transit infrastructure nationwide, a sector where projects invariably require public subsidy beyond user-fee revenues to cover capital and operating costs. Additionally, a key feature of second-generation Canadian transit PPPs is that they transfer very little demand risk to the private-sector partner and have employed a wide range of PPP models. This ensures that the public authority can seamlessly integrate service levels and fares on the transit PPP into the entire transit network, which is beneficial for users. Similar to road PPPs, it also reflects the fact that private investors are increasingly unwilling to assume significant revenue risk on Canadian transit PPPs. In the case of the Canada Line rapid transit project in Vancouver, for instance, only 10 per cent of the public authority's payment to the concessionaire is tied to ridership volume.

Fifth, second-generation Canadian PPPs have played no role as a screen against politically motivated infrastructure investment decisions. As noted above, most urban transportation PPPs in Canada use availability payments and do not transfer substantial demand or revenue risk to the private-sector partner. As such there is no incentive for investors to screen projects for financial viability or utility beyond the creditworthiness of the government making the availability payments. Moreover, as in the case of the Union Pearson Express airport rail link project in Toronto, Canadian governments have been willing to provide subsidies to PPP projects that are politically favoured, even when private investors demonstrate them to be uneconomical by refusing to invest without a government guarantee.

Overall, second-generation transportation PPPs in Canada reflect a learning of lessons from the first generation of projects, with mixed results. In terms of challenges, construction delays have been an issue on some recent urban transportation projects such as the Highway 407 tolled highway extension, the Eglinton Crosstown light rail line in Toronto, and the Evergreen rapid transit line in Metro Vancouver. Yet the financial risk transfer protocols in the PPP arrangements appear to be holding as the project costs to government have tended not to increase. Toll collection by the private-sector operator has not been without flaws. In Montreal, a class action lawsuit was successfully settled on behalf of users of the Autoroute 25 toll bridge who were incorrectly billed a service charge by the private operator of the tolling system. And auditor generals, academics, and opposition politicians continue to question the high cost of private finance in PPPs and whether it is sufficiently offset by real risk transfer to the private concessionaire (Siemiatycki 2015).

Nevertheless, second-generation Canadian PPPs have avoided some of the most significant pitfalls with transportation PPPs worldwide. In particular, the assignment of revenue risk to the public partner has allowed PPP facilities to be seamlessly integrated into the wider road and transit network, a major benefit for users, while facility availability risk has been effectively transferred to the private sector. And the recent PPP deals have been far more stable than their international counterparts. To date, no second-generation surface transportation PPP has faced a major contract renegotiation once it became operational, and there have been no concessionaire bankruptcies to date. A key factor is that

Canadian governments have generally retained demand risk and thus control over key infrastructure planning functions and rate setting, areas where frictions between the public authority and private concessionaire have arisen in past PPPs.

CONCLUSIONS

User fees charged on urban transportation PPPs remain a contentious topic in countries around the world. The Canadian experience highlights the tensions between the theory and practice of applying user fees on complex urban infrastructure PPPs. Despite the prospect that the rise of PPPs during the first wave of projects would inaugurate a wave of new user fee–supported infrastructure projects, the application of PPPs in the second wave of projects has in practice done little to spur the charging of user fees on urban highways or bridges that do not typically include them. Nor have second-wave PPPs contributed to a policy decision to charge higher user-fee rates on transit projects that are sufficient to achieve capital and operating cost recovery, a policy that would bolster government balance sheets but diminish equity of access to a critical public service.

In Canada during the second wave of PPPs, the decision to charge user fees on a transportation infrastructure project is a political choice that is made separately from the decision to deliver the project through a PPP. Canadian infrastructure project planners and politicians have recognized the political risk associated with the first wave of PPPs that sought to integrate user fees into the deal structures, in terms of conflicts over rate setting and the loss of long-term flexibility and control over the asset. And including user fees in Canadian PPPs or transferring toll-setting responsibility to the private sector increases public opposition to such arrangements, as they are seen as a form of privatization that puts profits ahead of the public interest.

Integrating user fees on Canadian surface transportation PPPs is a highly political decision, influenced by financial necessity, public opinion, and political will. As a result, recent urban road and transit PPPs have purposefully been structured in such a way as to maintain significant public control over rate setting and service levels. A key lesson from the second generation of Canadian PPPs is that by retaining revenue risk with the public authority, infrastructure project planners have created PPP arrangements that are more stable than in other parts of the world, while effectively transferring construction cost and availability risk to the private-sector partner.

Nevertheless, the political lure of privately funding high-quality public infrastructure through PPPs with user fees appears to be returning to the public agenda in Canada. In 2016, the federal government announced the formation of the Canadian Infrastructure Bank. This institution has been mandated to make investments in infrastructure projects in order to leverage additional private funds, which would be supported by user fees and other revenue streams. As the Government of Canada (2016) outlined in their fall 2016 Economic Statement, the aim of the Canadian Infrastructure Bank is to pursue "a great opportunity for the government to leverage its investments in infrastructure, by bringing in private capital to the table to multiply the level of [public] investment." As the plan for the Canadian Infrastructure Bank takes shape and is rolled out, time will tell whether Canada is entering a third wave of private involvement in infrastructure where the private sector is more deeply embedded in the planning, funding, ownership, and operations of major infrastructure assets. If this is the case, careful attention will be required to avoid the challenges that beset the first generation of PPPs in Canada.

NOTES

1 To provide an indication of the financial costs associated with PPPs, Blanc-Brude et al. (2009) find that PPPs in the road sector typically cost 24 per cent more upfront than traditionally procured projects due to higher financing, transaction costs, and risk transfer premiums. However, this cost premium in PPPs is meant to serve as an insurance policy against the risk of future cost overruns, which can be very large on major infrastructure projects.

2 PPP transactions tend to consist of 10 per cent equity (owned in part by the primary construction and operations contractors) and 90 per cent debt, while the special-purpose vehicle structure of the PPP concessionaire means that the parent firms are only exposed to lose their equity investment in the project.

3 One premium infrastructural service that has been delivered is the Union Pearson Express airport rail link in Toronto. Yet the design and exclusive service offering of this project was initiated by government, and it re-

ceived full public-sector funding when a private-sector concessionaire could not be found to undertake it as a free-standing PPP.

4 A toll is also included on the Port Mann Bridge project in Surrey, British Columbia, which was planned as a DBFO PPP but ultimately delivered as a design-build project when the private-sector concessionaire and the government were unable to reach a final agreement on the terms of a PPP.

9

Why We Should but Don't Pay the Right Prices for Urban Infrastructure

RICHARD M. BIRD

The greater part of such public works [as roads and bridges] may easily be so managed, as to afford a particular revenue sufficient for defraying their own expence, without bringing any burden upon the general revenue of the society ... Even those public works which are of such a nature that they cannot afford any revenue for maintaining themselves, but of which the conveniency is nearly confined to some particular place or district, are always better maintained by a local or provincial revenue, under the management of a local and provincial administration, than by the general revenue of the state.

Adam Smith, *The Wealth of Nations*, book V, article I

Adam Smith was right: whenever possible such local public infrastructure as roads and bridges, urban rapid transit systems, and water and sewerage systems should be paid for by those who use them, and most other local infrastructure should be financed and managed by the appropriate local government. Although some recent evidence suggests that there is considerably more support in both theory and reality for this classical benefit approach to taxation than standard public finance theory suggests (Weinzierl 2016a, b), much of the recent discussion of the infrastructure gap in Canada – as summarized, for example, by Slack and Tassonyi in this volume – ignores this ancient but sound advice and sometimes amounts to little more than a plea for someone else to pay the bills.

There are, as noted below, some reasons why higher-level governments should often make some contribution to some local infrastructure projects.[1] On the whole, however, Smith's arguments still hold, whether viewed through the usual economic lens focused on efficiency or with a broader political economy perspective that takes into account not only the apparently inherent human tendency to act less than fully rationally much of the time but also such specifics of the institutional context as how governments are structured, the incentives facing bureaucratic and political decision makers, and the constraints imposed on policy by legal, budgetary, or technological factors.

The conclusion of economic reasoning is clear: user charges can and often should be applied to the provision of many local public services and should also play a prominent role in financing the related infrastructure. The only real alternative source of revenue is taxation. Past, present, and future user-charge revenues may all be used to finance new investment – with past revenues being saved in reserves and spent for this purpose and present and future revenues used to secure and repay debt incurred to finance projects. Although taxes, unlike charges, allow the burden to be shifted from direct users to local taxpayers or even to provincial or federal taxpayers, in the end some past, present, or future taxpayer at some level has to pay the taxes used to finance the transfers, the borrowing, or any private financing used to finance investment.[2] No matter how infrastructure is financed, there is no free lunch. The bill must be paid either by implementing user charges or by taxing someone. Whenever feasible, user charges should be preferred, for reasons discussed briefly in the next two sections.

The remainder of the chapter focuses on the question posed in its title: why have most countries, including Canada, so conspicuously failed to heed Smith's sensible advice? The scanty literature bearing directly on this question offers a number of possible explanations of varying importance and persuasiveness ranging from technical problems in implementing the right kind of user charges to assertions that charges cannot finance large capital works to rather vague expositions about why people do not understand or like user charges and laments about their supposedly undesirable distributive effects. Many such arguments seem to rest more on anecdote and imagination than on evidence. Unfortunately, although in principle it should be possible to test some of the hypotheses raised later in the chapter to some extent with better data and well-designed experiments, only a little such evidence appears as yet to exist.[3]

Still, if one thinks it important to increase the rationality of the policy process and the efficiency of its outcome in terms of making the best use possible of scarce public resources, more attention needs to be paid to the essential role of user charges in shaping sound infrastructure investment policy. For this reason, although it may perhaps demonstrate little but the triumph of hope over experience, the concluding section suggests a few ways one may perhaps be able to sell the idea that user charges are the key to sensible infrastructure finance to the obviously skeptical and resistant audience found both in the policy community and in the public at large.

WHY USERS SHOULD PAY FOR INFRASTRUCTURE

The best way to encourage homeowners to better insulate their houses is to stop selling electricity below cost. The best way to encourage drivers to use public transportation is to have them assume the cost of the highways ... the simple fact of paying directly from their pockets pushes people to demand cheaper, better quality services.

Montreal Economic Institute (2003)

Economists have made such statements many times since Adam Smith wrote. Like him, they have mostly been right. There are many good reasons why people should pay fully for services, particularly the congestible services provided to easily identifiable users such as roads or water and sewerage that are usually provided (and often produced) by public sector agencies.[4] For example:

- From a simple *budgetary* perspective, services that are fully paid for by users are neutral; because they provide as much revenue as is spent on the services no additional taxes – almost all of which are inevitably distorting and hence reduce economic welfare – need to be levied to finance the service.
- From an *economic* perspective, when public-sector services fully cover the marginal social cost of providing them, resources will be as efficiently allocated as possible. In principle, people will rationally buy urban transit or water only up to the point at which the value they receive from the last unit they consume is just equal to the price they pay. Assuming one is willing to leave it up to each person to decide how much he or she values such services, then to ensure that society's scarce resources are allocated efficiently prices must cover the full marginal social cost of providing the service.

- From a *managerial* or administrative perspective, those responsible for providing a service financed by full-cost charges have good reason to employ the resources available (namely, those supplied by the users) as efficiently as possible to supply services at the level and quality that people are willing to pay for. They also have every incentive to adopt the most efficient and effective ways of providing such services.
- Finally, from a *political* perspective, assuming that political decision makers remain ultimately accountable to their constituents for the level and quality of services provided as well as for how well the managers they select to provide those services do their jobs, user-charge financing provides the information political decision makers need to assess the performance of managers as well as the information citizens need to assess the performance of politicians.

This rosy scenario rests on several critical assumptions unlikely to be fully satisfied by fallible human beings living in a changing, uncertain, and imperfect world. It is no surprise that even something as (relatively) simple as pricing water practice generally falls short of optimal. Kitchen (in this volume) shows that, although Ontario has substantially improved its water pricing in recent years, it still falls far short of full-cost pricing and does not even come close to pricing current usage on a marginal-cost basis.[5] Meloche and Vaillancourt (in this volume) show that Quebec is even further from any economic ideal in this respect. Kitchen and Tassonyi (2012) tell similar stories with respect to public pricing in Canada more generally. Even in Switzerland, which has perhaps taken the design and implementation of good user charging further than anywhere else, Dafflon (in this volume) shows that some localities still fall short of best practice, the divergence between reality and full-cost pricing being even greater with respect to pricing sewer services and especially solid waste disposal.[6]

To some extent the divergence between theory and practice may reflect technical or administrative difficulties in applying proper public prices as well as legitimate concerns about such complex and difficult issues as the distributive impact of pricing. More basically, however, the main reason so little attention has been paid in practice to the many good reasons for pricing appears to be because many people simply do not accept the basic economic rationale sketched above. Since one of the most pernicious results of poor pricing is to inflate artificially the apparent "need" for more investment in public infrastructure – for example; new investment in roads and transit to relieve congestion – the current emphasis on expanding such investment makes it especially important to reconsider carefully the arguments why users can and should pay (most of) the cost for most such services, and, by extension, for most such investment.[7]

Two economic arguments are commonly trotted out as explanations for the worldwide underpricing of transport-related services such as transit, roads, street services (lights, cleaning, and especially parking) as well as such other public services as water: economies of scale and externalities. For example, because public water supply has many characteristics of a natural monopoly, with average (and marginal) costs declining as output increases up to some point, marginal-cost pricing is often said to be inherently unsustainable because it results in deficits. This is one argument behind the common view that particular projects are simply too big to finance locally.[8]

In reality, relatively few water projects operate in the decreasing cost range; most are better characterized as increasing or constant cost in nature (Nauges and van den Berg 2008). Even when there are decreasing costs, making the case for less than full-cost pricing at the margin requires detailed consideration of the distortionary costs of possible alternative sources of finance. As Le Blanc (2007) correctly emphasizes, if water pricing does not cover full costs it is unsustainable anyway unless taxes are increased to cover continuing deficits.[9] Much the same can be said about most public services and the infrastructure needed to deliver them: if users do not pay, taxpayers must. Arguments against user-charge financing – assuming that the charges are properly designed – in the end thus amount to arguments for increased taxes (or, perhaps, reduced spending on something else), with the main variable being exactly who should pay such taxes and when.

Externalities raise more complex issues. For instance, important externalities are associated with road congestion, and one possible benefit associated with rapid transit infrastructure is that it reduces congestion to some extent. Although the size of such externalities depends heavily on time, mode, location, the responsiveness of demand at the margin, and how and how well road users are charged for the costs they impose on others, a careful study by Parry and Small (2009) concluded that taking such externalities into account, rapid transit fares in several US cities they examined should be subsidized substantially (e.g., more than 50 per cent off-peak). But no general conclusions can be drawn from such studies about the appropriate level and subsidization of infrastructure investment in rapid transit for two reasons. The first is simply because, as already noted, the results are highly case-specific. The second is that experience suggests that subsidized monopolies like rapid transit systems are all too often associated with such wasteful expenditures as "gold-plating" and overly generous wage policies. Those who benefit from such policies – the users, operators, and suppliers of rapid transit systems – are of course usually strong supporters of still more subsidies. Without receiving clearly demonstrated value in return, however, the rest of society should be less enthusiastic.

It is usually surprisingly difficult in practice to determine the results of alternative public pricing policies. As an example, several years ago Ontario considerably increased its charges for camping in provincial parks. One study (Sun and Jung 2012) concluded that the main (and intended) effect of this increase in user charges was to reduce the extent to which provincial government spending on parks was financed out of general tax revenues. However, a subsequent study (Eagles 2014) found that the major effect of increasing user charges (and reducing tax finance) was actually to increase total (tax plus charge) public revenues. Because park management and employees had to find new revenue if they were to keep their jobs, they did so by marketing their services more effectively and improving them (e.g., by implementing pre-registration for campsites). Eagles (2014) suggested that these efforts were as successful as they were in part because users were already used to paying something – there had long been nominal fees – and they were willing to pay more because services were better. In addition, demand was not very price-sensitive because there was not that much competition and the main competitive supplier (which in Ontario was actually another public agency, conservation areas) also charged user fees.

One reason it is often difficult to assess the effects of user charges is because as a rule neither the level nor the structure of most charges is set appropriately. Often, for example, the focus is solely on covering current operating costs rather than the full monetary costs including those related to investment (amortization, interest). As Dafflon and Daguet (2012) argue, it is essential to charge full costs in this sense.[10] If all inputs are secured from competitive markets, full financial costs may reasonably be assumed to correspond (more or less) to economic opportunity costs. Full-cost pricing will thus not only send the right signals to users and managers but also provide sufficient resources to finance the provision of the service at the economically correct level –

that is, the level at which the benefits to society are at least equal to the social costs of providing the service – without requiring additional budgetary support. When services are financed by full-cost charging it is thus no more difficult for public agencies to determine when a new infrastructure investment makes sense than it is for any business to decide on when and where to locate a new factory.[11] However, the story is far from over when the level of charges is set. Other important questions are when and whether marginal-cost pricing is desirable and feasible,[12] when and how public prices should be altered, and what weights should be attached to the equity dimensions – intergenerational, horizontal, and vertical – of public prices.

USER CHARGES VS THE REST

Dominic Barton, who heads Ottawa's Advisory Council on Economic Growth, said Canada lags far behind many countries in taking advantage of private financing to help fund large-scale projects, adding that infrastructure needs in Canada far exceed the capacity of governments to pay for them alone.

Lead article in the *Globe and Mail* (Toronto) (Curry 2016)

In saying this, Mr Barton was of course simply joining the large choir of those urging more private participation in infrastructure investment in some or all the ways discussed by Siemiatycki (in this volume). Nonetheless, although all levels of government and most people seem to agree that any significant expansion in public infrastructure will require increased private-sector participation, and they may perhaps be right in terms of the mechanics of getting good projects up and running soon at reasonable cost, the possible virtues of private participation have nothing to do with whether governments can pay. Governments do not pay for anything: taxpayers do, although the fiscal pain may sometimes be delayed by running deficits, perhaps for many years. How infrastructure investment is financed – except to the extent that users pay – is essentially about how we determine which taxpayers will ultimately pay how much and when. To the extent the private sector is involved in financing infrastructure, its contributions are not made for charitable reasons. In the end, taxpayers – or, preferably, whenever possible users (beneficiaries of the services provided by new infrastructure) – must still pay. Indeed, unless considerable care is taken in designing public–private arrangements taxpayers may sometimes even end up paying more via the private route than they would have if straight debt financing had been used.

In the end, the choice of who pays is simple: users or taxpayers. User charges when feasible – that is, when significant private benefits are reaped by readily identifiable users, whether in the form of water, waste disposal, transit, or roads[13] – are clearly superior to taxes for two reasons. First, collecting a dollar in taxes is economically more costly than collecting a dollar in user charges. The distorting nature of most taxes – the fact that they influence private decisions in ways that tend to reduce the level of resources available to the nation and its citizens as a whole – is well known to economists, if apparently to few others. Since Harberger's (1962) seminal study there have been countless measures of the size of the welfare losses imposed by taxes (see, e.g., the extended review of this evidence in Mirrlees et al. 2010, 2011). Although economists quibble about aspects of the numerous empirical estimates of such costs, most agree that because an additional dollar collected in taxes usually reduces welfare by more than a dollar – a common minimal estimate of the extra cost is in the range of 20–40 per cent[14] – the expenditures financed must also (at the margin, as economists always say) yield sufficient benefits to offset the costs associated with the taxes. While the weight one attaches to such concerns depends in part on one's values (particularly with respect to redistribution), and different people obviously have different views on such matters, it is surprising that so little attention is paid in public discussion to the overwhelming evidence that the social cost of taxes is more – sometimes quite a lot more – than the revenue they produce. Since properly set user charges impose no additional distortionary costs, they are the most socially efficient (cheapest) form of finance.

The second reason why user-charge financing is preferable is because willingness to pay user charges is one of the few ways in which users can clearly and unmistakably signal to public service providers when and where new infrastructure is needed. User-charge financing ensures that those responsible for providing public services are not only adequately financed but also encouraged to do so in the economically most efficient way possible. The essential role of a user charge is to apportion the current and capital costs of providing a public service to users in proportion to the benefit they obtain from the service. It is the public-sector equivalent of a market price and should be set as close as possible to the cost of providing a given service to a particular user in a particular place at a particular time (including the opportunity cost of the capital tied up in creating the infrastructure required to provide the service). User charge–financed public providers are in effect business enterprises – public utilities– whether organized and run by a government department or agency or by a separate enterprise (whether public or, as is true for water in many countries, a regulated private company).[15]

To put this principle into practice through user charges requires that two important conditions be satisfied. First, the normative value of charging for services in accordance to the benefit received must be accepted. In fact, as discussed below, an important reason why user charges are so seldom employed (or employed properly) even when feasible and desirable is because this value is not widely understood or accepted. Second, because good user charges should match the specific costs and benefits associated with services received by each individual user, considerable institutional, administrative, and legal preparation as well as substantial (and accurate) accounting information is required to design and implement a good system of user charges, as Dafflon (in this volume) nicely illustrates for the Swiss case.

It is only worth undertaking all this work if the prospective net gain from incurring these additional costs is sufficiently large. Most Canadian local governments have many, often one hundred or more, fees and charges of various types and sizes somewhere in their bylaws. However, relatively few of these levies are effective user charges in the sense just defined, and few of them should be. First, such charges can be employed only when services are received (and can be observed) by specific individuals – for example, transit use, water, sewers, solid waste removal and disposal, parking, direct use of park and recreation facilities, and the like.[16] Second, imposing user charges with respect to "natural monopolies" (such as those often created by regulation) needs to be watched carefully to avoid the kind of wastefulness mentioned briefly earlier.[17] Third, many small fees and charges imposed by governments produce little revenue and serve little economic purpose. Since the cost of getting such prices right likely exceeds any gain from doing so, most such nuisance levies should simply be abolished.[18]

A final important characteristic of a sound benefit-based user-charge system is that the revenue *must* go to the entity providing the service and be used solely for this purpose (Fox and Murray 2016). In contrast, environmental taxes intended simply to offset the negative externalities arising from private decisions by imposing the socially relevant costs are not logically connected to any particular expenditure activity, although of course those advocating for such levies often attempt to justify them in terms of how the revenues will be spent. In one sense, since the point is simply to impose the tax in order to discourage some activity considered to generate negative externalities, it does not matter how (or if) the revenue is spent. With user charges, however, it does matter. Not only should charge revenue flow directly to the providing entity, but cross-subsidization – flowing-user charge revenues to other purposes (e.g., via flowing funds to some other activity directly or through the local government general budget or using funds from some users to finance services to others) – is a bad idea.[19] Although cross-subsidization of some (e.g., lower-income or residential) users from revenues received from other users is common, the result is often to raise costs, increase misallocation, and obscure what is really going on. Some politicians and officials may, like those who benefit directly, prefer doing things this way. But since someone loses when scarce public resources are used in less than efficient ways the practice should be avoided. It is not a good idea to provide hidden and inefficient subsidies: if it cannot be done openly, should it be done at all?

Some infrastructure investments (e.g., streets and parks) may confer more generalized but still physically localized benefits. A case may be made for financing such investment at least to some extent through *ex ante* or *ex post* local levies or taxes. *Ex ante* levies like development charges, for example, are often imposed on new construction to cover such costs, with the funds being "saved" in reserves until spent on providing the required infrastructure. However, because such charges are seldom based on location cost differences, are not sensitive to usage, and are usually based on average costs rather than marginal costs in any case, they are more likely to encourage overbuilding and sprawl (Slack and Tassonyi in this volume) than to improve resource allocation. Charges that provide no incentive for existing residents to curb consumption or for new residents, once located, to do so serve little economic purpose other than to provide some funds to local budgets. *Ex post* land value increment taxes or other capture schemes like those discussed in Slack and Tassonyi (in this volume) may – much like plain old property taxes (assuming assessments are kept up to date) – not only provide funds but also have somewhat better incentive characteristics than development charges. They also tax those who actually benefit rather than those who will presumably benefit from future service provision. However, such levies are clearly less popular with local governments perhaps because not only do they not provide the same up-front budgetary lift as development charges (or for that matter land transfer taxes) but are also visibly imposed on local residents (and voters).

Understandably, most localities would prefer to fund local infrastructure investment by having someone else pay for it, thus saving them the pain of persuading either local users or local taxpayers to do so. But apart from a few critical network investments (e.g., a major transport hub), such externality concerns as the benefits accruing to non-residents are – or so the sparse evidence available suggests – as a rule considerably less important than much public discussion seems to assume. There are thus few good reasons why higher-level governments should step up and fund local infrastructure. Politicians and officials may nonetheless channel funds to lower-level governments especially for shiny new infrastructure, providing a site for an appropriate commemorative plaque and a good opportunity for a photo shoot. When they do so, however, they are unlikely to give locals a completely free hand in spending. As Martinez-Vazquez and Timofeev (2016) discuss, the net social benefits from intergovernmental capital transfers are invariably complex and difficult to assess in any country. Canada is no exception.

A sensible way for a local government or enterprise to finance a long-lived investment is often by borrowing (Kitchen and Tassonyi 2012). Borrowing does not provide any additional finance in the long run because it has to be paid back. The way to think about borrowing for infrastructure is thus not as a source of finance – Canadian governments at all levels have few problems in accessing the capital market – but rather to focus on how the loans are to be repaid. If a loan is paid through user charges, it is a non-distortionary source of finance and hence attractive even to economists (Bird 2005). Politicians, whose horizons are often relatively short, are generally keen to shift costs to the future. Harried local taxpayers are equally willing to put off to tomorrow the pain of paying taxes for debt service. Economically, it may make sense to shift some costs forward to the next generation to the extent benefits from the project financed flow to that generation.[20] It may also make sense as a way of "smoothing" tax increases over time to match the expected benefit flow from the project financed. But it never provides a way to dodge the main issue: who really pays?

Much the same can be said when it comes to the increasingly popular approach of involving private enterprises in financing public infrastructure through a variety of public–private partnerships (PPPs) as discussed in Siemiatycki (in this volume). Apart from federal airports

(Gooch 2016) it appears that little attention has been paid to privatization as such in Canada and that little "revenue risk" has been transferred to the private sector in Canadian PPP deals to date (Boardman, Siemiatycki, and Vining 2016). Since governments sometimes appear to turn to private-sector partners because they think the latter can do more and better than they could do themselves, it is perhaps implausible to expect them always to make the best possible deals from a public interest perspective. PPPs may sometimes be useful, not least because they may make user-charge financing (for debt service) more acceptable. But they provide no clear answer to the main question about financing infrastructure – who pays? – and may to some extent have confused matters by raising a range of other questions that tend to obscure this key issue.

Other issues may also be obscured when PPPs come into the picture. As stressed earlier, for instance, cross-subsidization is not good practice; it is equally not good policy to compel private agents acting under public contract to cross-subsidize certain users at the expense of others. If governments wish to redistribute income, they should do so directly. If they wish to give certain people more incentive to make use of certain services, they should subsidize users, not suppliers. The best way to design public infrastructure projects is to keep the decisions of (private) management focused on playing their contractual role efficiently (which the profit motive should do if the tricky issue of monitoring the return on capital when monopoly is involved can be resolved). Distributional issues should be left to government. Unfortunately, governments wishing to redistribute sometimes find it easier to achieve public acceptance by confusing the issue and appearing to load the costs on some "rich" private-sector actor – who of course will stay in the game only if it is sure that it will not in fact end up paying them. With such deals, governments get infrastructure and kudos; private players get paid; and the only losers are citizens who think they are getting something for nothing. The continued success of public lotteries suggests that many people are willing to pay for a dream that they understand is unlikely ever to become real. With a lottery, however, at least they know the price when they get in the game. The same cannot be said of some PPP proposals.

WHY USERS SELDOM PAY THE RIGHT PRICES
FOR WHAT THEY GET

The truth is often more complicated than the myth, which usually involves
considerable simplification. This puts the truth at a disadvantage because it is
harder to process, understand, and remember.

                                          Schwarz, Newman, and Leach (2016, 11)

Telling the truth about what needs to be done – relying on evidence, as
academics say – is always desirable in principle. As the passage just quot-
ed suggests, however, it is seldom easy to tell complex truths in ways
that will persuade people who are not already well primed to hear
them. Correcting false beliefs is difficult.[21] It takes careful planning and
hard and persistent effort as well as leadership to persuade people that
something they believe – for example, that user charges are unfair, regressive, and just another name for taxes – is wrong. This section discusses some of the problems that face those who advocate more and
better user pricing in the public sector.

  Broadly, there are three reasons why user charges are unduly neg-
lected: economic, technical, and political:

- Economic reasons, although often mentioned in the public discussion, are perhaps the least important reason for such neglect in developed countries like Canada, where there are well-established
  distributive mechanisms, well-functioning capital markets, and
  considerable technical expertise. The real economic problems are
  more often those now beginning to be discussed under the heading of behavioural economics (Congdon, Kling, and Mullainathan
  2011; Thaler 2015) and are frequently more political than economic in nature.
- Technical problems of various sorts in designing and implementing
  pricing schemes, although more important than is sometimes realized – for example, as mentioned earlier, when the cost of doing pricing right is sufficiently great that it is, in colloquial terms, simply not
  worth sweating the small stuff – are increasingly easier to resolve in
  many cases than they were before the arrival of the information age.
  When even rural farmers in Africa can buy and sell on their GPS-
  equipped mobile phones, the scope for effectively pricing, say, road
  usage in developed countries in which virtually everyone has such
  phones is obviously much greater now than it was ten years ago.

- In the end, especially in developed countries, the main reason so little use is made of user-charge financing seems almost invariably to be political, interpreting "political" broadly to encompass a wide range of issues from the obvious interest of some in obfuscating what is going on to the distributional concerns of others and, perhaps most basically, the different ways in which different people view and understand the concept of public provision.

Each of these aspects is discussed a bit further in this section. The most commonly cited economic argument against user-charge financing is that it is not desirable to finance public infrastructure in this way because the scale of the project is just too big for direct users to finance. This argument seldom makes sense. One reason is simply because the efficient scale of most public-sector facilities is not particularly large: see, for example, the evidence on water projects cited earlier (as well as in OECD 2009) and the broader evidence on scale economies reviewed in Slack and Bird (2013).[22] If those who benefit directly – whether local residents or not – are unable or unwilling to finance a project, the lesson one should usually draw is not that subsidization is required but that it is probably not worth doing at all. Of course, an additional consideration that is sometimes important is that the relevant costs reflect not only the physical environment and the specific characteristics of the infrastructure in question (and who determines those characteristics, with what objectives and trade-offs in mind) but also the institutional environment with respect to standards, regulation, and so forth within which it is expected to operate as well as how honestly and effectively the system is expected to be administered, although once again such complexities cannot be explored further here.

The best pricing system from an economic perspective is full-cost marginal-cost pricing. Assuming that all input markets are competitive or that adjustments moving the measured costs toward this target are considered feasible (Dafflon and Degault 2012) so that market prices reflect social opportunity costs, prices recovering full monetary costs (capital and current) will, on average, meet this standard, which, as Dafflon (in this volume) shows, is approximately true with respect to water in Switzerland. Such prices are found almost nowhere else, however. The user charges found in practice often, at best, recover only current operating costs. Even poorly designed user charges may be economically preferable to financing investments solely from grants or from such alternatives as a flat-rate connection charge (often tied to the property tax), but they are far from optimal. As Kitchen (in this volume) discusses with respect to Ontario, such alternative pricing systems as average incremental pricing – with different charges intended to finance access (the provision of, say, a water line), connection (connecting a particular user to the line), and usage (consumption) – and tariff rates that decrease or increase (sometimes after an initial low-priced lifeline block of usage) are also sometimes used and, if well-designed, may produce better results. However, even the most sophisticated charging systems seldom account adequately for all capital costs or vary sufficiently between locations to adjust for differences in cost – thus accentuating sprawl – or sufficiently with the time of use to encourage users to shift demand from peak to off-peak times. The reality of water pricing in most of the world still remains at least fifty years behind what we know is best in theory and can easily do in practice – if we want to do so.

Much the same can be said even more strongly with respect to other potential public prices. Technology now makes it relatively simple not only to impose appropriate full-cost prices on everything from street usage to sewers but even to vary such prices to match the short-run marginal social costs of providing a specific public service to a specific user in a given location and at a given time. Only with respect to electricity, which in most of Canada is provided and distributed by publicly owned and run utilities, provincial and local, has much effort been made to set proper prices along these lines. Unfortunately, Ontario's recent history of increasing the price of electricity in part to clean up past policy mistakes and in part to reduce carbon emissions provides a poor model of how to rationalize public pricing.[23] The resulting strongly adverse public reaction led to the introduction of subsidy programs intended to offset some of the impact (and, of course, at the same time to reduce the desired beneficial effects). As yet it is unclear how successful altering the pricing of electricity (as well as, by changing the regulatory rules, that of privately supplied natural gas) has been in achieving the intended objectives. But the poor way in which the province explained what it was doing, failing to persuade most people that it all makes sense and is good for them, means that many now view the increased prices as little more than a sort of hidden tax grab and a major adverse cost factor for businesses. This experience may perhaps make it even more difficult in the future to persuade people that it can make sense to price public services more sensibly. One shudders, for example, to think how any road-pricing scheme presented by those who gave Ontario its present set of energy prices would now be received.

Of course, even the best-designed and well-presented effort to introduce better pricing would require substantial and detailed prior work
to obtain the needed knowledge and understanding of the detailed production and cost functions of public services as well as a major sales effort, requiring detailed knowledge of market demand, in order to have
a chance of success. Even then it would still prove a hard sell to many
given the concrete, direct, and immediate costs and the inevitably more
nebulous, distant, and dispersed benefits. Political leadership of the
highest order – perhaps made more plausible by some highly visible
catastrophe – may be essential for success.

In some cases, as with water, where charging systems are already in
place, the necessary information is not only there but already largely
in our databases, although we seldom as yet make good use of it (Dafflon in this volume; Dafflon and Daguet 2012). With a little more
technology and more effort, much the same may also be said about
sewerage and solid waste treatment. In other cases, however, such as
road usage, we do not as yet collect the information, even though it
is now technically feasible to do so. Given the multiple uses and users
of roads and city streets, even with full information it would be a difficult task to devise and implement an appropriate charging system.
But we can certainly do something: for example, we could (as a few
cities do) price peak traffic flows in central cities or properly price
(and enforce) urban parking to reduce its significant contribution to
congestion. However, no one seems willing to focus on developing
and implementing such systems, let alone to face up to the task of
selling them to a resistant audience that has little reason to believe
experts, let alone politicians.

Proposals to – for instance – raise transit fares during rush hours or
to price access to the central business district or a specific highway differently when congestion is higher seem often to be viewed like suggestions to raise food prices during a famine – that is, as simply "not
right." But in economic terms – that is, in terms of ensuring that people get as much as possible out of scarce public resources – they are
right. If prices are not varied to encourage more even usage of facilities
over time, the result is inevitably increased pressure to build still more
public infrastructure to accommodate peak demand, diverting public
resources from other, more socially valuable purposes. Smart meters,
electronic tolling systems, and in general our vastly improved ability to
capture and utilize detailed usage information with respect to congestible public goods has increasingly made it possible to price right –

if we want to do so. No new skills are required to operate and live with such pricing systems. Airline pricing, for example, is already far more complex and variable than anything even the most finicky public pricing designer is likely to come up with. Firms like Amazon vary prices on a wide variety of items by the minute and no one seems to think anything of it. So far, however, governments have made very few moves to join the ongoing pricing parade.

The reason is not lack of economic understanding or technical competence. It is political: those in charge either do not want to price or they do not think they can sell people on pricing or, perhaps, both. At one level, this failure to act may perhaps be seen as just another manifestation of the classical political problem of reconciling conflicting interests. Individuals perceive, correctly, that they have no choice except to travel at peak hours. However, if we charged correct prices over time employers would, or so economists argue, necessarily have to adjust working hours or to pay more to keep staff. Economists are probably right in thinking this way. Well-functioning markets would eventually produce results that should leave people on average better off. But of course most people are not "average" – they are unique in where they live, where they work, the skills that they have, their contacts, and so on – so their lives (and relative positions to each other) may be drastically changed for the worse for years while the adjustment process goes on. People do not like change in any case, and they are understandably especially resistant to changes imposed from outside for reasons they do not grasp and with visible consequences that are, so far as they are concerned, mainly adverse.

Economists have taken much the same attitude with respect to adjustments to trade liberalization: yes, some people will likely lose their jobs, but all they have to do is to tough it out for a while and in the end everyone will be in a better world. As recent events have underlined, such blithe onward and upward arguments do not pay enough attention to the magnitude of the adjustments required, their uneven distributional impact, and the time, effort, and resources that need to be allocated for such changes to be made in an acceptably sustainable way. Much the same could perhaps be said about substantial alterations in the prices charged for such basic public services as roads. We might all be better off once all roads were sensibly priced; but some of us would have to change (or lose) our jobs, our houses, and our way of life, perhaps forever, in the course of moving there from here. Visions of a slightly better earthly paradise – less crowded commuting (road pricing) or cheaper goods (free trade) – even if one believes they will be achieved are unlikely to be persuasive to those who see such costs looming before them. Life is about transition, and successful policy design and implementation require much more attention to this critical question than it has usually received in either theory or practice.

One reason little attention has been paid to the transition issue is because it is often seen as essentially a distributional problem, and it is not in principle difficult to deal with the distributional problems associated with transitions. Mushkin (1972) noted long ago that smart cards could easily deal with any perceived distributional problems arising from policy-induced adjustments in behavioural patterns when it came to public pricing. The digital age has made it even easier. However, as a rule we do little or nothing along these lines. Even if we did, we would be neglecting what the next section shows is an even more important condition for success, namely, dealing with the overriding process issues that seem central to how most people receive proposed policy changes: was I consulted, were my views taken into account, does the proposal fit my view of what is right and true? People may simply not trust that either markets or governments will produce the promised results quickly enough or perhaps at all. Understandably, if changes are nonetheless pushed through, they may seek offsetting subsidies from governments or their employers (who will in turn then besiege the government for help), thus to some extent negating the expected beneficial effects of pricing. There are no easy solutions.

Rationalizing public prices is a difficult task. We can now in principle price most public services correctly regardless of who provides them, who produces them, who operates them, or who uses them or for what purpose. But we have not yet figured out how to persuade most people that it makes sense to do so. Broadly, there are two levels of political arguments against more economically rational user-charge policies. The most immediately obvious is simply that almost everyone affected is against them; at a deeper level, however, such resistance may reflect not simply self-interest but also deeper value-based conflicts:

• People who use particular services do not want to pay for them or, if they already do, to pay more. To some extent, this may reflect their belief that certain public services should be provided free for all as a matter of right or because they have already been paid for by general taxation.

- People who do not have access to the services do not see why they should pay for what others get or, if the aim is to charge for new services that will be extended to them, they do not see why they should pay more than those who have long benefited from similar services and paid less or nothing for them.[24]
- Those involved in actually providing the services – managers and workers (whether in the public or private sectors) as well as input suppliers and those providing ancillary activities – are usually against charging more because they suspect – often correctly – that one result will be to reduce demand for their services.[25] Or they may resist because as dedicated public servants they think what they do is an essential public service and that it is wrong to charge for it.
- Some in the central policy ministries may be more concerned about possibly reducing public revenues if the government goes too far down the charging path.
- Ideological opponents from the left are usually worried about the adverse distributive effects of charging or simply reacting to what they consider to be the improper "marketization" of public policy.
- Some from the right, even though they may not care that much about distribution, may still oppose charging and argue that the real answer is either to privatize the service or simply for government to get out of the business completely.

Given the resistance that user-charge proposals often generate, it is not surprising that the politicians who have to make the final decisions – and who seem often to look at charging as simply a question of revenue (Meltsner 1971) – may decide to leave things as they are. Alternatively, if they do decide to charge, to make doing so politically acceptable they may end up doing so in a hobbled and complex way with cross-subsidization here, special concessions there, and a complex financing structure that shifts costs outside the circle of direct beneficiaries (e.g., to the future). This approach may be successful in making the issue of who bears the costs sufficiently obscure to allow some charging to take place. But it may equally lend itself to "clientelism" and corruption. With or without such undesired accretions, politicized charging schemes are likely to reduce the ultimate social gains from improving public-sector pricing and infrastructure investment decisions over time. Bad experiences (e.g., energy pricing in Ontario) may also damage public trust in the capacity of governments to deliver on their promises. At the municipal level, where politicians have to live with their constituents, employees, and suppliers much more than they do at higher levels of government, it may be attractive to continue to take the easy way – to charge too little and in the wrong way and hence to end up providing what is often the wrong level and kind of services to the wrong people, while sometimes simultaneously begging for money from elsewhere to allow them to do even more of the wrong things – that is, things they cannot persuade their residents, the direct beneficiaries, to pay for.

CAN WE DO BETTER?

Effective advocacy, in tax or other policy areas, must be very clear about the objectives being sought, the costs and benefits of alternative options, what trade-offs are being made and, crucially, be prepared to respond to thoughtful lines of criticism. This task cannot, in a democracy, be left to experts ... it must always be led at the political level.

Pearl (2016, 410)

How might the case for public pricing be sold more effectively? Bazel and Mintz (2015, 2) correctly tell us that "a user-pay model would work to eliminate political influence, create revenue for infrastructure renewal, and facilitate an optimal allocation of infrastructure resources." So it would; and so economists have been saying for centuries. But almost no one seems to have been listening. One reason is, as Fenn (2016, 26) notes, that "linking the demand for infrastructure with ways to pay for it is a major political challenge. It can be a tough sell, if proposed in a political environment where the public is skeptical that its taxes, fees and fares are being put to best use. The 2015 defeat of the Vancouver region's transport sales tax referendum is eloquent testimony of this disconnect." Good pricing and a sound financial plan alone are not enough to get the right projects done; but without them they are unlikely to be done in a sustainable way. As the current apparent global revulsion with (relatively) free trade shows, economists do not have a good track record when it comes to persuading people that policies that seem obviously adverse to their immediate direct interests – and indeed often may be adverse at least for some time unless compensation is provided in some way – will be sufficiently beneficial in the long run to make the pain of adjustment worth bearing.

The usual answer of analysts to comments like these is simply to emphasize the need for better data, more transparent processes and pricing systems, and more education along the commendable lines set out in Slack and Tassonyi (this volume). But education alone is not enough. There are good reasons why people may not trust economists who tell them that charging is good for them – let alone governments that tell them it would be a really good thing for them to pay more for public services (Graser and Robinson 2016). An obvious reason mentioned earlier is that analysts almost never pay sufficient attention to so-called transitional issues, many of which may affect people's lives in the near future in a salient fashion and hence powerfully influence their reaction to proposed changes. Another reason is simply because almost never is sufficient attention paid to the need to sell proposals in the specific political context at hand. How people perceive proposed changes is explained to a considerable extent by a few key factors including framing and anchoring.

Anchoring is easier to explain and understand. People always and everywhere assess possible changes against their perception of present reality: they anchor their view of change to the status quo. As everyone in the budgetary game knows, what matters is not so much whether we do this or that right in some conceptual sense but rather precisely how we propose to change from whatever we are doing. User charges have a big hurdle to jump in this respect, especially if they charge for something that people now perceive as free. Nothing is of course really free when it comes to using scarce resources. But no one now has to pay out of pocket for pulling out of his or her driveway onto a city street, let alone to pay more for doing so if living in a congested downtown area or doing so at peak hour – you know, when you have to go to work or are trying to come home at the end of a long day. Good luck to those who must persuade people they should pay for the privilege of being stuck in rush hour traffic. Most people think that the cost of using their automobile is essentially what they pay for fuel and any parking charges. Period. Few factor in the much larger private costs of operating and maintaining a vehicle, let alone providing home storage for it and the more esoteric opportunity costs of commuting time. And perhaps no one but the occasional odd economist even thinks of the additional costs you impose on everyone else as a result of your commute.[26]

It is easier to think of increasing or restructuring user charges where they already exist, for example, with respect to parking, transit, water, or waste removal. In practice, however, it often turns out to be almost as difficult to change as to launch a charging system, particularly when it comes to moving from uniform (postage stamp) pricing to a more efficient cost-based system. Public pricing systems are almost invariably sticky in the sense that prices tend to stay where they are (Bird 1976). Those who are accustomed to pay a particular price seem to have a strong sense of entitlement and to resent and resist paying more in charges in much the same way that they resist paying more in property taxes.

One moral of the anchoring story is that it is better to start as one means to go on because it is so difficult to change things.[27] The problem, of course, is that governments almost never face a clean slate even with respect to brand-new infrastructure projects since the services such projects provide have their own pricing (or no-pricing) history. More generally, although we seldom consider pricing a completely new line of public activity, the mere fact that the public sector is involved may constrain the extent to which pricing is possible. The moment any policy change is characterized as affecting something seen as a public service, some people – perhaps many – immediately frame it in terms that imply that whatever it is should in principle both be paid for out of general public revenues (taxes) and made available free (of direct monetary payment) to all and sundry. To return to the Ontario energy case for example, many – and not simply the unions which have an obvious self-interest – think that the key problem dates back to the (partial) privatization of the electricity industry some years ago and that the way to resolve the problem is simply to recreate the good old days of the Ontario Hydro monopoly – even though it was largely the problems created by poor decisions made by that monopoly that led to its breakup in the first place (Dewees 2012). Looking back to an often mythical golden age in the past when one has problems with the present world is a common framing device.

Another important aspect of how people frame their reactions to policy changes relates to their notion of fairness. Sheffrin (2013, 225) notes that "a tax system is not simply a device for redistributing goods and services with the least social pain. It is also a system in which individuals express their values." Much the same argument may perhaps be applied to public pricing if only because at least some seem to consider charges paid to public entities as being just another way for the government to take away their hard-earned money. Sheffrin (2013) reports considerable evidence that when it comes to such matters the relevant frame is likely to be closer to what he calls folk justice than to the consequential equity (the effect of policy change on income distribution) that is usually the focus of technical analysts. A critical aspect of folk justice relates to process and procedure, specifically, the extent to which people feel that their voice has been heard and respectfully considered in developing and implementing any proposed policy change. Cases such as the reaction to energy pricing in Ontario discussed earlier, like the recent political upheavals in the Brexit vote and the recent US presidential election, provide some support for the proposition that those who wish to change the world need to focus more on what really shapes people's views about prospective policy changes than on how consistent the results may be with Rawlsian or other philosophical equity constructs. Those who want to improve policy outcomes, whether with respect to charging or anything else, need to pay close attention to ensuring that the process of policy design and implementation is right in the sense of producing results that make people in aggregate better off not only as measured by some abstract index of welfare but also, and more critically, that at least a viable coalition is visibly better off in terms of their own values and beliefs.

To illustrate, if a proposal is made to price water at something closer to its social marginal cost, one may perhaps imagine a mythical representative citizen having an internal dialogue along the following lines:

- Who are these experts who tell us that people like Joe who lives up on the hill (where it costs more to pump water) should pay more for water than people at the bottom of the hill?
- How can they say this is fair? Isn't it bad enough that poor people like those who can only afford to live up the hill already have to go up and down hill to get to work and even to get groceries while rich people like Jim who can afford to live at the bottom can just stroll to work and shop?
- Looking at it another way, though, since Jim and his family work for a living and pay taxes while most of Joe's family lie about the house doing nothing, perhaps it's only fair they pay more?
- Who knows? All I know is that no one asked my opinion, that I have no idea how they came to this weird conclusion, and I don't trust them anyway.

In addition to re-emphasizing the extent to which public consideration of user-charge proposals rests on both the status quo anchor and is usually framed only in terms of direct out-of-pocket monetary costs, two other important points may be drawn from this brief imagined soliloquy.

First, goods provided by the public sector – as water usually is in Canada – are sometimes considered somehow different in kind from those obtained from the private sector such as bread or housing. No one seems to worry much if the store at which Joe shops (because it is closer to him) charges more for bread than Jim's local high-class outlet. But most people seem to think that the water accompanying the bread should be the same price to both poor Joe and rich Jim.[28] Second, when something is provided by government, even if people accept not only that the costs of providing services to different people are different but also that people may choose to have somewhat different levels of service or different degrees of access to it, when it comes to changing prices, most discussion tends almost invariably to focus on the distributional effects even if the real reason for opposition (e.g., workers may fear losing their jobs if higher prices reduce demand for their services)[29] may be quite different and if the net impact of any distributive impact on inequality or poverty would be minuscule.

To the extent that opposition to good user-charge policy originates from such often vague arguments, it is seldom difficult to counter them. Such measures as making payments more convenient (Kim 2016),[30] measuring costs and benefits carefully and making people aware of them (De and Nag 2016), and – in cases where the distributive impact is sufficiently significant to warrant explicit attention – providing adequate compensatory offsets through direct transfers (e.g., adjustments in welfare payments and income-related tax credits, as was done when the GST was introduced for instance) are familiar and relatively effective responses. At least, that is what experts would say: as always, of course, getting most of the populace to agree may be difficult. People tend to focus on the clear and understandable truths that (1) we all need water, (2) the public sector is supposed to serve all of us, and (3) raising the price of water places a larger relative burden on the poor. They find it harder to grasp the offsetting truths that (4) subsidizing the price not only provides the greatest benefits to those who use the most water – big lawns and swimming pools – and encourages more people to use more water (Bird and Miller 1989) but as a result also means (5) that we are going to have to invest more in expanding the capacity of our water distribution system. Who among us can calculate the net outcome taking all these factors into account or assess the associated redistribution in the broader context of public-sector policy as a whole?

Even if one trusts that governments not only can but will offset undesired effects, there is no ready answer to those who think that the only fair way the public sector can or should do anything is by providing exactly the same type and level of service to everyone at no or (at most) the same cost. To the extent that the narrative frame (Akerlof and Snower 2016) within which charging issues are considered is that publicness implies that anything provided by the public sector should in principle be equally available to and provided freely to all, the problem is insoluble: everyone expects a service that no one is willing to pay for. The economic case for user charges is precisely that they establish the essential link between service received and payment and thus make it possible for people not only to see if they value the service sufficiently to pay its cost but also to evaluate the service and to adjust their usage as they see fit. While there is surprisingly little research on this issue, Sun and Jung (2012) found that imposing user charges on recreational facilities where users were identifiable, exclusion was feasible, and costs were measurable resulted in quantifiable and significant benefits to users. While the results varied depending on such factors as the costs of administration, externalities, and the importance of distributional issues, and it is far from simple to evaluate the elasticity of demand for most public services (Glaeser et al. 2015), such results are interesting. However, far more such studies are needed before we know enough about such matters to reach definitive conclusions.

Nonetheless, there may still be ways to deal with the most recalcitrant opponents of user charges. One may be to separate (unbundle) the financing issue as clearly as possible from the basic provision issue by subsidizing directly those who are to be subsidized. Only when subsidies (whether for distributional or, conceivably, development reasons) are kept completely distinct from questions of basic financing can the provision of public utility services, including investment in infrastructure, be made transparently financially sustainable while providing the right incentives to users, utility, and government. Moreover, subsidies should be directed to those targeted – that is, specific consumers – and not offered by, for example, requiring suppliers to provide them, as is commonly (and usually ineffectively and inefficiently) done (Serebrisky et al. 2009). Water, for example, may be considered by many to be a "social" rather than an economic good. Nonetheless, it is critical to separate the structuring and financing of such characteristics as universal access and distributive and health concerns from the basic problem of setting up and running a good water system (Le Blanc 2007).[31] Such things are easy for economists to say but they are seldom easy to estimate precisely. Even when good estimates can be made, in a policy context that seems increasingly strongly influenced more by the instantaneous, strong, and simplistic opinions of the many than by even the best reasoned (and hence generally complex and nuanced) conclusions of experts, even the best estimates may not prove persuasive to those who think they already know the right answers.

People are often right to be suspicious of promises to enact compensatory distributive policies – financed, for example, from the general budgetary revenues freed by charging the right prices for the private use of publicly provided services – because experience suggests that such policies are in fact seldom put in place. One reason may be that such concerns seem often to fade away after the initial decision is made. Many people may be strongly against a policy change in part at least on distributional grounds, but once the decision is made, little concern is usually evidenced about such matters. As Boardman, Siemiatycki, and Vining (2016) suggest with respect to public–private projects, it appears easier to introduce sound policies with respect to issues such as charging after a political decision is made to do something than before – an example perhaps of the continuing validity of the ancient adage that "it is better to ask forgiveness than permission."[32]

As noted in passing earlier, when it comes to nudging people to do the right thing in their own interest (Thaler and Sunstein 2008) the line between (more or less) Machiavellian manipulation of public opinion and the sort of libertarian paternalism envisaged by Thaler (2015) can be very thin. Good nudging of the second sort is intended to help people get what they – the people – really want, while bad Machiavellianism aims at getting them to go along with what someone else has decided is good for them (or at least for the nudger in question). It is not easy to draw a clear line between coercing or tricking people to behave in a different way and altering the context within which they view the policy in question so that they are more likely to make better decisions on their own. A recent brief comment on the (relatively limited) experience at the local level with nudge policies (Glowacki 2016) suggests that those who want to influence behaviour (or simply to sell ideas, whether with the good of the people or of themselves in mind) need to spend a lot more time and effort in understanding their audience than most governments seem to do.[33] As French and Oreopoulos (2016, 16) note in a comment on Canadian experience, would-be nudgers need to remember that "nudges cross many different boundaries such as economics, politics, and ethics, and must be considered carefully before being implemented." Simply being fully transparent and open to public scrutiny (Sunstein 2014) is unlikely to be good enough.

Students of tax reform should find such discussions familiar. Lejour (2016), for example, emphasizes that for tax reforms in OECD countries the line between idea and implementation is not straight but generally winding, from gathering the evidence (preferably by credible independent research) to placing the problem on the agenda, then devising some kind of solution that will deal with the problems that relevant groups consider possible, then waiting until the time is ripe for reform (e.g., a crisis) and finally pulling together sufficiently strong coalition support to get it through. Similarly, Brys (2011) stresses the importance of fitting any change proposal into the political cycle with respect to both timing and coalition building as well as designing proposals that will both be saleable in general as a desirable change in the status quo and able to accommodate such specific concerns as those of the most affected interest groups as well as being sufficiently robust to withstand the inevitable risks and uncertainties accompanying any significant policy change. To do so, one must, for example, be able to reframe distributional concerns to focus on the effects of the fiscal system as a whole rather than the particular changes being made – always a major problem – and also to sequence and bundle different measures so that they reinforce rather than conflict with each other within the critical constraints (e.g., constitutional, legal) that cannot be changed in the relevant time frame. All this is much easier to prescribe than to do, whether one is concerned with tax reform or reforming user charges.

Perhaps the only way short of catastrophe[34] that the issue of more rational user charging for congestible goods provided by public-sector agencies may get on the agenda and have a hope of being accepted is with respect to providing new infrastructure. We all live in the short run, and few of us spend much time thinking much beyond the immediate future. Only when something new is on the horizon can people see that they are, as it were, being asked to enter into a contract in the sense of agreeing to pay for some new benefits that they can actually see coming down the road.[35] So long as charging more means paying more for what people already get – or perhaps even paying more for services that are deteriorating as more users crowd in – the prospects for success are slim. To frame the question differently, so long as people think it is not necessary for their own welfare to pay higher prices for some service that they consider necessary to their well-being then even a famed (if seldom found) rational economic being let alone any real (fallible and limited) human being is unlikely to support radical changes in the status quo – unless those proposing such changes can tell a sufficiently strong and convincing story that resonates with his or her values, ideas, and interests.

Experience everywhere suggests that when it comes to raising public revenues there is invariably resistance. Most people think they already pay too much to government. If they are to be asked to pay more it should be as clear as possible that they are paying for something that they (through their political institutions) have chosen – presumably often only after many long and involved public discussions and arguments. To overcome such resistance to change requires that policy advocates be prepared to engage in prolonged, detailed, credible, and patient interaction with those who are expected to pay.[36] Officials need to be able to present clearly the costs and benefits of alternative options and the trade-offs being made, policy advocates need to understand in depth and respond adequately to at least the more thoughtful criticisms made, and politicians have to be prepared to carry the ball in the legislature and on the hustings. When it comes to user charges, one implication of this line of argument is that it is critical not only to direct revenues from user charges explicitly and strictly to providing the designated services but also to ensure that the payments are transparently separated from any other payments to government agencies such as property taxes or such other charges as water and sewerage bills.

As an example of what not to do, when Greece attempted in 2012 to push through a national property tax without the usual prolonged public arguments preceding such reforms, it attempted to make the new tax more palatable by collecting it with the utility bill: however, resistance to the tax turned out to be so great that not only did people not pay the new tax but many also ceased paying their utility bill (Sheffrin 2013). Instead of getting, as it perhaps hoped, two for one, the result was that the government ended up batting zero. Jacobs and Matthews (2015) found in several US studies that citizens were most likely to reject policy initiatives not because they did not want the services to be financed and not because they were unalterably opposed to all new taxes and charges but rather because they simply did not believe that governments were likely to deliver the promised benefits. Given their recent experiences, it is hardly surprising that many Greeks did not believe there was any reason for them to pay more over to their government.

From an economic perspective, it is critical to build into any rational charging system not only a sensible (economically appropriate) structure to the extent (politically) possible but also to ensure that adequate provision is made for full recovery of life-cycle costs including both the repayment of initial loans and adequate O&M (including replacement). To do so may, for example, require some form of indexing (to account for price-level changes) and more generally the establishment of clear and transparent procedures for setting prices initially and subsequently adjusting them in accord with future contingencies. Unless an appropriate price-adjustment process is built in from the beginning any new user charge system is all too likely soon to become as sticky as most such systems now are. The result is unlikely to be very close to any kind of theoretical optimum.

In the end, however, just as smaller, less efficient local governments may sometimes be better in political economy terms than even the most efficient larger regional governments (Hall, Matti, and Zhou 2016),[37] so even a charging system that is at best only half-way to perfection – for example, more rational parking charges and enforcement on city streets (Miller and Wilson 2015) instead of congestion tolls on city streets – is likely to be a far better and more sustainable way to finance new urban infrastructure than funds obtained either from on high (federal grants) or from such apparently free revenue sources as those that some seem to think PPP proposals offer. Users or taxpayers must always pay in the end, and user charges (whether channelled through PPPs, governments, or utilities) are clearly the best way to pay for new infrastructure when feasible. As much of the recent discussion of infrastructure finance argues, it is important to ensure that the relevant share of costs is recouped from non-residents and future residents and that both intergovernmental transfers and borrowing (directly or via PPPs) are appropriate financing tools for these purposes. However, not nearly enough attention has been paid to making it clear to all that in the end either users or taxpayers must pay, and that the case for charging users when feasible is not only the most efficient but also arguably the fairest way to do so.

Thinking more carefully about the role that better user pricing can play in financing the intended major expansion of infrastructure may be a good place to begin a new era in which public investments are made not in response to the noisiest or most influential prospective beneficiaries but rather where and when they represent the best use of public-sector resources. Public resources are not free, and more and better use of pricing where feasible is one of the best ways we know to ensure that governments use such resources as efficiently as possible in delivering the public services that we as a society want and are willing to pay for. Even a small start in this direction, perhaps by rationalizing water pricing, perhaps by pivoting some major new transport investments on a soundly based pricing strategy, would be more than most past governments have managed to do.

NOTES

I am grateful for helpful suggestions from Kyle Hanniman and Enid Slack as well as comments by other participants at the conference where an earlier version of this paper was presented.

1 The present discussion focuses mainly on large urban areas: as Slack and Kitchen (2006) note, there are good reasons for higher-level governments to play a larger role in providing infrastructure in more sparsely populated and often poorer rural regions.

2 For instance, the "availability payments" often used in Canada to cover the private debt incurred in PPP arrangements (Siemiatycki 2016) are usually financed from tax revenues.

3 For example, Steinmo (2016) makes a strong argument for more use of experimental methods in testing the "internal validity" of hypotheses about the political economics of public revenue policy, and a good recent example of such a study can be found in Jacobs and Mathews (2015).

4 Many important issues cannot be discussed here, such as the difference between public production and public provision, the level(s) of government that provide a service, and the organizational forms through which they do so (government department, subordinated agency, public enterprise, contracted private firm, etc.).

5 See also Fenn and Kitchen (2016).

6 Carratini, Baranzi, and Lalive (2016) provide further evidence on how far from economically optimal the prices imposed on waste are in most EU countries.

7 As De Mello and Sutherland (2016) emphasize, charges are especially desirable for congestible infrastructure because they both signal where new investment is needed and provide funding for it. We do not attempt here to classify investment in terms of what might be labelled its chargeability: for partial attempts to do so, none of which is wholly satisfactory, see

Bird (1976), Kessides (1993), Bird and Tsiopoulos (1996), and De Mello and Sutherland (2016).

8 In some instances the case can be made that the best way to deal with high fixed costs may be to spread them across a larger population – e.g., a regional (or provincial) rather than local government area (Ostrom 1972).

9 In principle, water pricing may also play a role in terms of internalizing externalities and encouraging innovation. However, there is little evidence that the first of these objectives has been taken into account anywhere (De Mello and Sutherland 2016) or that the second has as yet led to many positive results. Consider, for example, the recent move towards stormwater pricing in Ontario. Not only may the structure of pricing be criticized (Cairns, Arros, and O"Neill 2016) but whatever economic benefits might result from imposing more efficient user charges risk being offset by the continuing pressure to use the revenues to subsidize this or that currently favoured "green" policy (Aquije 2016). Economic arguments seldom support such earmarking of green taxes to green spending (Thirsk and Bird 1994). There may be a political economy case for such earmarking in some instances (Bird and Jun 2007) but it is quite different (and weaker) than the strong economic argument for earmarking properly designed service charges to spending on the service in question.

10 For a fuller account of how to determine and measure the production and cost functions of chargeable public services, see Dafflon (2013).

11 As Bird (2005) emphasizes, full-cost user pricing means that the distortionary costs of taxation do not need to be taken into account in applying traditional cost-benefit analysis to public-sector projects. However, such costs should be included when considering tax-financed projects, although this seems almost never to be done.

12 This point is not discussed further here, but see Bird and Tsiopoulos (1996, 1997) as well as the more fundamental theoretical treatment in Vickrey (1994).

13 As Dafflon (in this volume) mentions, similar arguments may be applied to education, health, and other "social" services provided by government, although this may raise more important distributional questions (Bird 1976). However, the present discussion is focused on physical (engineering) infrastructure.

14 See, for examples, the estimates reported by Baylor and Beausejour (2004), who conclude that increasing taxes on saving and investment is a particularly costly way to raise revenues in Canada, with payroll and consumption taxes being notably less costly. Johansson et al. (2008) report

similar results for OECD countries generally, adding the interesting conclusion that property taxes are the socially least costly way to raise revenue – a point that supports the case for financing infrastructure spending from local property taxes as the second-best (after user charges) way of financing local services and their supporting infrastructure.

15   This "benefit" model can usefully be extended to encompass most activities usually carried out by local governments by treating the local property tax as a sort of "generalized user charge" (as well as perhaps the most economically efficient form of general taxation available) although this point is not discussed further here (see Bird and Slack 2014).

16   Since automobile use on roads and streets is also individual and observable, in principle appropriate user charges could be applied in this case also although in fact this is seldom done and such relatively crude proxies as licence fees and fuel taxes are used instead: for a useful recent review of this subject, which is not further discussed here, see Kitchen and Lindsey (2013).

17   Similarly, if demand for some public service is essentially unrelated to its price – for example, everyone must register for health cards and they have to pay for the privilege – it may be called a fee but it is decidedly not a user charge as the term is used here. An additional obstacle that Canadian municipalities have to deal with in setting user fees is the legal and judicial obstacle course carefully described in Farish and Tedds (2014): if more and better user charges are to be used to finance expanded local infrastructure, some changes in the existing legal framework seem needed, although again this is not a matter that can be further discussed here.

18   For two quite different discussions that lead to this conclusion, see Fullerton (1996) and Bird (2006).

19   As Dafflon demonstrates in this volume, the Swiss take this point very seriously indeed.

20   See Heim (2015) for an interesting discussion of this process at work in two US cities over time.

21   For an interesting, and applicable, perspective on this problem, see Schwarz, Newman, and Leach (2016), who suggest why so many attempts to rectify false "myths" fail – for example, simply repeating something false in order to refute it reinforces the salience of the false argument to those who have already heard it, and the more times people hear something, even if they are told it is false, the more likely they are to believe it.

22   As Meloche and Vaillancourt note in the case of Montreal in this volume and Vickrey (1994) stresses more generally – see also the reference in

note 1 above to small rural areas – the decreasing cost argument may be relevant in some cases. But the point is that it is almost never critical to the question of whether or not to charge.

23 Dewees (2012); a more recent review of the Ontario experience (Morrow and Cardoso 2017) is no more favourable.

24 Dafflon, in this volume, notes this point has been important even in the outstandingly rational Swiss system.

25 Although remember the encouraging story told earlier about increased camping fees and the managerial reaction, which also dealt with the next point listed.

26 There is an increasing literature on the relevance of visibility or salience to taxation (Congdon et al. 2011): for a Canadian example, see Bird (2010a). Similar considerations are, as Finkelstein (2009) shows, perhaps even stronger with respect to such user charge issues as road pricing.

27 A good illustration is the Montreal case discussed by Meloche and Vaillancourt in this volume. A more positive historical tale from the perspective of good pricing is that told in the "Swiss way," discussed by Dafflon in this volume.

28 To underline that it is the way a product is delivered (by the public or private sector) rather than the nature (public or private) of the good that is considered most important, experience elsewhere (e.g., Egypt) suggests that when government makes itself responsible for supplying bread, its price becomes a major political issue and as a result is usually kept both uniform and below real cost.

29 There is no reason to doubt that teachers, doctors, and other public-sector workers may fervently believe that every additional dollar that flows into in their pockets improves education and health – just as most university professors think that spending more on universities obviously improves social well-being. But there is seldom any evidence supporting the belief that simply increasing expenditure on such activities necessarily improves the level or the quality of the service provided, let alone constitutes the best possible use of scarce public funds.

30 Note that by reducing the level of consciousness of the cost of expanding public-sector activities, increased convenience may arguably have its own down side.

31 As Dafflon notes in this volume, the same is true with respect to the classic "public good" use of water to deal with fires.

32 Carattini, Barazii, and Lalive (2016) similarly stress how different *ex post* and *ex ante* decisions may sometimes be.

33 Interestingly, to date most nudging experience seems to have been at the national level, with very few examples at the local level, where presumably people are closer to their governments (and vice versa).

34 Note the beneficial impact of the Walkerton disaster on water pricing in Ontario (see Kitchen in this volume).

35 For recent explorations of this fiscal contracting approach in different contexts, see Bird and Slack (2014) on local governments in developing countries and Bird and Zolt (2015) on national governments in Canada and the United States.

36 Examples are the long evolution of the Swiss way of charging for water described by Dafflon in this volume or the equally long evolution of most successful property tax reforms described in Slack and Bird (2014).

37 For some interesting empirical support for this argument, see Lassen and Serritzlew (2011).

References

Administration Fédérale des Finances (AFF). 2012. "Financement par les émoluments dans les cantons et les communes." Rapport et Document de travail, 30 October, version 1.1. Section statistique financière, Confédération suisse, Berne.

Akerlof, George A., and Dennis J. Snower. 2016. "Bread and Bullets." CESifo Working Paper No. 5747. February.

Albalate, Daniel, and Germè Bel. 2009. "What Local Policy Makers Should Know about Urban Road Charging: Lessons from Worldwide Experience." *Public Administration Review* 69(5): 962–74.

Alberta, n.d. City Charters. https://www.alberta.ca/city-charters.aspx.

– 2016. "Canada and Alberta Reach Agreement under New Federal Infrastructure Funding Programs." 1 September. http://www.alberta.ca/release.cfm?xID=43323FEE38AE2-91B7-11FE-2BECE0D757EC2086.

– Municipal Affairs. 2017. "Municipal Financial and Statistical Data." http://www.municipalaffairs.alberta.ca/municipal_financial_statistical_data.

– Municipal Affairs. n.d. "The Municipal Sustainability Inititative" (MSI). http://municipalaffairs.alberta.ca/msi.

Alm, James. 2011. *Municipal Finance of Urban Infrastructure.* http://econ.tulane.edu/RePEc/pdf/tul1103.pdf.

Althaus, Catherine, and Lindsay M. Tedds. 2016. *User Fees in Canada: A Municipal Design and Implementation Guide.* Toronto: Canadian Tax Foundation.

Althaus, Catherine, Lindsay M. Tedds, and Allen McAvoy. 2011. "The Feasibility of Implementing a Congestion Charge on the Halifax Peninsula: Filling the 'Missing Link' of Implementation." *Canadian Public Policy* 37(4): 541–61.

Altman, Roger C., Aaron Kelin, and Alan B. Krueger. 2015. *Financing US Transportation Infrastructure in the 21st Century*. Washington, DC: Brookings Institution Hamilton Project.

Altus Group Limited. 2008. *Financial Reporting Standards: An Overview of the Changing Accounting Standards Relevant to Public Sector Organizations*. Report prepared for the National Executive Forum on Public Property. http://www.publicpropertyforum.ca/library/public-property-forum-2008-ifrs-psab-discussion-paper-part-i.pdf.

Antunes, Pedro, Kip Beckman, Jacqueline Johnson. 2010. *The Economic Impact of Public Infrastructure in Ontario*. Ottawa: Conference Board of Canada. 10 March. 39 pp. http://www.conferenceboard.ca/e-library/abstract.aspx?did=3492.

Aquatera. 2014. *Aquatera Annual Report 2014*. http://aquatera.ca/images/uploads/our_company/Plans%2C%20Reports%20%26%20Information/annual2014.pdf.

Aquije, Daniela, D. 2016. "Paying for Stormwater Management." *IMFG Perspectives* 12. Toronto: Institute on Municipal Finance and Governance (IMFG), Munk School of Global Affairs, University of Toronto.

Arnott, Richard, and John Rowse. 2009. "Downtown Parking in Auto City." *Regional Science and Urban Economics* 39(1): 1–14.

Ashton, Philip, Marc Doussard, and Rachel Weber. 2012. "The Financial Engineering of Infrastructure Privatization." *Journal of the American Planning Association* 78: 300–12. doi:10.1080/01944363.2012.715540.

Bailey, Stephen, Peter Falconer, and Stuart McChlery. 1993. *Local Government Charges: Policy and Practice*. London: Longman Group.

Baldwin J., and J. Dixon. 2008. "Capital: What Is It? Where Is It? How Much of It Is There?" *Canadian Productivity Review*. Statistics Canada 15-206-X – No. 016. http://www.statcan.gc.ca/pub/15-206-x/15-206-x2008016-eng.pdf.

Baylor, Maximilian. and Louis Beausejour. 2004. "Taxation and Economic Efficiency: Results from a Canadian CGE Model." Department of Finance Working Paper 2004-10. November.

Bazel, Philip, and Jack Mintz. 2014. "The Free Ride Is Over: Why Citizens Must Start Paying for Much Needed Infrastructure." SPP Research Papers 7(14), (14), May. Calgary: School of Public Policy, University of Calgary.

– 2015. "Optimal Public Infrastructure: Some Guideposts to Ensure We Don't Overspend." SPP Research Papers 8(37). November.

Bird, Richard M. 1976. *Charging for Public Services: A New Look at an Old Idea*. Toronto: Canadian Tax Foundation.

– 2000. "Decentralization of the State." Lecture notes. Havana, Cuba, 6–10 March 2000.

- 2005. "Evaluating Public Expenditures: Does It Matter How They Are Financed?" In *Fiscal Management*, edited by Anwar Shah, 83–108. Washington, DC: The World Bank.
- 2006. "Local and Regional Revenues: Realities and Prospects." In *Perspectives on Fiscal Federalism*, edited by Richard M. Bird and Francois Vaillancourt, 177–96. WBI Learning Resources Series. Washington, DC: World Bank, 2006.
- 2010a. "Visibility and Accountability– Is Tax-Inclusive Pricing a Good Thing?" *Canadian Tax Journal* 58(1): 63–76.
- 2010b. *Local Government Finance: Trends and Questions*. http://ssrn.com /abstract=1659807.
Bird, Richard M., and Joosung Jun. 2007. "Earmarking in Theory and Korean Practice." In *Excise Taxation in Asia*, edited by Stephen L.H. Phua, 49–86. Singapore: National University of Singapore.
Bird, Richard M., and Barbara D. Miller. 1989. "Taxation, Pricing and the Poor." In *Government Policy and the Poor in Developing Countries*, edited by Richard M. Bird and Susan Horton, 49–80. Toronto: University of Toronto Press.
Bird, Richard M., and Enid Slack. 2014. "Local Taxes and Local Expenditures in Developing Countries: Strengthening the Wicksellian Connection." *Public Administration and Development* 34(4): 359–69.
Bird, Richard M., Enid Slack, and Almos Tassonyi. 2012. *A Tale of Two Taxes: Property Tax Reform in Ontario*. Cambridge, MA: Lincoln Institute of Land Policy.
Bird, Richard M., and Almos Tassonyi. 2001. "Constraints on Provincial and Municipal Borrowing in Canada: Markets, Rules and Norms." *Canadian Public Administration* 44(1):84–109.
Bird, Richard M., and Thomas Tsiopoulos. 1996. "User Charge Policy in the Federal Public Sector," International Centre for Tax Studies, Faculty of Management, University of Toronto, June.
- 1997. "User Charges for Public Services: Potentials and Problems," *Canadian Tax Journal* 45(1): 25–86.
Bird, Richard M., and Eric M. Zolt. 2015. "Taxes, Spending and Inequality in Canada and the United States: Two Stories or One?" *Osgoode Hall Law Journal* 52(2): 401–27.
Blais, Pamela. 2010. *Perverse Cities: Hidden Subsidies, Wonky Policy, and Urban Sprawl*. Vancouver: UBC Press.
Blanc-Brude, Frederic, Hugh Goldsmith, and Timo Valila. 2009. "A Comparison of Construction Contract Prices for Traditionally Procured Roads and Public–Private Partnerships." *Review of Industrial Organizations* 35: 19–40. doi:10.1007/s11151-009-9224-1.

Boadway, Robin, and Harry Kitchen. 2014. "A Fiscal Federalism Framework for Financing Infrastructure." Paper presented to the 2015 State of the Federation Conference, Queen's University, Kingston, 4–6 June.

– 1999. *Canadian Tax Policy*, 3rd ed. Toronto: Canadian Tax Foundation.

Boardman, Anthony E., Matti Siemiatycki, and Aidan R. Vining. 2016. "The Theory and Evidence concerning Public–Private Partnerships in Canada and Elsewhere." SPP Research Papers 9(12), March. Calgary: School of Public Policy, University of Calgary.

Boardman, Anthony, and Aidan Vining. 2012. "The Political Economy of Public–Private Partnerships and Analysis of Their Social Value." *Annals of Public and Cooperative Economics* 88(2): 117–41. doi:10.1111/j.1467-8292.2012.00457.x.

Bojorques, F., É. Champagne, and F. Vaillancourt. 2009. "Federal Grants to Municipalities in Canada: Nature, Importance and Impact on Municipal Investments, from 1990 to 2005." *Canadian Public Administration* 52(3): 439–55.

Boothe, Paul. 2007. "Accrual Accounting in the Public Sector: Lessons for Developing Countries." In *Budgeting and Budgetary Institutions*, edited by A. Shah, 179–202. Washington, DC: World Bank.

Borge, Lars-Erik, and Jorn Rattso. 2003. "The Relationship between Costs and User Charges: The Case of a Norwegian Utility Service." CESifo Working Paper No. 1033, Munich.

Bourdeaux, Carolyn, and Mels de Zeeuw 2015. "Connecticut Fiscal Comparisons." In *Final Report of the Connecticut Tax Panel*, vol 2. Hartford: Connecticut General Assembly. https://www.cga.ct.gov/fin/.

Breguet, B., and F. Vaillancourt. 2008. "Montreal's Public Transit System: Institutions, Financing and Prospects." In *Managing and Financing Urban Public Transport Systems*, edited by G. Guess, 259–93. Budapest: Open Society Institute.

Breton, Albert. 1996. *Competitive Governments*. Cambridge, UK: Cambridge University Press.

British Columbia. Ministry of Community Services. 2006. *Primer on Regional Districts in British Columbia*. https://www.regionaldistrict.com/media/28095/Primer_on_Regional_Districts_in_BC.pdf.

– Ministry of Community, Sport, and Cultural Development. n.d. "Local Government Statistics." http://www.cscd.gov.bc.ca/lgd/infra/statistics_index.htm.

– Ministry of Transportation. 2003. "Guidelines for Tolling." http://www2.gov.bc.ca/assets/gov/driving-and-transportation/reports-and-reference/reports-and-studies/planning-strategy-economy/mot_guidelines_for_tolling.pdf.

Brodhead, John, Jesse Darling, and Sean Mullin. 2014. *Crisis and Opportunity: Time for a National Infrastructure Plan for Canada*. Canada 2020 Foundation. Ottawa, 1 October. http://canada2020.ca/crisis-opportunity-time-national-infrastructure-plan-canada/.

Brown, Janice W., Robert Pieplow, Roger Driskell, Stephen Gaj, Michael J. Garvin, Dusty Holcombe, Michael Saunders, Jeff Seiders Jr, and Art Smith. 2009. *Public–Private Partnerships for Highway Infrastructure: Capitalizing on International Experience. US Federal Highway Administration*. http://international.fhwa.dot.gov/pubs/pl09010/pl09010.pdf.

Brueckner, Jan. 2015. "Decentralized Road Investment and Pricing in a Congested, Multi-Jurisdictional City: Efficiency with Spillovers." *National Tax Journal* 68(35): 839–54.

Brunori, David. 2012. "State Corporate Income Taxes." In *The Oxford Handbook of State and Local Government Finance*, edited by Robert D. Ebel and John E. Petersen, 333–51. Oxford and New York: Oxford University Press.

Brys, Bert. 2011. "Making Fundamental Tax Reform Happen." OECD Taxation Working Paper, No. 3.

Buchanan J. 1968. *The Demand and Supply of Public Good*. Chicago: Rand McNally.

Cairns, Stephanie, Pomme Arros, and Sara Jane O'Neill. 2016. *Incenting the Nature of Cities: Using Financial Approaches to Support Green Infrastructure in Ontario*. Toronto: Metcalf Foundation, May.

Canadian Municipal Water Consortium. 2015. "2015 Canadian Municipal Water Consortium Report: Section 2: Full Cost Recovery and Comparative Rate Structures." pp. 16–23. http://www.cwn-rce.ca/assets/resources/pdf/2015-Municipal-Priorities-Report/2015-Canadian-Municipal-Water-Consortium-Report-web.pdf?

Carratini, Stefano, Andrea Baranzi, and Rafael Lalive. 2016. "Is Taxing Waste a Waste of Time? Evidence from a Supreme Court Decision." Grantham Research Institute on Climate Change and the Environment, Working Paper No. 227, February.

CBC. 2015. "Bridge and Tunnel Tolling Plan Discriminates against Parts of Metro Vancouver, Mayor Says." http://www.cbc.ca/news/canada/british-columbia/bridge-and-tunnel-toll-would-discriminate-against-parts-of-metro-vancouver-says-dnv-mayor-1.3302228.

CCMF. 2007. Conference of the Cantonal Ministres of Finances, Swiss Harmonized Public Accounting System HPAS (*Modèle comptable harmonisé pour les cantons et les communes* MCH2) Berne. http://www.srs-cspcp.ch/en/ham2-n116.

City of Montreal. 2015. *Bilan 2014. Usage de l'eau potable*. Rapport annuel, Service de l'eau.

City of Toronto. 2015. "Report on Sections 37 and 45(9), Community Bene-
    fits Secured in 2013 and 2014." Staff Report to Planning and Growth
    Management Committee. Toronto, 31 August. http://www.toronto.ca
    /legdocs/mmis/2015/pg/bgrd/backgroundfile-83196.pdf.

City of Vancouver. 2016. *2015 Annual Report on Community Amenity Contri-
    butions and Density Bonusing.* Report to Vancouver City Council. Vancou-
    ver, 31 May, 2016. http://council.vancouver.ca/20160531/documents
    /a1.pdf

City of Victoria. 2016. *Animal Control and Licences.* http://www.victoria.ca/EN
    /main/city/bylaw-enforcement/animal-control.html.

Clark, David Allen. 2016. FY *2017 Department of Transportation Funding
    Streams.* Washington, DC: Office of the Chief Financial Officer of the Dis-
    trict of Columbia, 7 June.

Clayton, Frank. 2014. *A New Direction for Funding Growth-Related Water and
    Waste Water Infrastructure in the Greater Toronto Area and Hamilton.* Centre
    for Urban Research and Land Development (CUR), Ryerson University,
    Toronto.

College Board. 2016. *Trends in College Pricing, 2016.* New York: College Board.

Commerce Clearing House (CCH). 2015. *State Tax Handbook.* Chicago:
    Wolters Kluwer.

Congdon, William J., Jeffrey R. Kling, and Sendhil Mullainathan. 2011. *Policy
    and Choice: Public Finance through the Lens of Behavioral Economics.* Wash-
    ington, DC: Brookings Institution Press.

Conger, Brian, and Almos Tassonyi. 2016. "Financing Municipal Infrastruc-
    ture: The Basics." *Plan Canada* 56(2): 18–21.

Cory, Ehren. 2016. "Modern Public Infrastructure Project Delivery." *ReNew
    Magazine.* http://renewcanada.net/2016/modern-public-infrastructure-
    project-delivery/.

Cowan, S. 2010. "The Welfare Economics of Optional Water Metering."
    Economic Journal 120(545): 800–15.

Cruz, Carlos Oliveira, and Rui Cunha Marques. 2013. "Endogenous Determi-
    nants for Renegotiating Concessions: Evidence from Local Infrastructure."
    Local Government Studies 39(3): 352–74. doi:10.1080/03003930.2013
    .783476.

Curry, Bill. 2015. "Canadian Cities Lobby Ottawa for Increase in Public Tran-
    sit Funds." *Globe and Mail*, 30 March.

– 2016. "Infrastructure Plan May Include Tolls, Fees." *Globe and Mail*, 3 No-
    vember, p. 1.

Dachis, Benjamin. 2016. *Getting More Buildings for Our Bucks: Canadian Infra-
    structure Policy in 2016.* Toronto: C.D. Howe Institute. https://www

.cdhowe.org/sites/default/files/attachments/research_papers/mixed/
e-brief_225.pdf.

Dachis, Benjamin, and William B. Robson. 2015. *Building Better Budgets:
Canada's Cities Should Clean Up Their Financial Reporting. Commentary.*
Toronto: C.D. Howe Institute.

Dafflon, Bernard. 1998. *La gestion des finances publiques locales.* Paris:
Economica.

– 2006. "Real Property Management in the Swiss Communes." In *Managing
Government Property Assets: International Experiences*, edited by O. Kaganova
and J. McKellar, 201–30. Washington, DC: Urban Institute Press.

– 2009. "Les structures d'accueil de la petite enfance: une lecture du point de
vue de l'économie politique." In GIS-GRALE-CNRS, *L'action sociale des
collectivités locales, droit et gestion des collectivités territoriales*, 169–200. Paris:
Éditions Le Moniteur.

– 2010. "Local Debt: From Budget Responsibility to Fiscal Discipline." In
Forum, IEB's World Report on Fiscal Federalism 10, edited by N. Bosh and A.
Sollé Ollé. Barcelona. http://www.ieb.ub.edu/en/2012022056/fiscal-
federalism.

– 2013. *L'économie politique et la gestion territorial des services
environnementaux.* Agence Française de Développement, Document de
Travail 135, June.

– 2014. *Panorama des impôts en Suisse, du local au fédéral, entre équité et
concurrence: quels enjeux?* Éditions Domaine Public. www.domaine
public.ch.

– 2015. "Charging for Local Services: Why and How? A Critical Assessment
of Swiss Practices in the Last Two Decades." In *Interaction between Local
Expenditure Responsibilities and Local Tax Policy*, edited by J. Kim and
J. Lotz, 141–66. Seoul: Korea Institute of Public Finance/Copenhagen:
Danish Ministry of Social Welfare.

Dafflon, Bernard, and Sandra Daguet. 2012. "Local Environmental User
Charges in Switzerland: Implementation and Performance," *EuroEconomica*
5(31): 75–87.

Dafflon, Bernard, and François Vaillancourt. 2017. "Financement des
infrastructures et relations inter entités: pratiques internationales,
principes et réflexions sur le cas canadien." In *Le Québec économique*, edited
by Marcelin Joanis, 213–40. Quebec: Presses de l'Université Laval.

Dahlby, Bev, and Emily Jackson. 2015. "Striking the Right Balance:
Federal Infrastructure Transfer Porgrams, 2002–2015." SPP Research
Papers 8(36) (November). Calgary: School of Public Policy, University of
Calgary.

Dahlby, Bev, and Michael Smart. 2015. *The Structure and Presentation of Provincial Budgets* 8(25). Calgary: University of Calgary, School of Public Policy.

Dannin, Ellen, and Lee Cokorins. 2012. "Infrastructure Privatization in the New Millennium." In *The Oxford Handbook and State and Local Government Finance*, edited by Robert D. Ebel and John E. Petersen, 427–755. Oxford and New York: Oxford University Press.

Davis, Lance E., Jonathan R.T. Hughes, and Duncan McDougall. 1969. *American Economic History: The Development of a National Economy*, 3rd ed. Homewood, IL: Richard D. Irwin.

De, Indranil, and Tirthankar Nag. 2016. "Dangers of Decentralisation in Urban Slums: A Comparative Study of Water Supply and Drainage Service Delivery in Kolkata, India." *Development Policy Review* 34(2): 253–76.

De Mello, Luis, and Douglas Sutherland. 2016. "Financing Infrastructure." In *Decentralization and Infrastructure in the Global Economy: From Gaps to Solutions*, edited by Jonas Frank and Jorge Martinez-Vazquez, 146–70. New York: Routledge.

de Palma, A. and R. Lindsey. 2011. "Traffic Congestion Pricing Methodologies and Technologies." *Transportation Research Part C: Emerging Technologies* 19(6): 1377–99.

Dewees, Donald, N. 2002. "Pricing Municipal Services: The Economics of User Fees." *Canadian Tax Journal* 50(2): 586–99.

– 2012. "What Is Happening to Ontario Electricity Prices?" Sustainable Prosperity SP Background Paper, University of Ottawa.

Downing, Paul B. 1999. "User Charges, Impact Fees, and Service Charges." In *Handbook on Taxation*, edited by W. Bartley Hildreth and James A. Richardson, 239–62. New York: Marcel Dekker.

Drummond, Don, Chair of the Commission on the Reform of Ontario's Public Services. "Public Services for Ontarians: A Path to Sustainability and Excellence," 2012. http://www.fin.gov.on.ca/en/reformcommission/chapters/report.pdf.

Dupont, Diane P., and Steven Renzetti. 2001. "The Role of Water in Manufacturing." *Environmental and Resource Economics* 18(4): 411–32.

Dupont, Diane P., Steven Renzetti, et al. 2013. "Liquid Assets: Assessing Water's Contribution to Niagara." Niagara Region and Brock University. 80 pp. https://www.niagararegion.ca/living/water/pdf/NR-Liquid-Assets-Paper-2013-FINAL.pdf.

Eagles, Paul F.J. 2014. "Fiscal Implications of Moving to Tourism Finance for Parks: Ontario Provincial Parks." *Managing Leisure* 19(1): 1–17.

Ebel, Robert D., John E. Petersen, and Ha T.T. Vu. 2013. "The Great Recession:

Impacts and Outlook for US State and Local Finance. *Municipal Research Journal* (Spring /Summer): 33–77.

Elgie, Stewart, Michelle Brownlee, Sarah Jane O'Neill, and Mercedes Marcano. 2016. "Pricing Works: How Pricing of Municipal Services and Infrastructure Can Lead to Healthier and More Efficient Cities." Green Prosperity Papers, Metcalf Foundation. http://metcalffoundation.com/stories/publications/pricing-works/.

Engel, Eduardo, Ronald Fischer, and Alexander Galetovic. 2011. "Public–Private Partnerships to Revamp US Infrastructure." Discussion Paper 2011-02. Brookings Institution.

Environment Canada. 1991–2009. *Municipal Water and Waste Water Survey*. Ottawa, selected years from 1991 to 2009.

– 2011. *2011 Municipal Water Pricing Report*. Ottawa.

European PPP Expertise Centre. 2010. "Eurostat Treatment of Public–Private Partnerships." http://www.eib.org/epec/resources/epec-eurostat-statistical-treatment-of-ppps.pdf.

Farish, Kelly, I.E. 2006. "When Is a User Fee Actually a User Fee? Design and Implementation Challenges Faced by Canadian Municipalities." Master's thesis, University of Victoria, Victoria, BC. https://dspace.library.uvic.ca:8443/bitstream/handle/1828/3917/Farish_Kelly_MPA_2012.pdf?sequence=5&isAllowed=y.

Farish, Kelly, and Lindsay M. Tedds. 2014. "User Fee Design by Canadian Municipalities: Considerations Arising from the Case Law." *Canadian Tax Journal* 62(3): 635–70.

Federation of Canadian Municipalities (FCM). 2012. *Canadian Infrastructure Report Card*, vol. 1: *2012 Municipal Roads and Water Systems*. Ottawa: FCM.

Fenn, Michael. 2016. *Megatrends: The Impact of Infrastructure on Ontario's and Canada's Future*. Report prepared for Residential and Civil Construction Alliance of Ontario.

Fenn, Michael, and Harry Kitchen. 2016. *Bringing Sustainability to Ontario's Water Systems: A Quarter-Century of Progress, with Much Left to Do*. Study for the Ontario Sewer and Watermain Construction Association.

Finkelstein, Amy. 2009. "E-Z Tax: Tax Salience and Tax Rates." *Quarterly Journal of Economics* 124(3): 969–1010.

Fisher, Ronald C. 2016. *State and Local Public Finance*. 4th ed. London and New York: Routledge.

Fisher, Ronald C., and Robert W. Wassmer. 2015. "Analysis of State and Local Government Capital Expenditure During the 2000s." *Public Budgeting and Finance* 35(1) (January): 3–28.

– 2016. "Naming Rights as a State Revenue Generator." *State Tax Notes* (13 June).

Flyvbjerg, Bent, Nils Bruzelius, and Werner Rothengatter. 2003. *Megaprojects and Risk: An Anatomy of Ambition.* New York: Cambridge University Press.

Fortin, Michael, and Bruce Mitchell.1990. *Water and Waste Water Charges for Ontario: The User Pay Principle.* A report prepared for the Ontario Sewer and Watermain Construction Association.

Fougère, Danny. 2004. *L'approvisionnement en eau à Montreal: du privé au public, 1796–1865,* Quebec: Septentrion.

Found, Adam. 2016. *Tapping the Land: Tax Increment Financing of Infrastructure.* E-Brief. Toronto: C.D. Howe Institute.

Fox, William F. 2015. "Connecticut General Sales Taxation." In *Final Report of the Connecticut Tax Panel,* vol. 2, chapter 9, edited by Michael E. Bell and Robert D. Ebel. Hartford: Connecticut General Assembly. https://www.cga .ct.gov/fin.

Fox, William F., and Matthew Murray. 2016. "The Challenge of Operating and Maintaining Infrastructure." In *Decentralization and Infrastructure in the Global Economy: From Gaps to Solutions,* edited by Jonas Frank and Jorge Martinez-Vazquez, 305–23. New York: Routledge.

Frank, Jonas, and Jorge Martinez-Vazquez, eds. 2016. *Decentralization and Infrastructure in the Global Economy: From Gaps to Solutions.* New York: Routledge.

French, Robert, and Philip Oreopoulos. 2015. "Applying Behavioral Economics to Public Policy in Canada." NBER Working Paper 23671, September.

Fullerton, Don. 1996. "Why Have Separate Environmental Taxes?" In *Tax Policy and the Economy,* vol. 10, edited by James Poterba, 33–70. Cambridge, MA: MIT Press.

Gais, Thomas, Donald Boyd, and Lucy Dadayan. 2012. "The Social Safety Net, Health Care, and the Great Recession." In *The Oxford Handbook and State and Local Government Finance,* edited by Robert D. Ebel and John E. Petersen, 594–623. Oxford and New York: Oxford University Press.

Gardner, G. 1997. "Recycling Organic Waste." Worldwatch Paper 135. Washington, DC: Worldwatch Institute.

Garrett, Mark, and Brian Taylor. 1999. "Reconsidering Social Equity in Public Transit." *Berkeley Planning Journal* 13: 6–27.

Garvin, M., and Doran Bosso. 2008. "Assessing the Effectiveness of Infrastructure Public–Private Partnership Programs and Projects." *Public Works Management and Policy* 13: 162–78.

Geddes, Richard R. 2015. *America's Transportation Challenges: Proposals for Reform.* Washington, DC: American Enterprise Institute.

Gifford, Jonathan L. 2012. "Transportation Finance." In *The Oxford Handbook of State and Local Government Finance*, edited by Robert D. Ebel and John E. Petersen, 594–623. Oxford and New York: Oxford University Press.

Glaeser, Edward, Scott Duke Kominers, Michael Luca, and Nikhil Naik. 2015. "Big Data and Big Cities: The Promises and Limitation of Improved Measures of Urban Life." NBER Working Paper 21778, December.

Glowacki, Monika. 2016. *Nudging Cities: Innovating with Behavioral Science*. http://datasmart.ash.harvard.edu/news/article/nudging-cities-innovating-with-behavioral-science-833.

Gooch, Daniel-Robert. 2016. "Our Airport System Already Flies on Its Own, with a Few Exceptions." *Globe and Mail*, 9 September, B4.

Gordon, Tracy, Richard Auxier, and John Iselin. 2016. *Assessing the Fiscal Capacities of the States*. Washington, DC: Urban Institute.

Government of Canada. 2016. *Fall Economic Statement 2016: Chapter 2 – Investing in the New Economy*. http://www.budget.gc.ca/fes-eea/2016/docs/statement-enonce/chap02-en.html.

Government of Quebec. 2011. *Stratégie québécoise d'économie d'eau potable*
– 2015. *Rapport sur le coût et les sources de revenu des services d'eau*. Stratégie québécoise d'économie d'eau potable.
– 2016. *Rapport annuel de l'usage de l'eau potable 2014*. Stratégie québécoise d'économie d'eau potable.

Graham, Steven, and Simon Marvin. 2001 *Splintering Urbanism*. London: Routledge.

Gramlich, Edward. 1994. "Infrastructure Investment: A Review Essay." *Journal of Economic Literature* 32(3): 1176–96.

Graser, Dina, and Pamela Robinson. 2016. "A Recipe for Fiscal Trust." University of Toronto, IMFG Perspectives 13. Toronto: IMFG, Munk School of Global Affairs, University of Toronto.

Grimsey, Darrin, and Mervyn Lewis. 2004. *Public Private Partnerships*. Cheltenham, UK: Edward Elgar.

Grush, Bern. 2013. "Reduce, Rethink, Reform." *Thinking Cities* 1(1): 132–7. http://www.polisnetwork.eu/uploads/Modules/PublicDocuments/thinking-cities-issue-1-web.pdf.

Guasch, J. Luis. 2004. *Granting and Renegotiating Infrastructure Concessions*. Washington, DC: World Bank Institute of Development Studies.

Gulyani, Sumila. 2005. "Willingness to Pay for Public Services." In *Encyclopedia of Taxation and Tax Policy*, edited by Joseph C. Cordes, Robert D. Ebel, and Jane G. Gravelle, 471–2. Washington, DC: Urban Institute.

Haider, Murtaza, and Liam Donaldson. 2016. "Can Tax Increment Financing

Support Transportation Infrastructure Investment?" IMFG Paper 25. Toronto: IMFG, Munk School of Global Affairs, University of Toronto.

Hall, Joshua C., Joshua Matti, and Yang Zhou. 2016. "Regionalization and Consolidation of Municipal Taxes and Services." Working Paper No. 16-20. West Virginia University, Department of Economics.

Hamel, Pierre J. 2012. "Remettre en question les compteurs d'eau domestique." Colloque "Le service public d'eau potable à l'épreuve du développement durable." Grenoble.

Hanniman, Kyle. 2015. "A Good Crisis: Canadian Municipal Credit Conditions after the Lehman Brothers Bankruptcy." IMFG Paper 22. Toronto: IMFG, Munk School of Global Affairs, University of Toronto.

Harberger, Arnold C. 1962. "The Incidence of the Corporation Income Tax." *Journal of Political Economy* 70 (3): 215–40.

Heim, Carol E. 2015. "Who Pays, Who Benefits, Who Decides? Urban Infrastructure in Nineteenth-Century Chicago and Twentieth-Century Phoenix." *Social Science History* 39 (3): 453–82.

Henchman, Joseph. 2013. *How Is the Money Used? Federal and State Cases Distinguishing between Taxes and Fees.* Background Paper No. 66. Washington, DC: Tax Foundation, March.

Henstra, Daniel, and Jason Thistlethwaite. 2017. "Climate Change, Municipal Floods and Risk Sharing in Canada." IMFG Paper 30. Toronto: IMFG, Munk School of Global Affairs, University of Toronto.

Hirsch, W.Z. 1959. "Expenditure Implications of Metropolitan Growth and Consolidation." *Review of Economics and Statistics* 41(3): 232–41.

Hodge, Graeme, and Carsten Greve. 2010. "Public–Private Partnerships: Governance Scheme or Language Game?" *Australian Journal of Public Administration* 69: S8–S22. doi:10.1111/j.1467-8500.2009.00659.x.

Infrastructure Canada. 2016. *Building Strong Cities through Investments in Public Transit.* http://www.infrastructure.gc.ca/plan/ptif-fitc-eng.phpL.

Jacobs, Alan M., and J. Scott Matthews. 2015. "Policy Attitudes in Institutional Context: Rules, Uncertainty, and the Mass Politics of Public Investment." *American Journal of Political Science.* doi:10.111/ajps.12209.

Johansson, Asa, Christopher Heady, Jens Arnold, Bert Brys, and Laura Vartia. 2008. "Tax and Economic Growth." OECD Economics Department Working Paper No. 620, July.

Johnson, Lisa, and Tamra Baluja. 2015. "Transit Referendum: Voters Say No to New Metro Vancouver Tax, Transit Improvements." CBC News. 3 July. http://www.cbc.ca/news/canada/british-columbia/transit-referendum-voters-say-no-to-new-metro-vancouver-tax-transit-improvements-1.3134857.

Kaganova, O., and J. McKellar, eds. 2006. *Managing Government Property Assets: International Experiences*. Washington, DC: Urban Institute Press.

Kelleher, Maria, Janet Robins, and John Dixie. 2005. "Taking Out the Trash: How to Allocate the Costs Fairly." *Commentary*. Toronto: C.D. Howe Institute.

Kessides, Christine. 1993. "Institutional Options for the Provision of Infrastructure." World Bank Discussion Paper 212.

Kim, Julie. 2016. "Handbook on Urban Infrastructure Finance." New Cities Foundation. www.newcitiesfoundation.org/wp-content/uploads/2016/03/PDF.

Kim, J., and J. Lotz, eds. 2015. *Interaction between Local Expenditure Responsibilities and Local Tax Policy*. Seoul: Korea Institute of Public Finance/ Copenhagen: Danish Ministry of Social Welfare.

Kitchen, Harry. 2003. "Physical Infrastructure and Financing." Paper prepared for the Panel on the Role of Government in Ontario.

– 2006a. *A State of Disrepair: How to Fix the Financing of Municipal Infrastructure in Canada. Commentary*. Toronto: C.D. Howe Institute.

– 2006b. "Municipal Infrastructure Financing: A Prescription for the Future." Paper prepared for Infrastructure Canada, Ottawa. http://www.trentu.ca/economics/WorkingPaper/Kitchen_060206.pdf.

– 2007. "Financing Water and Sewer Systems in the GTA: What Should Be Done?" Report prepared for the Residential and Civil Construction Alliance of Ontario. www.rccao.com.

– 2010. "Principles and Best Practices for Funding, Financing, and Cost Sharing Metro Vancouver's Municipal Services." Discussion paper completed for Metro Vancouver.

– 2013. "Canadian Municipalities and the Recent Recession: What Have We Learned?" www.trentu.ca/economics/papers.php.

– 2015. "No Seniors' Specials: Financing Municipal Services in Aging Communities." IRPP Study 51, February. Montreal: Institute for Research on Public Policy.

Kitchen, Harry, and Robin Lindsey. 2013. "Financing Roads and Public Transit in the Greater Toronto and Hamilton Area." Report for the Residential and Civil Construction Alliance of Ontario. www. rccao.com.

Kitchen, Harry, and Enid Slack. 2016. "More Taxes for Canada's Largest Cities: Why, What, and How?" IMFG Paper 27. Toronto: IMFG, Munk School of Global Affairs, University of Toronto.

Kitchen, Harry, and Almos Tassonyi. 2012. "Municipal Taxes and User Fees." In *Tax Policy in Canada*, edited by Heather Kerr, Ken McKenzie, and Jack Mintz, 9: 1-9-34. Toronto: Canadian Tax Foundation.

Kneebone, Ron, and Ken McKenzie. 2003. "Removing the Shackles: Some Modest and Immodest Proposals to Pay for Cities." In *Paying for Cities*, edited by Paul Boothe, 43–77. Edmonton: Institute of Public Economics, University of Alberta.

LAC and Associates. 2015. "City of Ottawa – Water and Waste Water Rate Review Study," Annex 2.

Lassen, David Dreyer, and Soren Serritzlew. 2011. "Jurisdiction Size and Local Democracy: Evidence on Internal Political Efficacy from Large-Scale Municipal Reform." *American Political Science Review* 105(2): 238–58.

Lauzon, Léo-Paul, François Patenaude, and Martin Poirier. 1997. *La privatisation de l'eau au Quebec, 2e partie: Le cas de Montréal et du Québec.* https://unites.uqam.ca/cese/pdf/rec_97_privatisation_eau.pdf.

Le Blanc, David. 2007. *Providing Water to the Urban Poor in Developing Countries: The Role of Tariffs and Subsidies*, United Nations, Department of Economic and Social Affairs, Sustainable Development Innovation Briefs, Issue 4, October.

Leiringer, Roine. 2006. "Technological Innovation in PPPs: Incentives, Opportunities and Actions." *Construction Management and Economics* 24(3): 301–8.

Lejour, Arjan. 2016. "The Political Economy of Tax Reforms." Netherlands Bureau for Economic Policy Analysis, CPB Policy Brief/2-16/08.

Lenti, Erica. 2016. "Nope There's Still Not Enough Money to Fund Regional Transit Projects." *Torontoist*, 16 August 2016. http://torontoist.com/2016 /08/nope-theres-still-not-enough-money-to-fund-regional-transit-projects/.

Lindahl, Erik. 1958. "Positiv Losung, Die Gerechtigkeit der Besteurung (1919)." Translated as "Just Taxation – A Positive Solution." In *Classics in the Theory of Public Finance*, edited by Richard A. Musgrave and Alan T. Peacock, 168–76. New York: St Martin's Press.

Loxley, John. 2012. "Public–Private Partnerships after the Global Financial Crisis: Ideology Trumping Economic Reality." *Studies in Political Economy* 89: 7–37. doi:10.1080/19187033.2012.11674999.

Manahan, Andy. 2010a. "Presentation to the Standing Committee on General Government on Bill 72: The Ontario Water Opportunities and Water Conservation Act, 2010." Residential and Civil Construction Alliance of Ontario, Vaughan, ON.

– 2010b. "Will Patience Be Rewarded?" *WaterCanada.Net*, March/April.

Marlow, Justin. 2012. "Capital Budgeting and Spending." In *The Oxford Handbook of State and Local Government Finance*, edited by Robert D. Ebel and John E. Petersen, 658–81. Oxford and New York: Oxford University Press.

Martinez-Vazquez, Jorge, and Andrey Timofeev. 2016. "Capital Infrastructure and Equity Objectives in Decentralized Systems." In *Decentralization and Infrastructure in the Global Economy: From Gaps to Solutions*, edited by Jonas Frank and Jorge Martinez-Vazquez, 171–215. New York: Routledge.

Mayer, Andre. 2011. "Canada Lags in Use of Road Tolls." CBC *News*, 21 November. http://www.cbc.ca/news/canada/canada-lags-in-use-of-road-tolls-1.1012628

McHardie, Daniel. 2011. "Highway Transforms into 'a Poisoned Chalice.'" CBC *News*. http://www.cbc.ca/news/canada/new-brunswick/highway-transforms-into-a-poisoned-chalice-1.1041422.

McNichol, Elizabeth C. 2016. "It's Time for the States to Invest in Infrastructure." Washington, DC: Center on Budget and Policy Priorities, 23 February.

Meloche, Jean-Philippe. 2017. "Les infrastructures québécoises et leur poids dans les finances publiques." In *Le Québec économique*, edited by Marcelin Joanis, 113–39. Quebec: Presses de l'Université Laval.

Meloche, Jean-Philippe, François Vaillancourt, and Stéphanie Boulenger. 2016. "Le financement des municipalités du Quebec: comparaisons interjuridictions et éléments d'analyses." CIRANO. https://www.cirano.qc.ca/files/publications/2016RP-13.pdf.

Meltsner, Arnold J. 1971. *The Politics of City Revenue.* Berkeley: University of California Press.

Metro Vancouver. 2017. *2017 Budget in Brief.* http://www.metrovancouver.org/about/programs-budget/BudgetPublications/2017BudgetinBrief.pdf.

Miller, Sebastian, and Riley Wilson. 2015. *Parking Taxes as a Second Best Congestion Pricing Mechanism.* Inter-American Development Bank IDB – WP-614, October.

Mirrlees James et al. 2010. *Dimensions of Tax Design: The Mirrlees Review.* Oxford: Oxford University Press.

– 2011. *Tax by Design: The Mirrlees Review.* Oxford: Oxford University Press.

Montreal Economic Institute. 2003. "The Pros and Cons of Public Service User Fees." *Economic Note.* December.

Moore, Aaron. 2013. "Trading Density for Benefits: Section 37 Agreements in Toronto." IMFG Papers 13. Toronto: IMFG, Munk School of Global Affairs, University of Toronto.

Morrow, Adrian, and Tom Cardoso. 2017. "Ontario Power Play," *Globe and Mail,* 9 January, A8–A9.

Munnell, Alicia H., and Leah M. Cook. 1991. "Financing Capital Expenditures in Massachusetts," *Federal Reserve Bank of Boston New England Economic Review* (March/April): 3–29.

Musgrave, Richard A. 2005. "Fairness in Taxation." In *The Encyclopedia of Taxation and Tax Policy*, edited by Joseph C. Cordes, Robert D. Ebel, and Jane G. Gravelle, 137–8. Washington, DC: Urban Institute.

Mushkin, Selma J. 1972. "Designing a Credit Card Experiment." In *Public Prices for Public Products*, edited by Selma Mushkin, 407–8. Washington, DC: Urban Institute.

Mushkin, Selma J., and Richard M. Bird. 1972. "Public Prices: An Overview." In *Public Prices for Public Products*, edited by Selma Mushkin, 3–26. Washington, DC: Urban Institute.

National Council on Public Works Improvement (NCPWI). 1988. *Fragile Foundations*. Washington, DC: US Government Printing Office.

Nauges, Ulbrich Celine, and Caroline van den Berg. 2008. "Spatial Heterogeneity in the Cost Structure of Water and Sanitation Services: A Cross-Country Comparison of Conditions for Scale Economies." www.research gate.net/profile/Caroline_Berg/.

Netzer, Dick. 1992. "Differences in Reliance on User Charges by American State and Local Governments." *Public Finance Quarterly* 20(4) (October): 499–511.

Novaresi N. 2001. "Discipline budgétaire: étude de l'influence du référendum financier et des règles d'équilibre budgétaire sur les finances publiques des vingt-six cantons." PhD thesis, BENEFRI, Centre d'étude en économie du secteur public, Université de Fribourg, Suisse.

O'Connor, The Honourable Dennis R., Commissioner. 2002. *Part Two Report of the Walkerton Inquiry: A Strategy for Safe Drinking Water*. Toronto: Queen's Printer for Ontario. http://www.attorneygeneral.jus.gov.on.ca /english/about/pubs/walkerton/ and http://www.attorneygeneral.jus.gov .on.ca/english/about/pubs/walkerton/part2/Chapter_2.pdf.

OECD. 1998. *Household Water Pricing in OECD Countries*. Environmental Policy Committee, Paris, unclassified ENV/EPO/GEEI (98)12/FINAL. This is the updated version of the 1987 study.

– 2009. "Alternative Ways of Providing Water: Emerging Options and Their Policy Implications." Advance copy for 5th World Water Forum. www.oecd.org/env/resources/42349741.pdf.

– 2010. *Pricing Water Resources and Water and Sanitation Services*. Paris: OECD.

– 2015. *Revenue Statistics 1965–2014*. Paris: OECD Print.

Olmstead, S.M., and R.N. Stavins. 2009. "Comparing Price and Nonprice Approaches to Urban Water Conservation." *Water Resources Research* 45(4): 1–10.

Olson, M. 1965. *The Logic of Collective Action, Public Goods and the Theory of Groups* Cambridge, UK: Cambridge University Press.

Ontario Institute for Competitiveness and Prosperity. 2015. "Better Foundation: The Returns on Infrastructure Investment in Ontario." Working Paper 22.

Ontario Ministry of Infrastructure. 2016. *BuildingTogether – Guide for Municipal Asset Management Plans.* Toronto: Queen's Printer for Ontario. https://www.ontario.ca/page/building-together-guide-municipal-asset-management-plans.

Orszag, Peter R. 2008. "Investing In Infrastructure." Testimony before the Committee on Finance, United State Senate. Washington: Congressional Budget Office (CBO), 10 July.

Ostrom, Elinor. 1972. "Metropolitan Reform: Propositions Derived from Two Traditions." *Social Science Quarterly* 53(3): 474–93.

– 1990. *Governing the Commons: The Evolution of Institutions for Collective Action*. Cambridge, UK: Cambridge University Press.

O'Toole, Megan. 2012. Dalton McGuinty Dubs New $1B Highway 407 Extension 'the People's Highway." *National Post*. http://news.nationalpost.com/news/canada/dalton-mcguinty-dubs-new-1b-highway-407-extension-the-peoples-highway.

Parry, I.W.H., and K.A. Small. 2009. "Should Urban Transit Subsidies Be Reduced?" *American Economic Review* 99(3): 700–24.

Pearl, David. 2016. "The Policy and Politics of Reform of the Australian Goods and Services Tax." *Asia and the Pacific Policy Studies* 3(3): 405–11.

Pollock, Allyson, Jean Shaoul, and Neil Vickers. 2002. "Private Finance and 'Value for Money' in NHS Hospitals: A Policy in Search of a Rationale?" *British Medical Association Journal* 324(7347): 1205–9. doi:10.1136/bmj.324.7347.1205.

Raimi, Lukman, Adeniyi Fadipe, and Morufu Shokunbi. 2015. "Responsible Investment: An Alternative Funding Option for Roads-Bridges Management in Nigeria under the Public–Private Partnership Framework." *Journal of Economic Behavior* 5(1): 43–57.

Regan, Michael, Jim Smith, and Peter Love. 2010. "Impact of the Capital Market Collapse on Public–Private Partnership Infrastructure Projects." *Journal of Construction Engineering and Management* 137(1): 6–15.

Renzetti, Steven. 1999. "Municipal Water Supply and Sewage Treatment: Costs, Prices and Distortions." *Canadian Journal of Economics* 32(3) (May): 688–704.

– 2009. "Wave of the Future: The Case for Smarter Water Policy," *Commentary*. C.D. Howe Institute, Toronto.

Renzetti, Steven, and Joseph Kushner. 2001. "The Under Pricing of Water Supply and Sewage Treatment." Mimeograph, Economics Department, Brock University.

Reynaud, Arnaud, Steven Renzetti, and Michel Villeneuve. 2005. "Pricing Structure Choices and Residential Water Demand in Canada." *Canadian Water Resources Journal* 41(11): 1110–24.

Richardson, Pearl. 2005. "User Charges, Federal." In The *Encyclopedia of Taxation and Tax Policy*, edited by Joseph C. Cordes, Robert D. Ebel, and Jane G. Gravelle, 456–8. Washington, DC: Urban Institute.

Roumboutsos, Athena, and Stephane Saussier. 2014. "Public–Private Partnerships and Investments in Innovation: The Influence of the Contractual Arrangement." *Construction Management and Economics* 32(4): 349–61. doi:10.1080/01446193.2014.895849.

Schwarz, Norbert, Eryn Newman, and William Leach. 2016. "Making the Truth Stick and the Myths Fade: Lessons from Cognitive Psychology." https://behavioralpolicy.org/article/making-the-truth-stick-the-myths-fade-lessons-from-cognitive-psychology/.

Serebrisky, Tomas, Andres Gomez-Lobo, Nicolas Estupinan, and Ramon Munoz-Raskin. 2009. "Affordability and Subsidies in Public Urban Transport: What Do We Mean, What Can Be Done?" *Transport Reviews* 29(6): 715–39.

Shaoul, Jean, Anne Stafford, and Pamela Stapleton. 2006. "Highway Robbery? A Financial Analysis of Design, Build, Finance and Operate (DBFO) in UK Roads." *Transport Reviews* 26(3): 257–74. doi:10.1080/01441640500415243.

Sheffrin, Steven M. 2013. *Tax Fairness and Folk Justice.* Cambridge, UK: Cambridge University Press.

Shoup, Donald C. 2006. "Cruising for Parking." *Transport Policy* 13: 479–86.

Siemiatycki, Matti. 2006. "Message in a Metro – Building Urban Rail Infrastructure and Image in Delhi India." *International Journal of Urban and Regional Research* 30(2): 277–92. doi:10.1111/j.1468-2427.2006.00664.x.

– 2010. "Delivering Transportation Infrastructure through Public–Private Partnerships: Planning Concerns." *Journal of the American Planning Association* 76: 43–58. doi:10.1080/01944360903329295.

– 2011. "Urban Transportation Public–Private Partnerships: Drivers of Uneven Development?" *Environment and Planning A* 43: 1707–22. doi:10.1068/a43572.

– 2015. Reflections on Twenty Years of Public–Private Partnerships in Canada. *Canadian Public Administration* 58(3): 343–62. doi:10.1111/capa.12119.

– 2016. *Creating an Effective Canadian Infrastructure Bank*. Report prepared for the Residential and Civil Construction Alliance of Ontario. Vaughan, Ontario.

Siemiatycki, Matti, and Jonathan Friedman. 2012. "The Trade-Offs of Transferring Demand Risk on Urban Transit Public–Private Partnerships." *Public Works Management and Policy* 17(3): 283–302. doi:10.1177/1087724X 12436993.

Sjoquist, David L. 2015. "Diversifying Municipal Revenue in Connecticut." In *Final Report of the Connecticut Tax Panel*, vol. 3. Hartford: Connecticut General Assembly. https://www.cga.ct.gov/fin/.

Sjoquist, David L., and Rayna Stoycheva. 2012. "Local Revenue Diversification: User Charges, Sales Taxes and Income Taxes. In *The Oxford Handbook of State and Local Government Finance*, edited by Robert D. Ebel and John E. Petersen, 406–28. Oxford and New York: Oxford University Press.

Slack, Enid. 2002. *Municipal Finance and the Pattern of Urban Growth. Commentary*. Toronto: C.D. Howe Institute.

– 2010. "Provincial–Local Transfers in Canada: Provincial Control Trumps Local Accountability." In *General Grants versus Earmarked Grants: Theory and Practice*, edited by Junghum Kim, Jorgen Lotz, and Niels Jorgen Mau, 318–44. Seoul: Korea Institute of Public Finance / Copenhagen: Danish Ministry of Interior and Health.

– 2015. "Local Finances and Fiscal Equalization Schemes in Comparative Perspective." In *Das Teilen beherrschen, Analysen zur Reform des Finanzausgleichs*, edited by R. Geibler, F. Knupling, S. Kropp, and J. Weiland, 283–312. Germany: Nomos.

Slack, Enid, and Richard M. Bird. 2013. "Does Municipal Amalgamation Strengthen the Financial Viability of Local Government? A Canadian Example." *Public Finance and Management* 13(2): 99–123.

– 2014. "The Political Economy of Property Tax Reform." OECD Working Papers on Fiscal Federalism No. 18, April.

– 2015. "Financing Regional Public Transit in Ontario: The Case for Strengthening the Wicksellian Connection." Paper presented to the 2015 State of the Federation Conference, Queen's University, Kingston, 4–6 June.

Slack, Enid, and Harry Kitchen. 2006. "Providing Public Services in Remote Areas." In *Perspectives on Fiscal Federalism*, edited by Richard M. Bird and Francois Vaillancourt, 123–39. Washington, DC: World Bank Institute.

Slack, Enid, Almos Tassonyi, and David Grad. 2015. "Fiscal Health of Ontario Large Cities: Is There Something to Worry About?" In *Is Your City Healthy? Measuring Urban Fiscal Health*, edited by Richard M. Bird and Enid Slack

Toronto: Institute on Municipal Finance and Governance, University of Toronto.

Small, Kenneth A., and Erik T. Verhoef. 2007. *The Economics of Urban Transportation*. New York: Routledge.

Smetanin, Paul, et al. 2014. *Ontario Infrastructure Investment: Federal and Provincial Risks and Rewards*. Commissioned by Residential and Civil Construction Alliance, Vaughan, ON, July 2014. 36 pp. http://www.rccao.com/news/files/RCCAO_Ontario-Infrastructure-Investment_July2014-WEB.pdf.

Smith, Adam. 1937 [1776]. *An Inquiry into the Nature and Causes of the Wealth of Nations*, edited by Edwin Cannan. New York: Modern Library.

Smith, Patrick J., and Kennedy Stewart. 2009. "British Columbia." In *Foundations of Governance: Municipal Government in Canada's Provinces*, edited by Andrew Sancton and Robert Young. Toronto: University of Toronto Press.

Soliño, Antonio, and Jose M. Vassallo. 2009. "Using Public–Private Partnerships to Expand Subways: Madrid-Barajas International Airport Case Study." *Journal of Management in Engineering* 25: 21–8.

Statistics Canada. 1988–2008. *Financial Management System*. Statistics Canada, catalogue no. 68F0023X. http://www5.statcan.gc.ca/olc-cel/olc.action?objId=68F0023X&objType=2&lang=en&limit=0.

– 2008–2014. *Government Finance Statistics*, table 385-0037.

– 2016. "Population by Year, by Province and Territory as of July 1, 2016" (table), CANSIM (database). Last updated 28 September 2016. http://www.statcan.gc.ca/tables-tableaux/sum-som/l01/cst01/demo02a-eng.htm.

Steinmo, Sven. 2016. "Historical Institutionalism and Experimental Methods." In *The Oxford Handbook of Historical Institutionalism*, edited by Tulia Falleti, Orfeo Fioretos, and Adam Sheingate, 1–19. Oxford: Oxford University Press.

Steiss, Alan Walter. *Local Government Finance: Capital Facilities Planning and Debt Administration*, 62. http://www-personal.umich.edu/~steiss/page 62.html.

Strategic Alternatives et al. 2001. "Financing Water Infrastructure." Issue Paper 14. Commissioned by the Walkerton Inquiry, Toronto.

Sun, Rui, and Changhoon Jung. 2012. "Does User-Charge Financing Reduced Expenditure Levels for the Charge-Financed Services?" *American Review of Public Administration* 42(2): 170–85.

Sunstein, C.R. 2014. "Nudging: A Very Short Guide." *Journal of Consumer Policy* 34(3): 583–8.

Swain, Harry, Fred Lazar, and Jim Pine. 2005. *Watertight: The Case for Change in Ontario's Water and Waste Water Sector*. Report of the Water Strategy Expert Panel. Queen's Printer for Ontario. 96 pp. http://www.probe international.org/EVfiles/Watertight-panel_report_EN.pdf.

Tassonyi, Almos T. 1997. "Financing Infrastructure in Canada's City-Regions." In *Urban Governance and Finance: A Question of Who Does What?* edited by Paul A.R. Hobson and France St-Hilaire, 171–200. Montreal: Institute for Research on Public Policy.

– 2002. "Municipal Budgeting." *Canadian Tax Journal* 50(1): 181–98.

Tassonyi, Almos T., and Brian W. Conger. 2015. "An Exploration into the Municipal Capacity to Finance Capital Infrastructure." SPP Research Papers 8 (38), November. Calgary: School of Public Policy, University of Calgary.

Thaler, Richard H. 2015. *Misbehaving: The Making of Behavioral Economics.* New York: W.W. Norton.

Thaler, Richard H., and Cass R. Sunstein. 2008. *Nudge: Improving Decisions about Health, Wealth, and Happiness.* New Haven, CT: Yale University Press.

Thirsk, Wayne R., and Richard M. Bird. 1994. "Earmarked Taxes in Ontario: Solution or Problem?" In *Taxing and Spending: Issues of Process*, edited by Allan M. Maslove, 129–84. Toronto: University of Toronto Press.

Thuronyi, Victor. 2005. "Tax." In *Encyclopedia of Taxation and Tax Policy*, edited by Joseph C. Cordes, Robert D. Ebel, and Jane G. Gravelle, 375. Washington, DC: Urban Institute.

Tiesman, Geert, and Erik.-Hans Klijn. 2002. "Partnership Arrangements. Governmental Rhetoric or Governance Scheme?" *Public Administration Review* 62(2): 197–205. doi:10.1111/0033-3352.00170.

Tindal, C. Richard, Susan Nobes Tindal, Kennedy Stewart, and Patrick J. Smith. 2012. *Local Government in Canada*, 8th ed. Toronto: Nelson Education.

Torrisi, G. 2009. Public Infrastructure: Definition, Classification and Measurement Issues. *Economics, Management and Financial Markets* 4(3): 100–24.

Treff, Karen, and Deborah Ort. 2013. *Finances of the Nation 2011.* Toronto: Canadian Tax Foundation.

– 2014. *Finances of the Nation 2012.* Toronto: Canadian Tax Foundation.

Turgeon M., and F. Vaillancourt. 2002. "The Provision of Highways in Canada and the Federal Government." *Publius* 32(1) (Winter): 161–80.

Ulbrich, Holley H., and Steven Maguire. 2005. "Infrastructure Financing." In *The Encyclopedia of Taxation and Tax Policy*, edited by Joseph C. Cordes, Robert D. Ebel, and Jane G. Gravelle, 204–6. Washington, DC: Urban Institute.

Urban Land Institute and Ernst and Young, 2010. *Infrastructure 2010: Investment Imperative.* Washington, DC: Urban Land Institute.

US Census Bureau. 2002. Census of Governments, vol. 4, no. 2. *Finances of Special District Governments: 2002*. Washington, DC. https://www.census.gov/prod/2/gov/gc92-4/gc924-2.pdf.

– 2006. Census of Finance and Employment. *Classification Manual*, Washington, DC. https://www2.census.gov/govs/pubs/classification/2006 _classification_manual.pdf.

– 2013. Census of Governments. *Individual State Descriptions: 2012*. Washington, DC. https://www2.census.gov/govs/cog/2012isd.pdf.

– 2014. Census of Governments, *State and Local Government Summary Report, 2012*. Washington, DC. https://www.census.gov/govs/local/.

– 2016. Census of Governments. *State and Local Government Finances*. Washington, DC: https://www.census.gov/govs/local/.

US Bureau of Economic Analysis. Fixed Assets Tables. 20/24/2016. Last Revised 2002. www.bea.gov/national/faweb/AllFATables.asp.

– 2016. *Public Education Finances, 2014*, Washington, DC, https://www.census .gov/library/publications/2016/econ/g14-aspef.html.

US Congressional Budget Office (CBO). 2015. *Public Spending on Transportation and Water Infrastructure, 1956 to 2014*. March. www.cbo.gov/ publication/49910.

US Department of Transportation. 2014. *Highway Statistics, 2014*. Washington, DC: US Department of Transportation.

Vecchi, Veronica, Mark Hellowell, and Stefano Gatti. 2013. "Does the Private Sector Receive an Excessive Rate of Return from Investments in Health Care Infrastructure? Evidence from the UK." *Health Policy* 110(2–3): 243– 70. doi:http://dx.doi.org/10.1016/j.healthpol.2012.12.010.

Vickrey, William S. 1972. "Economic Efficiency and Pricing." In *Public Prices for Public Products*, edited by Selma Mushkin, 53–72. Washington, DC: Urban Institute.

– 1994. *Public Economics*. Edited by Richard Arnott, Kenneth Arrow, Anthony B. Atkinson, and Jacques H. Dreze. Cambridge: Cambridge University Press.

Wallace, Sally. 2015. "The Evolving Financial Architecture of State and Local Governments." In *The Oxford Handbook of State and Local Government Finance*, edited by Robert D. Ebel and John E. Petersen, 156–75. Oxford and New York: Oxford University Press. https://www.cga.ct.gov/fin/.

Walton, Gary M., and Hugh Rockoff. 2013. *History of the American Economy*, 12th ed. Independence, KY: Cengage Press.

Watson and Associates. 2016. *PSAB 3150 vs. Asset Management_0*. Mississauga: Watson and Associates Economists Ltd. http://www.ofntsc.org/sites /default/files/PSAB%203150%20vs%20Asset%20Management_0.pdf.

Watson and Associates and Dillon Consulting Ltd. 2012. *Towards Full Cost Recovery: Best Practices in Cost Recovery for Municipal Water and Waste Water Services.* Toronto: Association of Municipalities of Ontario.

Weinzierl, Matthew. 2016a. "Revisiting the Classical View of Benefit-Based Taxation." Harvard Business School, Working Paper 14-101, revised March.

– 2016b. "Popular Acceptance of Inequality due to Brute Luck and Support for Classical Benefit-Based Taxation." NBER Working Paper 22462, July.

Wood, James. 2016. "New Report Raises Idea of Tolls to Help Pay for Alberta Roads." *Calgary Herald*, 13 January. http://calgaryherald.com/news/politics/new-report-raises-idea-of-tolls-to-help-pay-for-alberta-roads.

World Bank. 2016. "Public–Private Partnerships in Roads." PPPIRC. http://ppp.worldbank.org/public–private-partnership/sector/transportation/roads-tolls-bridges/road-concessions.

Yerly N. 2013. "The Political Economy of Budget Rules in the Twenty-Six Swiss Cantons: Institutional Analysis, Preferences and Performances." PhD dissertation, Faculty of Economic and Social Sciences, University of Fribourg.

Youngman, Joan. 2011. *TIF at a Turning Point: Defining Debt Down.* Cambridge, MA: Lincoln Institute of Land Policy.

Yuan, X.-X., and J. Zhang. 2016. "Understanding the Effects of Public–Private Partnerships on Innovation in Canadian Projects." Ryerson Institute for Infrastructure Innovation. http://www.ryerson.ca/content/dam/riii/ryerson-construction-innovation-2016.pdf.

Zakaria, Fareed. 2011. *The Ryan Budget: A Test of Character for Obama.* CNN Cable Network News. 7 April. https://fareedzakaria.com/?s=the+ryan+budget.

Contributors

RICHARD M. BIRD is professor emeritus at the Rotman School of Management, University of Toronto, and senior fellow at the Institute on Municipal Finance and Governance. He is the author of "Below the Salt: Decentralizing Value-Added Taxes," in *Handbook of Multilateral Finance* (Edward Elgar, 2016).

BERNARD DAFFLON is professor emeritus in the Faculty of Economic and Social Science, University of Fribourg, Switzerland. His research interests are fiscal federalism, decentralization and local finance, deficit and public debt rules, and the use of the benefit principle in financing environmental policies.

ROBERT D. EBEL is consultant to US state and local governments at Local Governance Innovation and Development (LGI-D). A former deputy chief financial officer for the Washington, DC, government, he is the co-editor with John E. Petersen of the *Oxford Handbook of State and Local Government Finance* (2012).

HARRY KITCHEN is professor emeritus in the Department of Economics, Trent University. He is the co-author with Michael Fenn of "Bringing Sustainability to Ontario's Water Systems: A Quarter-Century of Progress, with Much Left to Do," a study for the Ontario Sewer and Watermain Construction Association (2016).

JEAN-PHILIPPE MELOCHE is associate professor in the School of Urban Planning, Université de Montréal. He is the author of "A Sizeable Effect? Municipal Council Size and the Cost of Local Government in

Canada," co-authored with Patrick Kilfoil, in *Canadian Public Administration* (2017).

MATTI SIEMIATYCKI is associate professor in the Department of Geography and Planning, University of Toronto. He recently published "Canadian Pension Fund Investors in Transport Infrastructure: A Case Study," in *Case Studies in Transport Policy* 3(2) (2015).

ENID SLACK is director of the Institute on Municipal Finance and Governance and adjunct professor at the Munk School of Global Affairs, University of Toronto. She recently published "Sustainable Development and Municipalities: Getting the Prices Right" in *Canadian Public Policy* 42, Supplement 1 (2016).

ALMOS T. TASSONYI is executive fellow and director of the Urban Policy Program at the School of Public Policy, University of Calgary. He is the author of "An Exploration into the Municipal Capacity to Finance Capital Infrastructure" with Brian Conger, School of Public Policy, University of Calgary, SPP Research Papers 8(38) (2015).

LINDSAY M. TEDDS is associate professor in the School of Public Administration, University of Victoria. She is the author, with Catherine Althaus, of *User Fees in Canada: A Municipal Design and Implementation Guide* (Canadian Tax Foundation, 2016).

FRANÇOIS VAILLANCOURT is professor emeritus at the Université de Montréal. His research interests include fiscal federalism and the economics of language. He recently wrote "Fiscal Health of Québec Municipalites," with Jean-Philippe Meloche and Matthieu Strubb, in *Is Your City Healthy? Measuring Urban Fiscal Health* (IMFG, 2015).

YAMENG WANG is a consultant with the World Bank. She recently wrote "Recent Developments in Corporate Tax Policies in the European Union and in the U.S. States" with Joann Weiner, John Alvarino (George Washington University), and Elliott Dublin (Multistate Tax Commission, 2016).

Index

Switzerland, 194–5, 200, 210–11n11; in United States, 146, 151, 156

Spadina subway extension, Toronto, 216

Spain, 219–20, 229

special assessments, 35, 51n23, 139; in United States, 142

special districts in United States, 163, 165, 177n19

special-purpose vehicle (SPV) company, 213

specific benefit taxes, 142

spillover effects. *See* externalities

sprawl, urban, 39, 76, 129, 247

state of good repair, 47

State Route 91 Express Lanes, California, 228

Statistics Canada, 26, 53n37, 122–3, 125, 128; definition of family unit, 65; definition of infrastructure, 89

Stavins, Robert, 104

Steinmo, Sven, 267n3

Stewart, Kennedy, 124

Stockholm, 34, 109–10

stormwater: fees or levies for, 30, 50n15, 84, 151; management of, 13–14, 70, 75; pricing models for fees, 55, 62, 74–5, 268n9; in Switzerland, 211n13

Strategic Investment Fund, 94

street lighting, 25, 34, 106

subsidies, 12, 24; hidden, 6; unintended, 28

Sun, Rui, 262

surpluses, government, 15, 17, 116

sustainability: fiscal, 55, 83, 85; system, 84; water, 55–6, 85. *See also* Municipal Sustainability Initiative

Sutherland, Douglas, 267n7

Swain, Harry, 56

swimming pools, 95

Swiss Harmonized Public Accounting System, 197

Swiss National Bank, 182

Switzerland, 9, 17, 105, 115, 241, 246; infrastructure financing in, 178–211

Sydney, Australia, 109–10, 226

tariff, multi-part, 14

Tassonyi, Almos, 29, 44–5, 238, 241, 247

taxes: progressive vs regressive, 121; social cost of, 245; in Switzerland, 184, 205, 209n2; tax competition, 205; tax credits, 19; tax design, 24, 205; types of in United States, 142. *See also* consumption taxes; excise taxes; gasoline tax; income tax; land transfer taxes; payroll taxes; property tax; sales tax; specific benefit taxes

tax increment equivalency grants (TIEGs), 36, 52n28

tax increment financing (TIF), 35–6, 51–2n26

taxis, 149

Tax Policy Center, 167

Tedds, Lindsay, 34, 118–19, 122, 135

telecommunications infrastructure, 90

Tennessee, 173

Texas, 228

Thaler, Richard, 263

Thunder Bay, Ontario, 64

time-of-day charging/pricing, 29, 34, 48, 73

Timofeev, Andrey, 248

tipping fees for garbage, 31